THE JOY OF CONVERSATION

Published by Utne Reader Books
1624 Harmon Place
Minneapolis, MN 55403
First edition.
Second printing, 1997.
ISBN: 0-953816-0-9
The Joy of Conversation: The Complete Guide to Salons / by Jaida n'ha Sandra;
preface by Eric Utne, introduction by Jaida n'ha Sandra.
Manufactured in the United States of America.

THE JOY OF CONVERSATION
The COMPLETE GUIDE to
SALONS

by
JAIDA N'HA SANDRA
and the Editors of Utne Reader

AN UTNE READER BOOK

Acknowledgments

My first thanks to all those salon members who have shared their homes and memories with me over the years. Although I cannot list them all, I am particularly indebted to Avaren Ipsen and Victoria Woolley of The Lowry Hill Salon, Judith Bell of The Loring Neighborhood Salon, and all my friends at the Berkeley Creativity Salon. Steven Grover and Alan Lipton, thank you for keeping the salon alive while I went off to write this book. My love also to my housemates at the Tree House. You allowed the salon to happen.

Thanks must go to all my friends and colleagues who made this California woman welcome and helped me survive the long Minnesota winters. Special thanks to John and Lori, owners of the wonderful Coffee Gallery in Minneapolis. Therein a good half of this book was written. Susan Burr, thank you for insights and information on the meetings of the Friends. My optometrist Herb Monroe has always helped me see my way more clearly, figuratively as well as literally. My gratitude also to the *Utne Reader* staff for generously answering questions and sharing resources. Jules Inda, Carolyn Adams, Griff Wigley, Patti Cich, and Elizabeth Larsen all provided enormous support. Above all, thank you Eric Utne for seeing my potential and taking a gamble on an unknown author.

This book was composed to the tunes of Peter Apfelbaum and the Heiroglyphics, Paul Kelly and the Messengers, Jai Uttal, Jah Wobble, Michelle Shocked, Buffy Sainte-Marie, and Alicia Corbet and Jay Basso's great unknown band, Tea and Sympathy. Thank you, Peter Apfelbaum, for a genius that continues to inspire, and Alicia Corbet, for a voice well worth braving any Minnesota winter night to hear.

Finally, this book is dedicated to my two fathers: Gary Bethke, who welcomed me home when I seemed farthest from home, and Leslie Gerber, who has unfailingly believed in my ability to realize any dream. I love you both.

—Jaida n'ha Sandra

Cover Art: Lynn Rowe Reed
Book design: Ken Hey and Tony Goshko
Additional editing: Greg Linder
Art research: Martha Coventry

Contents

Preface by Eric Utne vii

Introduction ix

HISTORY

Remembrance of Conversations Past: A Brief History of Salons   1

1. Origins: From Ancient Greece to the Twentieth Century 3
2. Conversation American-Style: The Twentieth Century 23

PART I

Foundations: Building Your Own Salon   33

3. Getting Organized: First Steps 35
4. The Salon Site: Choosing a Meeting Place 51
5. Finding People: Building Your Membership 65

PART II

Big Talk: Conversation and Leadership   85

6. Choosing Topics: Deciding What to Talk About 87
7. Conversational Skills: The Art of Successful Conversation 103
8. Leadership and Rules: Facilitating the Process 125

PART III

Variations on a Theme: Other Directions for Salons   149

9. Book Clubs and Study Circles: Education and Involvement . . . 151
10. Councils: Friends, Palavers, and Talking Sticks 171
11. Creativity Salons: Conversation at Play 191
12. E-Salons: Conversations on the Net 211

PART IV

The Open Circle: Salons and Community   227

13. Extended Family: Building Community in Your Salon 229
14. Salons in Society: Making a Difference 247

Appendices 255

Bibliography 259

Eric Utne

A Minneapolis coffeehouse/bar is filled with diffuse mid-morning sunlight. Tapestries and colorful paintings hang on the walls. The aromas of coffee and muffins waft through the air. Some twenty media junkies stir in a loose circle of well-worn, comfortable old chairs, each of a different design. A three-hour discussion/debate/jam session is launched with the question: "What have you been thinking and obsessing about lately?" Thus begins the *Utne Reader* Salon.

Salons are the most stimulating aspect of producing the *Utne Reader*. When the coffee's strong and the chemistry's right, our conversations seem to tap directly into the zeitgeist. One person's ideas inspire another's and another's. Each contributes his or her own piece to something larger. By making explicit what may have been, prior to the salon, only flickering at the edges of our awareness, these heady gab sessions turn into something transcendent—conversational and conceptual jazz.

In the March/April 1991 issue of *Utne Reader*, we published a cover section called "Salons: How to Revive the Endangered Art of Conversation and Start a Revolution in Your Neighborhood." At the end of the section, we ran a little ad inviting those readers who'd like to participate in salons to send us their names, addresses, and daytime phone numbers. We promised to introduce them to other *Utne* readers in their neighborhood who wanted to get together.

We expected 1,000 to 1,500 responses. We received over 8,200. Within a year, nearly 20,000 people had joined *Utne Reader's* Neighborhood Salon Association.

Since then, the salon phenomenon has turned into a movement. Thousands of book clubs, church circles, office work groups, and even dinner parties, inspired by the articles in *Utne Reader*, have transformed themselves into salons or one of the various permutations, like councils (more meditative, with the emphasis on listening and speaking from the heart) or study circles (more intensive and goal oriented). Hundreds of newspapers and radio and television stations have reported on the development of these salons in their communities. Some of these media, like the Minneapolis *Star Tribune*, the Spokane *Spokesman-Review*, and Wisconsin Public Radio, have even started salons of their own.

Since our distant ancestors first gathered around the fire, most cultures have had some social form like the salon. It's just basic to being human—people need to get together and talk over the things they care about and believe in. In the United States, television and the accelerated pace of modern life seem to be the principal forces that undermine such gatherings. The current resurgence of salons may herald a turning point in American history. As more and more people turn off their tubes and reach out to each other, direct, person-to-person, community-based democracy can begin to flourish once again.

Indeed, salons could be the antidote for the sense of alienation and malaise that currently infects much of America. They're fun. They're glamorous, and evocative of seventeenth-century Paris. And yet they're as simple to produce as a coffee klatsch. I believe they might even change the world. Are you up for a cultural revolution?

We hope *The Joy of Conversation* will serve to inspire and guide you as you conduct your own salon. Please let us know what works for you and what doesn't. What activities and roles has your group devised, and in which direction is your salon evolving? We would like to include your experiences in future editions of this book.

—Eric Utne

To converse is human. To salon is divine.

I wrote this book because I am a salon-keeper. I founded the Creativity Salon in Berkeley, California, in July of 1990, so I could get together with people every month to have fun with art and performance projects. I called it a "salon" because no other word so aptly describes regular, informal gatherings held in one's home.

Hosting a salon was part of my effort to connect with a community. I had spent several years in Japan, where I was impressed by the family and community support each individual seemed to receive. My return to the United States brought with it a shocking awareness of isolation. I decided not to travel again until I had carved out a "home" in my own culture. The Creativity Salon was part of this effort. It was a way of reaching out to a wider circle of acquaintances and building, over time, a "community of memory."

A year later, the regular members of the salon told me it had become a touchstone in their lives. Within two years, over seventy people were included on my list of interested participants. Strangers and acquaintances outnumbered close friends, but we were all connected through our neighborhoods, our workplaces, our lovers and families, and our shared experiences at the salon.

I had come to know a more diverse group of people. I had a wider circle of supportive and trustworthy friends than ever before. And, for the first time, I believed in my ability to have an impact on other people's lives and the larger society. The salon was a success.

The other, at first more important, reason for starting a salon was to practice creativity in a setting where I needn't fear judgment of my efforts. I had been struggling with writer's block ever since I first decided to try getting published. I knew my awestruck regard for other people's genius was stifling me, but I didn't know how to get over it and simply enjoy writing. The salon was an experiment in approaching art playfully. By starting a group where criticism was not allowed, I hoped to subdue my internal critic.

In this respect, too, the salon succeeded. I became able to take greater and greater creative risks. I began to write again, sending articles and stories to publishers without freezing at the prospect of rejection slips. That lightheartedness made it easy for me to write a quick letter about salons to the *Utne Reader* magazine. The letter resulted in a fairy-tale sequence of events, culminating in my first break as a professional writer.

As it turned out, I was not the only one interested in salons. Eric Utne's obsession with rebuilding community in America had led him to a fascination with salons—the topic of the cover section of the March/April 1991 issue of the magazine. I read the salon issue eagerly, and I was delighted by the optimism of the editors and authors, who suggested that salons might "change the world one evening at a time."

Letters to the editor in the *Utne*'s next issue made it clear that such enthusiasm was not universal. Many people regarded salons as gatherings of chatty elitists who were uninvolved with the real problems of society. This didn't jive with my understanding of historical salons, or with the projects we were undertaking in our salon. I wrote a letter describing our socially active Creativity Salon, which became an article in the "creativity issue" of the *Utne Reader*, published a year later.

I also drew up casual notes for a possible book about the history of salons, their social potential, and how to organize them. Eric Utne had been thinking along the same lines. He first asked me to create an expanded article on the Creativity Salon, which appeared in the Neighborhood Salon Association newsletter. Then he asked if I was interested in writing the first book to be published by the *Utne Reader*—this one.

––––––––––

At its heart this book is about conversation—the most basic, most varied, and occasionally the most elevating of all human activities. Of course, the ability to converse is not unique to humans—chimpanzees do it, dolphins do it, even parakeets and poodles manage to make themselves understood by one another. But humans have made conversation the defining experience of our social identities. Conversation is the sea we swim in. Conversation is the way we convey information, inspire each other, and achieve

Jaida n'ha Sandra

understanding. Conversation is the way we display our prowess, knowledge, and refinement. Conversation is the way we challenge, amuse, and amaze each other. Conversation is the music we make when we commune. But not all conversation is created equal. Some talk, though right and proper, is small. Cocktail chitchat, locker-room bravado, office gossip, and talk show repartee come to mind.

Then there's the salon. Salons are gatherings where people talk "big talk," talk meant to be listened to and perhaps passionately acted upon. Salons are incubators where ideas are conceived, gestated, and hatched, sometimes in a matter of minutes or hours. Salons are the frontiers of social and cultural change. Salons are the concert halls where conversation is presented in virtuoso style. They're going on all over America right now. In living rooms and suburban church basements, in coffee shops and pubs and parks, friends and neighbors are coming together to engage in un-small talk. They're talking about community, democracy, technology, and love. They're reading each other poetry and making music together. They're forming eco-teams, cohousing groups, and letter-writing clubs. They're cultivating their creativity, reviving the art of conversation, and quite possibly changing the world.

Because there is no one best way to conduct a salon, this book attempts to be descriptive rather than prescriptive. It provides a series of choices. It tries to answer questions: How do you find members for a salon? Where do salons meet? When? How often? Should you bring food? What do you do with the kids? Who's going to call everyone? Do you collect money? How do you choose topics? What happens if the group members argue too much? How come some people don't speak up? Is the salon diverse enough? Why aren't your members more intimate? Can you visit other salons? Should you go camping together? What if you want to take action on the issues you've discussed? Should you bring in speakers? Are rituals important in a salon?

In fact, each choice makes a salon unique. A willingness to experiment keeps the salon alive.

Unlike other groups, salons are not necessarily set up to achieve goals. This makes some people a little uneasy. They can't quite understand how sitting around talking is going to do anyone much good. Americans favor activities that are supposed to make them stronger, smarter, more beautiful, richer, and generally more satiated than they were before—or activities that will make the world less hungry, less poor, less noisy, less dirty, less angry, less scary, less barren. The salon makes no such promises. But the absence of specific goals does not mean that salons serve no purpose.

Several years ago, I interviewed a Tibetan Buddhist monk about the life of Tibetan refugees in Nepal. When the subject turned to education, he asserted that Nepalese were, on the whole, better educated than Americans. Because at that time only nineteen percent of the adults in Nepal could read, I was quite taken aback. When I asked the monk to explain, he said that the Nepalese got more of an education because they discussed everything that was going on in the world. "If only one person [in a family or village] can read," he said, "everyone knows what that person knows. Nepalese talk about everything a lot, in restaurants, on buses. Everybody gets together and passes information to each other." In his experience, Americans seemed to know little about anything except their jobs, and they rarely talked to anyone about matters of consequence.

Anybody now living in the United States who reads, owns a television or radio, or has a computer encounters more information than has been available at any other time in history. But we risk ignorance when we choose to receive information passively. In forming their opinions, many Americans rely more upon experts and media sound bites than upon their own life experiences. Those of us who analyze information extensively are often in highly specialized fields, and we may block out information irrelevant to the particular work at hand. To the world's detriment, we ignore the

"We have in the salons . . . a place to awaken and strengthen the natural, almost genetic, abilities of community and step out of the blurring pace of modern life into a quiet eddy where talk, plain and simple, has the power to open new doors. **"**
—Chris Cone, member of the Stanley Street Salon

interactions of whole systems. Even those of us who try to keep up with all the latest trends in business, politics, the arts, environmental practices, and discoveries in science never catch up completely, and rarely have time to put the pieces together. There is simply too much information for any one person to digest.

As my Tibetan acquaintance implied, talking with others is one way out of this bind. Salons encourage probing the complexities of our world. They are educational in the best sense, moving beyond statistics and facts toward genuine understanding. Salons naturally tend to leave specialization behind and move in the direction of synthesis. At salons, people search for meaning and come to trust their own ability to evaluate all the information that is thrown at them. The most exciting experience at a salon is finding yourself saying something with conviction that you hadn't previously realized you'd known or believed. In the moment of speaking, you discover your own wisdom.

In salons, we have the chance to talk over the things we are privately concerned about, to grasp the views of those who have had experiences different from our own, and to arrive at some understanding of where we can go from here. The resurgence of salons is a hopeful sign. It means people believe that what they think is important and useful, even if they are not experts. Salon conversations bind people together. We gain the skills of democratic participation. We learn how to organize something and keep it running. We practice abandoning no-win dichotomies and finding consensus. We gain the confidence to interact with the larger world, knowing there are others who support our actions.

Important changes don't often occur as a result of sudden, earth-shattering events. They happen in increments, through a slow buildup of fragile, almost imperceptible experiences. Gradual alterations in attitudes and opinions add up, until you find yourself doing something you know you wouldn't have done a year ago, five years ago, a decade ago. Salons are communities wherein such tiny alterations occur and evolve into something meaningful.

And so, for these reasons and many others, this book is about the place and the process called the salon.

HISTORY

Remembrance of Conversations Past:

A Brief History of Salons

Origins:
From Ancient Greece to the Twentieth Century

I have been delighted in the course of my research to meet the men and women of the salons. They have spoken to me across centuries, encouraging me with their determination to educate and express themselves, inspiring me with their love of humanity and their compassion for human failings. I admire their desire for great and meaningful friendships, their support for one another's deepest values and ambitions. I am astonished by the breadth, subtlety, and complexity of their thoughts, as well as the intensity of their involvement in the world.

Most inspiring of all has been the salon participants' ability to bring all kinds of people into fellowship. Salons, like most informal conversational groups, have tended to be egalitarian. In these groups, people who might elsewhere have been socially ostracized were included—provided they could offer wit, intelligence, charm, and literary or political insight. Sadly, ironically, these remarkable human qualities have often been regarded by societies at large as suspect, or even dangerous.

I am amazed by the range of topics that has occupied people who attended salons. They eagerly debated the fundamental philosophical ideas that were transforming their society. They grappled with questions of human rights and liberties; with the conflicts between church, state, and science; with education, feminism, sexuality, law, and developments in the arts and sciences. Passionate conversation has often led to passionate action, to lives risked and sometimes sacrificed in efforts to achieve social and political change. It's my hope that the chosen examples will encourage you to toss your talents and your dreams into the half-public, half-private arena called the salon.

A complete history of conversational groups—that is, small, informal but regular meetings held for the purpose of general discussion—would require an entire book.

f I would travel 500 leagues to talk to an intelligent man."

—Salon-keeper Germaine de Staël

It would include groups in every country, from the *diwaniyeh* of Kuwait to Latin American *tertulia*. It would describe every gathering where speaking has become both an entertaining art form and a means of acquiring a political voice, as in the Maaori *hui*, the African *palaver*, and the American town hall. It would begin with early history, perhaps with the Ancient Greek *symposia*, and proceed to the modern Swedish study circles. It would include creative, playful activities that have fostered conversation, among them quilting, card playing, musical performances, and word games.

While many of these groups and activities will be described, this book cannot encompass a complete history. Instead, I will present an overview of one group conversation format known as "the salon." The historical salons serve as precedents, and as examples of the wide impact that small conversational groups can exercise upon politics and society.

The First Salons

The precursors of European salons were the symposia of Ancient Greece. Symposia, like salons, took place in private homes, in special rooms built for the purpose. These rooms, called *andron*, were present in every house, from those owned by the wealthiest Athenians to those of the poorest farmers, illustrating the importance of symposia to Greek cultural life. During gatherings in the andron, six to eight guests ate, drank, and discussed everything from local gossip to politics and philosophy. The six or eight guests were sometimes entertained by professional musicians or dancers, but more often they amused themselves by reciting poetry and dramatic passages, or by singing hymns, love songs, and drinking songs.

Egalitarian both in subject and membership, the symposia brought together people from many occupations, including philosophers, farmers, actors, poets, doctors, craftsmen, mathematicians, geographers, painters, historians, and politicians. This mix of people encouraged creative exchanges between members of different disciplines, and kept the more powerful members of society in healthy contact with ordinary citizens. The symposia were not egalitarian with respect to women and other non-citizens (slaves, children, foreigners). However, at least one woman, Aspasia, the foreign wife of Pericles, started her own symposium.

The Ancient Romans imitated the symposia with their somewhat more decadent banquets. Again, people of all ranks dined together while discussing current news events and showing off their talents. Banquets were so commonplace that they often escaped the scrutiny that suspicious Roman emperors accorded men's clubs and fraternities. The seemingly innocuous nature of general conversation later helped salonists foment the French Revolution, because men were allowed to speak freely in conversational circles run by women.

The Roman habit of welcoming artists and writers into homes of the elite continued throughout the centuries in Italy. Later, the French royalty became envious of Italian arts and scholarship. French kings returned from wars in Italy with writers and scholars in tow, determined to set up their own circles. Wealthy wives of merchants and royal women residing away from court began to imitate this new fad. The result was the birth of the French salon.

Sixteenth-Century Literary Circles

The French salon came about as a result of changes in society. Most of the nobility were uneducated and illiterate, and so ill-suited for dealing with the emerging monetary economy. Many of them ended up in poverty and moved to court, where they had the leisure and opportunity to amuse themselves with conversation. Commerce also made it necessary for the nobility to hire and do business with scholars and middle-class merchants, which increased the amount of contact between previously separated classes of people.

People throughout Europe had begun to question the chivalric ideal, which protected and idolized women, as well as the misogynist mainstream of Christian philosophy, which stated that women were agents of the devil and had no souls. Women became freer to act as companions of men. By the sixteenth century a few royal women, including Queen Anne, had established themselves as social leaders, inviting scholars to their court circles. The examples set by these women paved the way for other women to begin holding salons.

Meanwhile, middle-class and low-ranking members of the nobility began to hold literary circles in their homes. These were often comprised of scholars who hoped to win employment at court writing poetry, teaching, practicing law, or performing secretarial work. They gathered in small, mutual support groups based on common interests and ambitions. Jean de Morel's home was central for such people.

In 1541, thirty-year-old Jean de Morel left Switzerland and took a job in Paris as a tutor. Two years later, he married Antoinette de Loynes, a well-educated young woman

"The freest, most spirited, most instructive conversation that ever was. . . . There is no daring notion in politics or religion that is not put forward and debated as to its pros and cons. "

—Abbé Morellet, describing Baron d'Holbach's salon

who shared many of her husband's intellectual interests. The couple welcomed into their home and advised many of the unemployed poets, lawyers, and diplomats who had come to Paris seeking work. Jean de Morel used his influence with the author and patroness Princess Marguerite to gain pensions for his most talented friends. His house was praised as "le premier salon littéraire de Paris."

As the landed gentry became poorer and the merchants became richer, class distinctions continued to erode. By the mid-1600s, an individual could be middle class, or even poor, but if sufficiently witty, worldly, and interesting, would receive invitations to salons that the royalty frequented. This social change did not occur immediately or graciously. Most aristocrats had no desire to mix with the bourgeois. It was one thing to keep poets around as pets, but quite another for monied commoners to hold their own literary circles and mimic royalty. Nobles were outraged when "she whose pomp and attire had attracted the eyes of almost all the court" turned out to be "a seller of used clothing from a mediocre retail shop or a mere dealer in fresh fish." Some court circles were established specifically to exclude commoners. Salons, where no one paid attention to rank, were regarded as corrupt and an especially bad influence on women.

The noblemen who opposed such mixing had reason to fear the influence of salon gatherings, for the egalitarianism of open conversation was emboldening members of all social classes. In these early salons, a democratic philosophy developed that would in fact change the world.

Madame de Rambouillet and the Polite Society

Catharine de Rambouillet's salon set the tone for the seventeenth century and was started in opposition to the court salons. Disgusted by the decadence of palace life under Henry IV, Mme. de Rambouillet left court in 1607 to live in her own house nearby. Her salon, called by her guests "the sanctuary of the Temple of Athéne," remained open until her death at the age of seventy-seven in 1665. By then she had established a standard of polite behavior, inspired countless women to set up their own salons, profoundly affected French literature, and established the foundation for a French social

66 Politeness does not always inspire goodness, equity, complaisance, gratitude, but it gives at least the appearance of these qualities and makes man seem externally what he ought to be internally."

—La Jean de Bruyére

activity that would persist for another two centuries.

Wealthy, beautiful, and of royal blood, Madame de Rambouillet is almost a stereotype of the classic salon-keeper. But her fortunate circumstances alone do not explain her great influence. Most importantly, she was an independent woman driven by the desire to mold society into a form she found acceptable. She was able to realize this ambition through her ability to appreciate and handle people, and through her willingness to befriend foreigners and bourgeoisie.

At the time, society offered little outlet for a woman's talents and intelligence, but Madame de Rambouillet refused to accept social and intellectual isolation. She used her artistic skills to create a salon that was delightful and entertaining. She welcomed to her home anyone she considered intellectually worthy and well behaved. This last criterion was strict. She flatly rejected those who did not meet her standards of politeness. But because she expected her guests to behave virtuously and chose them wisely, the opinions of her regular corps came to be taken seriously by the rest of the world. The ambassador and writer Louis de Rouvroy Saint-Simon later described the group as a "tribunal with which it was necessary to count, and whose decisions upon the conduct

A SALON BY ANY OTHER NAME

Although Morel's mid-sixteenth century open house was referred to as a literary salon, these kinds of half-private/half-public gatherings would not generally be called 'salons' for another century. Even Madame de Rambouillet's circle was not called a salon, as it did not meet in her living room. Her guests sat around her bedside (ruelle); the room was called the Chambre Bleu because of its blue walls and drapes. For a time *ruelle* came to mean the conversational gathering itself. In *Watteau's Painted Conversations*, art historian Mary Vidal writes, "The word salon was not generally used to designate this type of social meeting until the end of the seventeenth century. Up to that time the social group or the place where they met would have been called by a variety of other names: ruelle, cabale, cabinet, réduit, alcôve, compagnie, société, cour littéraire cercle, assemblée."

That is, you might have named your salon after the room in which it took place: bedroom, bedside, living room, nook, or alcove. Or you might have called it by whatever term you preferred to describe a group of people: cabinet, company, society, literary court, circle, or assembly. Later salons became known satirically as *bureaux d'esprit*, or offices of wit. Whatever the term, the activities were essentially the same.

and reputation of people of the court and the world had great weight."

The renowned Cardinal Richelieu so feared the salonists' opinions that he asked Madame de Rambouillet to pass along everything that was said in her salons. Catharine diplomatically refused, pointing out that everyone knew of the friendship between them, and so no one would dare speak badly of him. By turning aside intrigue with a compliment, she employed a tactfulness that was increasingly emulated throughout the salons. Simply asserting a standard of decency and grace was then a social revolution, one that eventually spread to all classes.

Madeleine de Scudéry: An Early Feminist

Mademoiselle de Scudéry

After Madame de Rambouillet's death, her friend Madeleine de Scudéry took over the "Hôtel de Rambouillet." Initially, many factors counted against her by the standards of Parisian society. She had grown up in the countryside, had remained unmarried, and was considered exceptionally homely. Yet the salon she started at the age of sixty became so famous that its regular meeting day, Samedi (Saturday), was known as her day.

What "The Illustrious Sapho" (Madeleine's favorite nickname) *did* have was an education, thanks to an uncle who had encouraged her to complete training in women's accomplishments as well as in studies usually reserved for men (including Spanish and Italian, in which she became fluent). Her skill as a writer, particularly in thumbnailing the character of her friends, sparked a fashion in pen portraits. These were highly complimentary essays on salon habitués, and they were all the rage for several decades. In her descriptions of salon dialogue, it becomes evident that she and her friends delighted in jokes and verbal play, especially puns.

Through the salon, Madeleine was able to express and find support for ideals that would later be considered feminist. She thought little of "light and coquettish women whose only occupation is to adorn their persons and pass their lives in fêtes and amusements—women who think that scrupulous virtue requires them to know nothing but to be the wife of a husband, the mother of children, and the mistress of the family; and men who regard women as upper servants, and forbid their daughters to read anything but prayer-books." The best kind of woman, she said, was one who "knows a hundred things of which she does not boast, that she has a well-informed mind, is familiar with fine works, speaks well, writes correctly, and knows the world."

Madeleine was not alone in her views. People at salons debated whether women and men were essentially the same or entirely different, although women were assumed virtuous by nature. Unable to conclude the argument, both male and female feminists at the salons became proponents of women's rights. A number of well-known writers declared that it was a form of tyranny to prevent women from taking part in government. Marriage was considered oppressive, a waste of the minds of women who could instead be serving their country.

The salons gave women a public voice and social influence. Salon women became increasingly well-educated as their male guests suggested books for them to read and encouraged them to learn more languages. Their leadership roles in salons gave women reason to imagine that they could become leaders in public life. Salon-keepers subverted the norms simply by holding salons, but it was not until the eighteenth century that women moved from admiring and inspiring men to realizing their own ambitions in the public sphere.

Salons of the Philosophes

By the early 1700s, salons were as numerous as women who had the time and resources to host them. Eventually there were hundreds throughout Paris and the provinces. Directories were published to assist foreign visitors who wished to participate. Through these conversational gatherings, women orchestrated the dissemination of radical theories, political rumors, and social gossip. Women were able to make or break the political careers of men, and could insist that developing ideas on human rights must be aired.

The most important movement supported by the eighteenth-century salons was the Enlightenment, a rationalist, materialist, humanist philosophy that directly threatened both the church and the state. The Philosophes, also called the Encyclopédists,

François-Marie Arouet Voltaire

included Voltaire, Jean-Jacques Rousseau, Jean Le Rond d'Alembert, Denis Diderot, and others. These influential thinkers propounded in writing their radical notions of liberty and equality, and argued their beliefs in the ubiquitous salons. Although the Philosophes were satirized, imprisoned, exiled, and tortured, their ideas spread through the salons into the general population. By the end of the century, they would foster a complete social and political revolution.

Each of several salons was proclaimed *the* rallying place for the Philosophes. Each featured nearly the same guests; each covered essentially the same topics; and each attempted to become the center of the new philosophy. However, each salon was unique, due to the distinctive character of each salon-keeper. One of the salons was run by a man—an eccentric misanthrope from Germany named Baron d'Holbach. An ardent materialist easily converted to atheism, d'Holbach devoted himself to the Philosophes, introducing them to members of the aristocracy who might support their ideas. He also penned several hundred articles for their great project, the *Encyclopédie ou Dictionnaire Raisonné Des Sciences, des Arts et des Métiers*. The first volume of this revolutionary encyclopedia was published in 1751, immediately stirring up a storm of political controversy.

Madame Geoffrin

D'Holbach held his dinners on Thursdays and Sundays, so they would not conflict with the other favorite philosophical gatherings at Madame Geoffrin's home. The wealthy, generous, and unpretentious woman welcomed the Philosophes, but worried about their dangerously unbridled speech. She once offered a great deal of money to a friend on the condition that he would burn a paper he had written. When he protested eloquently that he was unafraid, she heard him out, then asked, "How much more do you want, M. Rulhière?"

Madame Geoffrin instituted a great salon innovation when she subdivided hers into two nights, each with its own character and purpose. Her Wednesday night salon became notorious as a "fortress of free thought," due to the presence of Philosophes and scholars, while her Monday dinners were reserved for artists, art scene

THE SALON-KEEPER WHO LOST HER HEAD

At least one salon woman followed her political convictions to the guillotine. Madame Roland and her husband were members of the Girondists, a group of moderate Republicans, all of whom were executed during the French Revolution. The group had begun by meeting a few times each week to discuss the terrible problems facing the government. Madame Roland was the only woman present. At first she listened quietly, mending clothes as the men ranted. Soon, however, she grew frustrated with their "say much but do nothing" attitude. Her eloquent insights and earnest sincerity convinced them to take action. Madame Roland began helping them make plans, many of which accelerated the beginning of the French Revolution. As the person in charge of the Republican/Girondist headquarters, she was executed during the portion of the revolution called "the Terror."

While in prison, Madame Roland did not negotiate to save her own life. Instead, she wrote pages of justification for the Girondist views she had helped shape. She was executed in 1793. Her last words: "Oh, Liberty! What crimes are committed in thy name!"

poseurs, foreign dilettantes, and any celebrities she ran across. This was a break with tradition, for until then polite society did not mix with artists, considering them crude drunkards fit only for cafés, bars, and cabarets.

Geoffrin was an exception to the witty, critical, even cynical persona that had become fashionable. She chose an uncluttered life and considered herself happy due to "the truthfulness of my disposition, the naturalness of my mind, and the simplicity and variety of my tastes." Yet despite her good nature, she made enemies—rivals such as Madame du Deffand, who sought to win the Philosophes to their own salons.

Madame du Deffand was famous for wit alone. She was not wealthy and tended to be stingy, so not even the possibility of free, high-quality food can explain the popularity of her salon. In fact, her cook was known to be one of the worst in France. One guest complained that "there was only a difference of intention" between du Deffand's chef and another who had been executed for poisoning several members of the family that employed him.

> 66 A young author would bring his new play or poem, his moral story or didactic essay, to read to the literary experts, who, in polished phrase and witty epigram, or with a silence more damning than faint praise, would make or mar the success of the work."
>
> —Janet Aldis, *Madame Geoffrin: Her Salon and Her Times, 1750-1777*

Like many women of the time, Madame du Deffand was frustrated by the limitations imposed upon her because of her gender. Growing up, she was a highly intelligent, imaginative, and headstrong girl. But neither living in a convent nor a later marriage encouraged her abilities. Throughout her adult life she had attacks of ennui, a kind of saturating boredom that was a common complaint of women at the time, and this made her capricious and sharp. She made friends easily, but quickly abandoned them when they began to seem dull. She grew as quickly bored with books as with people, and was often chided by close friends for merely skimming important works she then critiqued in oft-repeated, damaging epigrams. She professed disdain even of the Philosophes' ideas, yet her salon was considered one of the most exciting in all of France, thanks to her brilliant if cynical abilities as a conversationalist. The salon was her only avenue of self-expression, and her only distraction from the agony of boredom.

Despite Madame du Deffand's bitter wit and sharp commentary on their work, the Philosophes might have thanked her in retrospect for one great service she performed—the introduction of Julie de Lespinasse to Parisian society. Julie was a poor, illegitimate country relative whom Madame du Deffand hired as a companion. She quickly became beloved of the Philosophes. Where Madame du Deffand belittled them, Julie was all rapt attention, winning their devotion.

Madame du Deffand initially enjoyed the accolades Julie received, thinking that the praise reflected favorably on her. Later she became increasingly jealous, especially of Julie's friendship with the mathematician and philosopher d'Alembert, whom Madame du Deffand had stolen from Madame Geoffrin's circle. When du Deffand discovered that her most prized guests were meeting in Julie's small rooms to talk freely before attending her own more constrained salon, she fell into a rage, saying she would "no longer feed the snake in my bosom." In 1764, after ten years of unpaid service, Julie was forced to move out.

Her salon friends rallied to support her. They donated furniture and set up small pensions to keep her going. Madame Geoffrin, who had not yet met Julie but loved d'Alembert and despised du Deffand, sold three paintings from her collection to pay for Julie's apartment; they later became close friends. Julie wrote in gratitude that the mentorship first of Madame du Deffand and then of Madame Geoffrin had taught her "how to speak and how to think."

Julie de Lespinasse was plain, sickly, too poor to feed her guests, and had no literary talent. Yet her salon remained open daily from five to ten P.M. for twelve years. Her guests were devoted to her, perhaps because she truly loved and revered them. The Philosophes dubbed her their Muse; her salon was called the "Laboratory of the Encyclopédia." Philosophers, historians, and economists mingled freely there, settling literary questions and making or breaking political reputations. People came to her small apartments to gossip, to challenge, to be inspired. They left fired with hope for revolution.

These four salons illustrate the wide range of possibility for modern conversational groups. Baron d'Holbach disliked people, but was able to use his influence and talents to support a group project. Madame Geoffrin subdivided her salon to focus on specific activities and topics, and in the process introduced a previously ostracized group to high society. Madame du Deffand's success rested on conversation and wit, while Julie de Lespinasse was loved because she cared for others and treasured their ideas. The pitfalls of jealousy, rivalry, and censorship are present in these examples, but so is the extraordinary potential for private discussion groups to spread new ideas and influence society.

Salons supported social change by making it increasingly acceptable for women to receive an education, write books, choose their own sexual and marital partners, and take an active role in politics. As French society began to prepare itself for outright revolution, a few salon women stepped into the political limelight, risking exile and execution for their beliefs. One of these women was Germaine de Staël.

Germaine de Staël: A Salon in Exile

Germaine de Staël grew up in a salon hosted by her mother, Madame Necker. As a child, her closest friends were adults such as Diderot and d'Alembert, whose ideals she took to heart. She learned the philosophy of liberation at their feet; as an adult, she was determined to be both politically involved and sexually free.

Through the speeches she heard from the great thinkers of her time, Germaine acquired a lifelong taste for politics and oratory. In 1786, only twenty years old, she married the Swedish minister to France, Baron de Staël, and became an ambassadoress

"Every woman here has two authors planted in her house, and heaven knows how carefully she waters them! "

—Sir Robert Walpole, on a visit to Paris

herself. She immediately took over her mother's salon and started a second salon at the Swedish embassy.

Her father, Monsieur Necker, was now head of state. Germaine was wealthy, idealistic, and living in a rapidly changing society. Wit and politeness had become obsolete. Insight, passion, imagination, theory, and oratory mattered, and she excelled in all of these areas. By 1789 France was on the eve of the French Revolution, and Germaine de Staël was at its core.

Germaine was determined to win love through her eloquence and charm. No delicate beauty, she made the most of her voluptuousness by exposing her generous arms and bosom at every opportunity, even receiving guests in her bedroom while she was being dressed. She continued this practice until her death, scandalizing the more prudish generation of the nineteenth century.

Germaine de Staël

When Germaine became pregnant by a lover with her first child, she fled to her father's home, threatening suicide rather than reconciliation with her husband. Eventually, she won a promise from Baron de Staël that he would leave her alone for the rest of their lives—a not uncommon solution at a time when divorce was unknown.

As the French Revolution began, the revolutionaries suppressed all private gatherings, including salons. The government had ignored them as inconsequential because they were run by women, but the men who had plotted the overthrow of the government in women's living rooms knew better. Every private group became suspect, and people who attended them risked denunciation, exile, or prison. Germaine fled France for the duration of the war.

Upon her return to Paris she was at first enthused about France's new leader, the Italian Napoleon Bonaparte. But she soon realized that he opposed freedom and human liberation, and so turned against him. Her reconvened salon drew all of Bonaparte's enemies, becoming a center of opposition to his policies and his schemes of world domination. Madame de Staël's eloquence had great influence upon the men who gathered there, and many of them were leaders under the new Constitution.

Before long, her salon was not the safest place to pass time while in Paris. Napoleon understood the behind-the-scenes power wielded by salons. A salon led by a woman of Germaine's intellect and connections might conceivably destroy him, and he made it plain that anyone attending her gathering was in danger. The last straw came when Germaine asked her current lover, the French-Swiss writer Benjamin Constant, to read a speech that was extremely critical of the government. Benjamin warned her that it would end her social career, saying, "Your salon is filled with people who please you; if I speak tomorrow, it will be deserted. Think of it." Typically, she replied, "One must follow one's convictions." Benjamin was right. Her salon stood empty from then on.

In 1803, Napoleon put her on a list of "permanent conspirators" and sent Germaine and Benjamin into exile. She fled her beloved Paris for a mansion on the shores of Lake Geneva, remaining there until Napoleon himself was exiled a few years before her death in 1817. Germaine was heartbroken by exile. She began writing novels in which she explained her views to the public, and she tried unsuccessfully to win amnesty from Napoleon. She also traveled throughout Europe, and for several years held a splendid, round-the-clock salon, but reports by Napoleon's spies ultimately made visiting her salon too dangerous.

Salons and the Romantic Period

After the French Revolution, women began to lose their stature in French society. English men's clubs, which dated back to the fifteenth century, became the "new" model for socializing in Europe. The clubs were intentionally apolitical; they excluded women in their charters and met outside of private homes. Salons had emphasized mutual support and egalitarianism, but club members preferred to be left alone or to cultivate convivial, shallow associations with others who were much like themselves. Nineteenth-century French women were not allowed to walk the streets unescorted, visit restaurants, or view sports events. Their gatherings, with a few exceptions, became a trivial social activity known as "the Day."

Women established certain days during which they would remain at home to receive visitors. On their days off, they participated in other Days—sometimes feeling obliged to visit as many as fifty women's homes during the week. Playing solitaire in groups became popular as a means of whiling away the long afternoons. Conversation had lost its fire. The Day became a burdensome round of obligations rather than a source of enlightening conversation; it eventually deteriorated to just an hour a week or a couple of hours monthly, then faded out altogether during World War II.

But with the demise of the old salon came a new kind of conversational gathering. Ambitious literary men, deprived of the once-powerful women's network, began holding their own group discussions. These men seldom felt the necessity for lavish entertainment; thinking and talking were all that mattered in their circles. The Romantic writer Charles Nodier offered his guests only sugar-water for refreshment, candles for lighting, and the floor for seating. Nevertheless, such men became social leaders in their own right, and men have continued to host salons and other private social groups through the twentieth century.

The Romantic Period also saw the spread of conversational gatherings throughout Europe and the Americas. The salon proved itself an important venue for people whose ideas or circumstances had isolated them from the larger society. The groups were often run by women who had been barred from both men's groups and conventional women's society—women stigmatized because they were divorced, Jewish, foreign, poor, overeducated, known for taking a lover or being a lesbian, suspected of spying, or had offended some royal personage. These women, unbound by convention and shunned by society, felt free to welcome everyone else on the fringe, including artists, writers, philosophers, students, and radical politicians. The more innovators they attracted, the more exciting their salons became. Because of their growing fame, they drew other intellectuals and visitors who were previously unwilling to risk their reputations. These unconventional women gained an increasing degree of social influence. Nowhere was this more apparent than in the early nineteenth-century Jewish salons of Germany.

Rahel Levin

Rahel Levin: A Light in the Attic

"The Learned Coffeehouse" and many other German salons began to forward the ideals of human rights that were sweeping through the rest of Europe, allowing Jews to begin coming out of isolation. Among all of Berlin's salons, the gathering run by Rahel Levin was to become the most popular.

Rahel was poorly educated. She lived in a tiny attic apartment on little money, and she considered her appearance "unpleasantly unprepossessing."

In addition, she deeply resented the fact that being Jewish prevented her from joining the learned society of Germany. She wrote: "It is as if some supramundane being, just as I was thrust into this

> "Everyone would really be original if people did not collect undigested ideas in their heads and give them out again undigested. **"**
>
> —Rahel Levin

world, plunged these words with a dagger into my heart: 'Yes, have sensibility, see the world as few see it, be great and noble, nor can I take from you the faculty of eternally thinking. But I add one thing more: Be a Jewess!' And now my life is a slow bleeding to death."

Instead of surrendering, Rahel transformed her despair into fuel for socializing. Unable to participate openly in society, she brought the world to her door. Her garret became the most sought-after meeting place of upper- and middle-class aristocrats—Jews and Christians alike—as well as actors, writers, philosophers, and other emancipated women.

Rahel insisted that there would be no social distinctions made in her attic; that only personality and intellect counted. Sometimes this rubbed visiting royalty the wrong way. Her fiancé, Count Finckenstein, was unable to cope with the social neutrality of her circle, where he was exposed as a rather useless, intellectually inferior man. Although Rahel would have become a wealthy countess and a Christian by marrying him, his inferiority at the salon put her off. Finckenstein cancelled the engagement—a relief to both of them.

Rahel Levin's greatest gift was her curiosity. A guest at her salon in 1801 wrote that her glance "seemed to pierce my soul. I should not have cared to meet it with a bad conscience." He goes on to describe a gathering at which *everything* was discussed, including "the boldest ideas, the deepest thoughts, the cleverest witticisms, the most capricious fancies, all strung together by careless chit-chat. All were animated and at their ease, all seemed equally ready to listen or to talk." He was most impressed by Levin herself: "I heard from her some really inspired utterances, wonderful sayings often in a few words only, like lightning flashes, which went to one's heart."

Rahel's witty epigrams, which she called "harsh truths of the attic," were repeated throughout Germany, influencing a generation's opinions about life and art. From the time she was thirty years old until her death, Rahel Levin (later Varnhagen) demonstrated that a social outsider could place herself at the center of intellectual society.

The Bluestockings of England: Women of Principle

While German women such as Rahel Levin made the most of their intellectual abilities, English women were more reluctant to reveal the same capacities. "Learned women" in England had to expect ridicule. They were considered likely to be unclean,

66 If she wants to go and libel me in foreign parts,
the frontiers are open to her."

—Napoleon, upon sending Germaine de Staël into exile

living in a fantasy world and, worst of all, promiscuous. It was said that women could become crazy with lust from reading. At the least, they would become ill from the strain of study and would be much better off devoting themselves to their husbands.

The fear of being considered too educated made women shy away from studying, lest their reputations be ruined. The learned and intelligent Lady Grey, for example, when invited to see some electrical experiments, quickly took her leave, hoping others would not think her a "Préciuse, Femme Sçavante, Linguist, Poetess, Mathematician, & any other name." In the end, most women who craved education chose a middle ground: They studied, but they remained so virtuous that no one could attack them. Besides shunning any sexual liaison or hint of passion, they restricted their salons to literary topics.

These principled women became known as the Bluestockings. The term was coined by salon hostess Mary Montagu, in a joking reference to a scholar friend who absentmindedly wore blue stockings to a social function where everyone else wore white stockings. She and other women began applying the term to their gentlemen friends and mentors, the special men who ignored society's contempt and willingly discussed serious topics with women. The word evolved to include the women themselves, as well as the philosophy espoused at their salons. Outsiders used it as a term of ridicule aimed at educated women who gathered in groups. Their ridicule backfired. The word was so easily remembered that it soon made the women's groups famous. They were gossiped and written about. *Bluestocking* eventually came to mean simply any woman with intellectual interests.

The Bluestockings succeeded in neatly separating learning from sin, but there was a downside to their conventionality. Their salons were boring. They looked askance at wittiness, enforcing a commonsensical approach that made conversation a serious, quiet, and restrained affair. Nonetheless, the Bluestockings were good-hearted, sincere, and determined women who did not succumb to the rivalries and gossip that had plagued French salons.

Elizabeth Vesey was an exception to the typical stuffiness of the Bluestockings. She was a tiny, wrinkled old crone with an ear trumpet. Delightfully informal and affectionate, Elizabeth was a wizard at breaking up cliques. Her disinterest in collecting celebrities and her genuine enthusiasm allowed her guests to drop their usual formality. She arranged surprises for them. On one occasion, she invited an atheist from Paris to discuss his views; another time, she demanded that everyone cut up colored papers to glue on her bedroom windows. She made certain that people of different tastes and personalities met one another by breaking each roomful of people into small groups, insisting that guests rotate in and out of the groups.

The Bluestockings were both patrons and students of scholars. Through their literary circles, they financially supported new writers (male and female), promoted the writers' work, and introduced them to publishers and critics. Male authors might deride the learned women whose opinions counted for so much, but they could not afford to ignore them. By implementing a strict moral code but tempering it with a deep reverence for friendship, the Bluestocking men and women proved that both genders could mix as equals in chaste but intellectually passionate friendship.

Ottoline and Emerald: Society Hostesses

At the turn of the twentieth century, learning was no longer such an intimidating issue for women. The range of personalities, activities, and styles of conversations had become broader than at any other time in history. The idea of holding meetings in the evenings at regular times was abandoned. Instead, wealthy society hostesses opened their country homes to visitors for whole weekends, or sometimes for weeks or months in the summertime.

One of these English society hostesses was Ottoline of Garsington. Ottoline recalled in her memoirs how Londoners "used to rush in on a Friday or Saturday, some by motorbikes, some by train, and crowd around the table, and then clamour for towels and bathing suits large and small, and run down to bathe in the old fish pond, and afterwards sit or lie on the lawn endlessly talking, talking. And then in the evening play games, act charades, or dance until I thought the old oak floor would fall through." These enthusiastic young talkers gathered at her home to express, among other things, their anti-war philosophy. Bertrand Russell, Aldous Huxley, and D. H. Lawrence were regulars. They spent days and years at Garsington, arguing their beliefs about philosophy, human nature, politics, and literature. Aldous Huxley later satirized the gatherings in his novel, *Crome Yellow*.

Following World War I, the most important English hostess was actually a transplanted American. Originally Maud Burk, she married Sir Bache, changed her first name, and became Lady Emerald Cunard. For a long time, she was ignored by proper English society women, but many later became fascinated by the novelty of an American salon in London. Her gatherings frequently lasted all weekend and were filled with journalists, explorers, scholars, sculptors, poets, and painters. Lady Cunard tolerated politicians and businessmen only if they were philanthropists to the arts.

"Exile is a tomb where only the post arrives.

—Germaine de Staël

If conversation slowed during the long hours, she asked her guests to sing or perform parlor tricks. Harold Acton, a devoted guest, remembers her as

Ottoline of Garsington

a remarkably vivacious woman who "turned conversation into champagne." This talent, combined with her eclectic array of guests, produced "flawless occasions when poetry melted into music and music crystallized into poetry again." Nothing fazed Lady Emerald, and she greatly enjoyed introducing incompatible people to one another. When she later lived at Carlton House Terrace, the Prince of Wales was a frequent visitor, knowing that there he could escape the machinations of his parents, who were trying to marry him off to various princesses. Lady Emerald once arranged for the prince to meet an interesting friend of hers. Her friend arrived in a strange mood, took out a small gun, and placed it on the table in front of him. Alarmed that he planned to assassinate the prince or possibly commit suicide, Lady Emerald casually picked up the pistol and remarked, "Oh, what an elegant object. Is it loaded with black pearls?" and dropped it into her purse.

Her ability to inspire and entertain remained intact long after she had spent her fortune supporting hungry artists and musicians. The bombing of her house during World War II forced her to move into a small apartment where, as Harold Acton recalls, "The war was all around us, bursting and crashing above and below; yet it failed to penetrate that seventh-floor apartment or pollute the conversation."

Other Countries' Conversations

Germany, France, and England are not the only places where open discussion groups proliferated in the early twentieth century. Beginning in 1921, for example, the *Patecnici* gathered weekly in Prague, Czechoslovakia. These "Friday Men" met weekly at Karel Capek's home at five p.m. They originally planned to discuss art and literature, but the salon was so diverse that topics soon included science and politics. The multilingual Capek invited people from many countries, helping them feel at ease by talking to them in their own language. If the conversation stalled, Capek invariably introduced a new subject guaranteed to stir up his guests.

In Spain, groups called *tertulia* closely paralleled salons. These gatherings remain standard social fare in Spain and Latin America today. They were initially named for meetings of *tertuliantes*, or followers of the second-century Christian intellectual and orator, Quintus Septimius Florens Tertullianus. Later, the term *tertulia* came to signify the upper circle or gallery in theaters, where the educated classes and clergymen sat. By the eighteenth century, the word held essentially the same meaning as a literary clique or salon, as intellectuals and nobility gathered in private homes to talk.

In the early nineteenth century, tertulia were common among the middle class; they were held in cafés and the offices of literary magazines. One of the first such public tertulia was a revolutionary group that met at La Fontana de Oro, or "Golden Fountain" Cafe. In his comic novel of the same name, Benito Pérez Galdós described one of the problems associated with holding revolutionary salons in public places: "The radicals pigeonholed themselves in The Golden Fountain, and those who were not radicals were driven out. Finally, it was decided that the sessions would be secret, so the club was moved upstairs. Those who were seated below were paying customers, drinking coffee or chocolate; they heard the frightening uproar from above in the heated moments of discussion and some, fearing that the ceiling would cave in on them along with the whole political heap, took to the hills, abandoning their inveterate custom of frequenting the café."

Probably the best-known twentieth-century tertulia is the one frequented by the beloved Spanish author Ramón Gómez de la Serna, who met with his friends for decades at the Pombo Café in Madrid. Writers and artists gathered every Saturday night to talk, doodle cartoons, read each other's manuscripts, and write. Some came by personal invitation; others dropped by out of curiosity as the fame of the Pombo tertulia spread. As countries in Latin America erupted in revolution, refugees including the poet Pablo Neruda and the muralist painter Diego Rivera found their way to the artistic haven of the Pombo.

"As one switches the radio to a different station, she instantly transposed the conversation into a livelier and more volatile rhythm. With an inspired inconsequency, a calculated attempt, as it were, to appear scatter-brained, her words flitted brightly around the table, settling here, there, and everywhere in the course of their erratic and restless flight. **"**

—Lord Kinross on Lady Emerald Cunard

Ramón, ingenious and imaginative, directed the loud, argumentative discussions and wild speculations. He always preferred his own tertulia to being the guest of honor at French salons, where he detected snobbery. He felt that the French treated him as a performing animal. Ramón continued to sponsor the Pombo tertulia whenever he was in Madrid until, falling into obscurity after a brief period of fame, he became too poor to pay the tab. His tertulia came to an end shortly before revolution broke out in Spain. At that time, political discussions were outlawed.

The Middle East has its own tradition of structured conversation. In Kuwait one might be invited to a *diwaniyeh*. Diwaniyeh, like "salon," refers both to the gathering and the gathering place—a room used for no other purpose. Men (women have separate diwaniyeh if they have any) gather there on a regular basis, usually once a week on a specified morning or evening. If the diwaniyeh belongs to a member of the ruling class, it may be as big as a squash court and filled with expensive and beautiful Persian rugs. A more modest diwaniyeh may resemble a library, the walls lined with bookcases. The diwaniyeh is theoretically open to anyone, but it is usually attended by a core group of men who share similar social standing, religion, age, and education. The favored topic is politics; some Kuwaitis argue that, as a forum for criticism, the diwaniyeh is a pillar of the country's democracy.

As the twentieth century progressed, the visible center of salon culture shifted to the New World, to the country where tribal councils and town meetings had laid the foundation for democratic talk and decision making. The conversational candle began burning brightly in the United States—particularly in the nation's largest metropolis, New York City.

Conversation American-Style:
The Twentieth Century

It is ironic that in the United States, the hotbed of democracy, egalitarian salons were virtually unheard of until the early twentieth century. Ironic, too, that the first "American" salons actually took place in France.

Gertrude Stein: An American in Paris

Paris had become an obligatory stop on the global pilgrimage of writers, artists, anarchists, and others who were searching for perspective in an unstable world. As if responding to a social need, the first American-run salons were held in this city, where American women seeking greater social freedom settled and began to host conversational gatherings for their artistic friends. Among these expatriates, Gertrude Stein was and is the most famous.

The Stein home at 27 rue de Fleurus was a stopover for virtually every visitor to Paris for two decades. The salon came about because people kept dropping in at unpredictable hours to see the collection of modern art owned by Gertrude and her brother Leo. Gertrude was trying to write a book at the time, and these visits became disruptive. "It was not to be written with people coming and going at all hours, and so the Saturday evenings evolved out of necessity and only after nine o'clock," she later wrote.

At the appointed hour, Gertrude would show people into the studio. There, Leo would entertain them with long expositions on modern art while Gertrude held back. Journalist and frequent salon guest Hutchins Hapgood described her as "generally silent, but with a deep warmth that expressed itself in her handclasp, her look, and her rich laughter." Like many good salon-keepers, Gertrude remained in the background, rarely asserting herself but making her presence felt and setting the tone for a pleasant

> **"** If you are way ahead with your head you naturally are old-fashioned and regular in your daily life."
>
> —Gertrude Stein

Gertrude Stein

evening of conversation. She could be very funny, and visitors invariably commented on her beautiful contralto laugh. Gertrude's opinions, when offered, were sharp and clear.

Whether because of Gertrude's generosity or the astounding and disturbing paintings she and Leo collected by then-unknown painters like Matisse, Cézanne, Gauguin, and Picasso, people from all parts of Europe and America eagerly attended her salon. The studio was packed every Saturday evening. Gertrude described the crowd, many of whom were Hungarians, as coming in "all sizes and shapes, all degrees of wealth and poverty, some very charming, some simply rough and every now and then a very beautiful young peasant. Then there were quantities of Germans, not too popular because they tended always to want to see anything that was put away and they tended to break things. . . . Then there was a fair sprinkling of Americans . . . some painters and occasionally an architecture student would accidently get there . . . people came and went, in and out." Her openness to visitors, her willingness to welcome anyone and everyone, is one of the defining features of the traditional salon.

Mabel Dodge: New York Evenings

Just as travelers brought tertulia from Spain to South America, so visitors to France brought salons to North America. The 1910s were a time of radical change in every aspect of life in the United States. Industry, politics, the arts, and social behavior were undergoing enormous upheaval. Young adults began to undertake long pilgrimages to Chicago, New York, Paris, and back again, looking for a way to assimilate the changes taking place in society. They drifted from coffeehouses to speakeasies to art colonies to salons to studios, seeking inspiration and meaning in these way stations, searching for a milieu in which they might discuss their lives.

From 1912 to 1914, one of the best-known salons was hosted by Mabel Dodge in

New York. Her home was the center of a subculture where sheltered, upper-class visitors flocked to encounter laborers and criminals, and anarchist radicals had an opportunity to skirmish with their oppressors. At Mabel's open house, people came to cross-fertilize ideas, rally support for radical political action, argue their views into clarity, and fill up on good free food.

Mabel had first lived in Europe, there becoming an experienced hostess. But, as was common for wealthy young women, she had grown suicidally bored with her life, left her husband, and come to New York, where she affected a European disdain for Americans. New York's high society returned her scorn, excluding her because she was twice-divorced, wore peculiar, long gowns and turbans, and talked mysticism. She was on her own until she met Hutchins Hapgood, an aging journalist who shared her mystical leanings but had far more life experience and had developed a taste for inhabitants of the underworld. Hutchins found her "completely innocent of the world of labor and of revolution in politics, art, and industry," but eager to learn. He began bringing an assortment of interesting characters to her apartment at 23 Fifth Avenue. As Max Eastman (editor of *The Masses*, who didn't care for salons or Mabel) later put it, "A cult arose among them of making friends with criminals."

Her ennui proved a boon. It drove her to live more fully, to open herself to every encounter. This in turn led to an extraordinary tolerance of others and a fearlessness in welcoming absolutely anyone to her home. Thieves and murderers, New York's intellectual elite, the unemployed, strikers and scabs, wealthy poseurs, socialists, unionists, anarchists, suffragettes and birth control advocates, poets, lawyers, artists, psychics, government officials, and psychoanalysts—all were habitués of Mabel's "Evenings." At least once a week, but sometimes two or three nights a week, New York gathered in her home. Sitting on the floor or leaning against the wall, sprawled before the fire or stretched across her couches, they gathered. Birth control advocate Margaret Sanger recalled: "Their clothes may have been unkempt, but their eyes were ablaze with interest and intelligence. . . . Each knew his own side of the subject as well as any scholar. You had to inform yourself to be in the liberal movement. Ideas were respected, but you had to back them up with facts."

Mabel Dodge

Once Mabel established a topic or asked a speaker to start with a short lecture, she rarely said anything. Plain, plump, and silent, she attracted others through what Max Eastman described as a "magnetic field in which people become polarized and pulled in and made to behave very queerly. Their passions become exacerbated; they grow argumentative; they have quarrels, difficulties, entanglements, abrupt and violent detachments. And they like it—they come back for more."

Mabel explained the popularity of her Evenings more modestly, saying they simply filled an empty niche in New York's social scene. "There were so many people with things to say, and so few places to say them in. There seemed to be no centralization in New York, no meeting place for free exchange of ideas and talk. So many interesting people only meeting each other in print! So I thought I would try to get people together a little and see if it wouldn't increase understanding if they would all talk among themselves and say what they thought. And I think I did . . . some who had been enemies for years in the hateful half-truth of newspaper columns came more and more to understand one another as they aired their views together in the open." The group that gathered for her salons combined forces behind several causes, including gaining the right to vote for women, bringing modern art to New York, and a pageant held to make the unreported plight of a group of striking workers public knowledge.

On occasion, Mabel's willing experimentation led to awkwardness or worse. An Evening devoted to a discussion of sexual equality ended abruptly when a young woman named Babs enthusiastically endorsed free love by announcing that she was available to any man in the room. Another night, eight of Mabel's friends innocently decided to try peyote, a substance that an anthropologist friend had brought after studying Native American rituals. For a time the effect was very pleasant and mysterious, as the friends serenely meditated and chanted. But the Evening ended in disaster when one girl became frightened and ran out of the building. They spent the rest of the night hunting for her, and finally telegraphed her father to tell him his daughter had suffered a nervous breakdown.

Mabel ended her salon and left New York in 1914. Wartime hysteria had made her gatherings increasingly dangerous, and she had received threats from the police. Later, some of her friends were tried for sedition or deported. In 1915 Mabel moved to New Mexico, where her home became an art colony visited by the likes of artist Georgia O'Keeffe and controversial author D. H. Lawrence. But the time when great art was intertwined with great politics in her salon had ended.

The Algonquin Round Table: Home Away from Home

As struggling artists and writers—people who had neither the room to accommodate huge groups nor the money to feed them—began holding salons, gatherings in public places became increasingly popular. Consequently, many American salons have been held in cafés, libraries, magazine offices and, in at least one case, a hotel. This latter was the Vicious Circle, a group of creative personalities including writers Dorothy Parker and Alexander Woollcott, humorist Robert Benchley, actor Alfred Lunt, novelist Edna Ferber, playwright George S. Kaufman, and others. These sophisticates met for lunch nearly every day from 1920 on at the Algonquin Hotel in New York City. Frank Case, the manager and later owner of the hotel, eventually provided them with their own large, round table in the hotel's Rose Room; as a result, the group was dubbed the Algonquin Round Table by gossip columnists and hangers-on.

Dorothy Parker

The Vicious Circle was not comprised of heavy drinkers or hedonists. The members were hard-working men and women with high standards for themselves and the world. They despised affectation and snobbery, but they hated shoddy work, false sentiment, and the Establishment even more vehemently. They attacked the objects of their loathing with unrelenting humor, and their witticisms were widely quoted (and misquoted). They roamed together, even when they were not lunching at the Algonquin. Evenings they often went out for a show or to play poker or charades in one another's apartments. Playwright Noel Coward, taken aback after running into the entire group three times at three different places in the course of a day, remarked: "But don't they ever see anyone bloody else?" Although they plainly preferred their own company, they gladly welcomed anyone new into the group, provided he or she could keep up with their sense of humor, had no pretensions,

"One more drink and I'd have been under the host. "
—Dorothy Parker

The legendary Algonquin Roundtable

and worked at his or her craft diligently. The Round Table was a place to share ideas and news, as well as a place to relax. Participants eagerly took up one another's causes. The women in the group were ardently in favor of women's suffrage; some of them wrote and demonstrated actively. The females expected exactly the same standards of friendship and camaraderie as the men, without gentlemanly condescension. When the Vicious Circle dispersed it was because fame, work, and the changing times separated the old group members. But while it lasted, it was a true salon—eclectic, friendly, creative, and democratic.

The Harlem Renaissance: Salons, Dances, and Suppers

Just as Jews in Germany found a social outlet in conversational gatherings, so African-Americans in New York found in salons an effective means of promoting their artistic endeavors and ideas. While many white American artists and writers fled to Paris, black Americans were busy asserting black culture and literature in the United States. Their salons were as varied as any in history. Langston Hughes recalled that "at the James Weldon Johnson parties and gumbo suppers, one met solid people like Clarence and Mrs. Darrow. At Dr. Alexander's, you met the upper-crust Negro intellectuals like Dr. DuBois. At Wallace Thurman's, you met the bohemians of both Harlem and the Village. And in the gin mills and speakeasies and night clubs between 125th and 145th, Eighth Avenue and Lenox, you met everybody."

The Harlem salons perpetuated the best literary salon tradition of hooking writers up with critics, editors, and publishers. Harlem's house rent dances, salons, and high society parties were part of the social round in which writers listened to one another's works being read aloud, discussed the ideologies of their literature, and found patrons. Lana Turner, a salon-keeper living in Harlem today, recalls that: "Their salons were full of the painters of the day, the musicians of the day, the writers of the day. Not only did they come together to talk about their work, they did it so often and so frequently and informally, it was more tantamount to borrowing sugar next door for an apple pie you're baking."

Sometimes they ended up at hair-straightening heiress A'Lelia Walker Robinson's mansion at Irvington-on-the-Hudson for a lavish, upper-crust party. A'Lelia started a literary salon called The Dark Tower on the upper floor of her house, specifically to provide young writers with food and contacts in the publishing world. On the other hand, salonists might go to writer Jessie Fauset's home for evenings of talking literature, reading poetry aloud, and conversing in French. As poet Langston Hughes put it in his autobiography, *The Big Sea*, such get-togethers also allowed salonists to escape from white "faddists momentarily in love with Negro life."

Langston Hughes

But the center of the Harlem Renaissance was writer and poet Wallace Thurman's apartment on 136th Street. Hughes portrays Thurman as a brilliant, critical, and bitter man who was never pleased with his own writing: "A strange kind of fellow, who liked to drink gin, but didn't like to drink gin; who liked being a Negro, but felt it a great handicap; who adored bohemianism, but thought it wrong to be a bohemian. He liked to waste a lot of time, but he always felt guilty wasting time. He loathed crowds, yet he hated to be alone. He almost always felt bad, yet he didn't write poetry." Some of Harlem's most important writers—and *all* of Harlem's young hopefuls—flocked to his house, leading Thurman and Zora Neale Hurston to mockingly refer to the salon as "Niggerati manor."

This was probably the last time in history in which salons blossomed as part of a whole community, as just one dimension of a social life among friends who regularly worked and played together. All of Harlem was a setting and an inspiration to the

"It was the period when the Negro was in vogue. I was there. I had a swell time while it lasted. But I thought it wouldn't last long. 99

—Langston Hughes,
The Big Sea: An Autobiography

writers. The importance of the problems to be discussed, the volatile and vital mood of the place, the sense of being part of a larger group and a time of meaningful change— these elements constitute the fertile soil of all great salons.

Modern Salons: Here, There, Then Everywhere

Following the social disruptions of the Great Depression and World War II, salons became virtually extinct as a regular social activity. The word fell into disuse, except to indicate the places where women go to get their hair done. Many discussion groups were spawned in the 1960s and 1970s, but most had an agenda for specific political or social change. These activist and civic groups are important to our history, but they were limited in scope and different in tone from the usual salon. Conversations were purposeful, and were dedicated to tactics rather than theory. Even the later and still-popular personal growth groups had goals that, for the most part, precluded the wide-ranging, lighthearted mood of the traditional salons.

Nevertheless, a few people maintained the salon tradition, usually with a circle of artistic or wealthy friends. Luba Petrova Harrington held a salon during the 1960s in her New York apartment. Writer John Berendt remembers her "ability to draw even the most reticent grump into lively conversation." Her lively group of regular guests included ex-king Peter of Yugoslavia, *New Yorker* cartoonist Charles Addams, Doubleday president John Sargent, *Harper's* editor Willie Morris, jazz bassist Charlie Mingus, and "assorted artists, writers, hippies, movie directors, blue bloods, and deadbeats."

Any group of friends that meets regularly can become a salon without much fore-thought. The Thinkers and Drinkers, a salon in New Jersey that lasted nearly ten years,

❝ Salons still exist, but the conversational aesthetic has vanished. Cocktail parties are not salons. The talk that takes place at cocktail parties with its discontinuities and roving eyes cannot be called proper conversation. Talk shows might pass as a species of salon if they were less self-conscious and plug-oriented, but the quality of intelligence on talk shows is diluted. While it abounds in sharpness, it often lacks the creative direction of good salon conversation.❞

—Stephanie Mills in *CoEvolution Quarterly*, 1974

got its start in the early 1960s when friends at a cocktail party remarked to one another, "We never really talk." Four couples decided to start meeting for discussion, with each couple taking a turn at hosting and choosing the evening's topic. Cofounder Barbara Neal, now in her seventies, recalls that, "After a few years, we knew what everybody thought about everything." The Thinkers and Drinkers then began inviting guest speakers and guest couples, in order to liven things up and broaden the range of opinions.

Sometimes salons have started with outside support or funding. In the early 1970s, activist and ecologist Stephanie Mills received a Point Foundation grant to hold a salon in Stockholm during the U.N. Conference on the Human Environment, where "eco-freaks," poets (Gary Snyder and Michael McClure), residents of the Hog Farm commune, Native American and white members of the Black Mesa Defense Fund, and other activists were arriving from the United States for environmental consciousness-raising. "All I wanted to do was give dinner parties," Mills admits. "Almost within minutes, funding was available for me to join the gang and set up the salon." She hosted a number of salons in Stockholm, built around various environmental topics.

Stephanie Mills

Back in Berkeley, the Point Foundation again provided funds for Mills "to bring people together who wouldn't necessarily meet, to provide them with a leisurely, gracious environment in which to become acquainted and intelligently converse, to encourage skylarking." Her account of the history of these salons, published in *CoEvolution Quarterly* magazine, planted the seed for the rebirth of salons throughout the United States in the 1990s.

In 1974 Eric Utne, then a young editor, was captivated by Mills's article. He especially liked the word *salon*, with its historical associations and the combined implications of glamour and revolution. The next year, he started what he called "New Age Salons," irregular parties that enabled print and broadcast journalists to "meet their peers and schmooze." It was not so much a true salon as a crush of people, fifty to a hundred, in a large room, but they affirmed Utne's notion that "bringing people together and getting them to talk about the stuff they care about and believe in" is important and enjoyable.

He returned to the salon idea in 1984, as he was starting his new magazine, the *Utne Reader*. This time he asked "certified media junkies from various perspectives" to read a number of alternative magazines, then gather once a month to discuss which material ought to be reprinted in the *Utne Reader*. Soon Utne realized that the people were more fascinating than whatever they were reading. "I began asking them what they were thinking and obsessing about. That question seemed to trigger some interesting conversations." The *Utne Reader* Alternative Press Reading and Dining Salon became a way of "tapping into the zeitgeist," as Utne puts it, and a continual source of new ideas for the magazine.

In 1991 Utne took modern salons a giant step further by reintroducing the word "salon" into the vernacular. The March/April 1991 issue of the *Utne Reader* included several articles on salons. A small advertisement in the issue invited readers to "meet up to 25 other people in your neighborhood (town, bioregion)" by starting or joining a salon, a study circle, or a council. Readers who sent in their names and addresses would receive, without charge, a list of people in their zip code who were equally interested in forming a salon.

The response was staggering. Within a few months, 8,000 people had joined the Utne salons. Within 16 months, 13,000 people had signed up. With the help of a grant from the Surdna Foundation, the *Utne Reader* formed the community service-oriented Neighborhood Salon Association to handle the paperwork. The NSA and the magazine then published a small pamphlet called "The Salon-keeper's Companion" and periodic newsletters to help salon members organize their salons. The salaries and supplies involved in handling so many requests required charging new members a lifetime sign-up fee of $12.

By August of 1993, over 20,000 people had signed up and formed more than 325 salons nationwide. Dozens of articles in the press publicized the phenomenon, and many other organizations began holding discussion groups among their members, readers, or listeners. As Utne had hoped, the salon concept was quickly disseminated far beyond readers of the magazine.

In all likelihood, people responded to the idea because vital, meaningful conversation was missing from their lives. Whether they were looking for friends, anticipating debate, or wanting to diversify their experiences, salons clearly addressed a need that many people had not even articulated until they saw the invitation in the *Utne Reader*. The modern American salon is really just one more meeting place among many, one part of the movement to regain a sense of community and to bring people back into democratic participation in their country. This is the task of the next century—one that has just begun. Every person who has taken the risk of starting a conversational group is now making history.

PART I

Foundations:

Building Your Own Salon

THREE

Getting Organized:
First Steps

Why not organize all this accidental, unplanned activity around you, this coming and going of visitors, and see these people at certain hours. Have Evenings! . . . Get people here at certain times and let them feel absolutely free to be themselves, and see what happens. Let everybody come! All these different kinds of people that you know, together here, without being managed or herded in any way! Something wonderful might come of it! You might even revive General Conversation!
　　　　　—Journalist Lincoln Steffens to Mabel Dodge

Something wonderful *does* emerge from every successful salon, no matter what its genesis. Organizing a private conversational group can be as simple as inviting visitors to drop by at a regular time. On the other hand, the birth of a salon can be quite complex, with regulated topics, carefully selected lecturers, and planned entertainments. Modern salons conduct their activities in a variety of ways, and most salons go through periods of greater and lesser complexity as the needs of the people who attend them change.

Who Makes the Initial Decisions?
Few salons arise spontaneously. Someone must be willing to arrange the time, place, and activities. In some cases, this may be one person who has decided to host a salon; in others, three to six organizers may make most of the decisions and set the tone for the group. The full membership of a group may even become involved from the start in planning and sharing responsibilities. Each start-up scenario will influence the future of the salon.

The least complicated way of setting up a salon is by having one person make all the initial decisions. If you consider yourself a competent, socially savvy, energetic person with a healthy ego, and if you have a reasonably sized living room, a number of friends, and plenty of entertaining ideas, you may want to run the salon yourself. Your personality and interests will determine the mood and goals of the salon; the number of people attracted will depend upon how inspiring they find your vision. In any case, you will be able to shape the salon to suit your needs, just as I deliberately shaped my first salon as an experiment in creativity and building community.

There is a significant downside to assuming sole responsibility for a group. While you don't have to reach an agreement with anyone else about how to conduct the salon, you end up doing all or most of the work yourself. You may find, as I did, that by the time the salon happens, you are worn out from making the preparations; or you may be so busy trying to put everyone at ease that you never relax and enjoy yourself. If particular evenings seem disappointing, you may feel so discouraged that you are reluctant to continue the salon. Worse—and this is a personality flaw I discovered in myself—you may overcompensate by trying to exert greater control over how others participate. You risk losing participants when people begin to resent your rules and suggestions.

In most cases, sharing the decision making and preparations with a core group of people is more viable. When I instigated my second conversational salon, I was living in a new city where I didn't know anyone, so I assembled a small group from the

66 Someone on the list called and arranged a gathering. About six of us arrived at the meeting place, but not the person who called us. He had told one of the people to relay the message to the group that he didn't want to be the leader. So there we sat, and there wasn't anybody to facilitate, so another woman and I tried to get something going, get something organized, discuss how it could be structured. I said, 'Nobody wants to be a facilitator full-time, so why don't we take turns facilitating and coming up with the topics?' I agreed to do the first topic, and I did it on creativity."

—Minneapolis salonist Judy Bell, describing her salon's start-up meeting

Neighborhood Salon Association's list for my zip code. One woman who lived in a good-sized house offered to let us all meet there. I called everyone who had offered to help organize and told them when and where our planning meeting would be held. (Others using a similar list have sent out postcards.) The people I contacted, all of us strangers, met to discuss the practical aspects of running a salon. The entire discussion lasted only two hours; at the end, two of us agreed to create a flyer. We sent it to friends and everyone else on the NSA list, inviting them to the first actual meeting of the salon.

When a small group makes the decisions, negotiations can proceed quickly. The group process is less daunting than setting up a new venture on your own, and it creates a reliable base of members who continue to share responsibility. Anyone who joins the salon later has agreed, in a sense, to abide by the standards and structure set up by the initial group. However, we did describe our plans at the first salon session, asking everyone for other suggestions or preferences.

Most people who don't like the way a salon is set up will simply drop out, rather than confronting the "old-timers" with different ways of doing things. This is especially likely if the core organizers are perceived as an elite, unwilling to hear other members' opinions. As long as the core members and others like the salon, the attrition may not matter, but if some of the initial organizers move away or drop out, there may be no one else willing to assume responsibilities. The salon could then peter out.

If there is a disadvantage to this approach, it may lie in the fact that salons run by a group sometimes lack the overriding vision and resolve that a single, inspired person can bring to the task of keeping a salon in motion.

The third organizing possibility involves inviting everyone who has expressed interest in your decision-making meeting to participate. A relatively large group of twenty or thirty people can work together in defining your new salon—in fact, there are some advantages to this process. Salons that begin with the full participation of all members tend to last the longest and develop the greatest degree of intimacy. These groups are often the ones that come up with the most innovative ideas for running their salons and handling interactions. They are usually deeply committed to building consensus. They are the most likely to extend their relationships outside of the salon—to camp and go to movies together, to share resources. In short, they are likely to build a community.

On the other hand, trying to create a salon that accommodates the views and desires of two dozen people is certainly the riskiest approach. The negotiations involved can be so difficult that the salon never gets organized. Everyone may have quite different ideas about what they want from a salon, what kind of structure it should have, and how much commitment and time they want to put into it. You may need two or three sessions to hash out the details, and people who just wanted to join a salon may quit in disgust. If you choose to accelerate the process by voting rather than trying to achieve consensus, you may lose people who feel that their concerns are being ignored. In most cases, only a few people ultimately have the energy and commitment necessary for running a salon, and these people end up forming a core group anyway.

Each of these start-up methods can work with the right group of people, but the salons started by small groups tend to get off the ground most efficiently and amicably. For purposes of discussion, I'll assume that your salon is being organized by a small group of three to six people.

The Planning Meeting

I would like to stress the importance of a salon finding its own voice. Guidelines and suggestions will be valuable, but every group of people has unique wants and needs. Respect these, and the salon will work for you.
        —Richard Rogers, member of Salon Realité, Washington, D.C.

Your first meeting will be devoted to getting to know each other a little, finding out how each person envisions the salon, and making practical decisions. The following fundamental questions should be considered:

- What kind of salon do you want?
- When and where will you meet?
- Do you want to serve food?
- How do you handle expenses?

In addition, you will probably find yourself discussing more complex topics that will have a greater long-term impact on your salon. These may include:

- How can you build your membership?
- How should you choose topics?
- Who's in charge of what?

This is more than enough territory to cover in one meeting, especially if you don't know each other very well. If you feel the necessity of setting ground rules for salon interactions, you might schedule a second meeting specifically to discuss group dynamics. Meanwhile, keep in mind that even simple factors such as where you hold the salon or whether you serve food can affect the tone, rhythm, and success of your salon.

Arriving at thoughtful, agreed upon answers to these questions can make future organizational meetings easier, or even unnecessary.

The first meeting inevitably sets a tone for the salon itself. I suggest keeping it as informal as possible. Allow time for socializing, and take breaks during the decision-making process. If the group is large, or if a few people hold views that are markedly different from the majority viewpoint, the discussion may get bogged down. There are a few ways to handle a stalled or contentious discussion.

One approach involves scheduling a second meeting and inviting an experienced salon-keeper to facilitate, or to talk about what works in his or her salon. Because so many salons have formed in all parts of the country, you may have a relatively easy time finding someone willing to mentor a start-up group. The NSA provides a directory of salon contacts nationwide. If you can't find a salon-keeper in your area, you could consider hiring a trained mediator to help move the discussion along.

"The Sculleys, the Jensons, the Walkers, Freddy, Joan, Don, and the Bowes. Oh, well, Madame de Staël had to start somewhere."

Some groups have resolved differences by handing out a questionnaire explaining various options to everyone in the group, then tabulating the responses and discussing them at a second planning meeting. If you're really organized, you might send the quiz out in advance of the first meeting and have the results summarized beforehand. A playful group might consider randomizing the parameters, perhaps drawing suggestions from a hat or rolling a die to choose between different possibilities.

As a final alternative, you can decide to settle on one salon format temporarily. Follow up by holding an organizational meeting after three to six salon sessions, to decide whether you need to change anything. If a trial period is agreeable but you still can't decide which format to choose, or if people are simply so eager to start the salon that they have no patience for planning, I recommend adopting the following basic format to start with:

- Hold a basic conversational salon, choosing one topic for each meeting.
- Choose one weekday evening per month (e.g., every first Tuesday), and plan on meeting for about two hours. Stick to the same day and time.
- Meet at the same person's home each time. Ideally, the home should be centrally located and offer a living room large enough to seat fifteen people (on the floor is okay).
- Choose a topic for the first salon by brainstorming a list of subjects, then voting. Allow people to vote for as many topics as they like. When you've isolated one that everyone is interested in, you've found your topic. Keep the list for next time, though.
- Choose someone to make and send flyers announcing the place, time, and topic of the first salon meeting. This person can also act as facilitator for the initial session. At the end of each meeting, ask for a volunteer to create the next flyer and facilitate the next salon.
- Collect one dollar per person, and give the proceeds to whomever is handling the mailing.
- Bring potluck snacks and beverages, but don't plan any major meals.
- Encourage people to invite friends. Add them to your mailing list.
- Think twice about starting your salon during the summer months. In many parts of the country, people are busy with family outings, vacations, gardening, sports, and other outdoor activities in summer. It's often best to start a salon in early autumn or late winter, when schedules are more stable and people are amenable to being indoors.

You may be wondering about the rationale behind these recommendations. In the remainder of this chapter and the next, we'll take a more detailed look at the questions frequently addressed during a planning meeting.

What Kind of Salon?

I have held to the hope that someday in another place I would walk through a door into a golden room filled with bright and glancing talk. No subject there would be too abstruse, no liaison too dangerous. Everyone would have read everything and thought the great thoughts.
　　—Raymond Sokolov, *Native Intelligence*

Following introductions, you might start your planning meeting by answering one or two questions in a round, such as:

- Why do you want to be in a salon?
- What do you hope will emerge from the salon in the future?
- What other groups have you participated in, and how would you like this one to be different?

However the questions are phrased, the aim is to get an overview of the philosophy and expectations of the group. Gauge whether the group as a whole prefers a high degree of structure or would rather be as casual as possible. Do people want to remain acquaintances who share conversation, or do they hope to find friends and form a community? Do they prefer a straightforward discussion group, or are they open to other activities and outings?

It's not necessary for everyone in the group to share the same expectations—nor is it likely that they will. This round allows everyone to hear a variety of perspectives and possibilities. It initiates the process of binding the members together, which in turn simplifies the practical decision making that follows. Next begins the process of arriving at consensus and adopting, through discussion, a format that everyone can "live with." You may want to talk about alternatives to general conversation salons, such as study circles, councils, and creativity salons, which are explained in later chapters. None of these formats are rigid or mutually exclusive. Many salons combine aspects of all of them and vary their focus over time. When you've decided in a broad sense what kind of salon you want, your group is ready to make practical arrangements. For now, I'll assume you've decided to set up a traditional salon devoted primarily to holding conversations.

Society for the Encouragement of Thinking, Stockton, California

When? How Often?

Our talk began with luncheon, reached a climax at tea, and by dinner we were staggering with it. By five o'clock in the morning we were unconscious but still talking.
—Margaret Anderson, My *Thirty Years' War*

The first question most salons address is when to meet. This may be a simple decision to make, because it depends almost entirely on how constrained your schedules are. There are quite a few factors involved, however, including how often you get together, whether to vary the meeting days, and the amount of time you allow for each discussion.

Early salons were conducted in a culture of leisure that afforded participants time to meet daily, or to hang around together for weeks or months on end in country mansions. Nowadays, though, the majority of working people and parents consider even a weekly commitment too much of a strain on their schedules. Consequently, most modern salons meet biweekly or monthly.

A monthly meeting is the easiest to set up, and it's the frequency I recommend to most start-up salons. Choose a single day of the month that works for people in your group, such as the third Tuesday or first Friday, and stick to it. Most salons meet weekday evenings after work. Some meet Sunday afternoons. Very few meet on Saturdays, as a Saturday session seems to fragment the weekend. My preference is meeting on Friday evening, so people don't have to fret about getting up for work the next morning. The guests at my Friday night creativity salon say they sometimes hesitate to come when they are worn out from the workweek, but by the time they leave they feel revitalized and eager for the weekend. Friday night is the traditional meeting time for the Spanish and Latin American salons called tertulia.

You may want to check with the NSA to determine when other salons in your area meet, then set yours up for a different day or week. This ensures that people who want to attend more than one salon won't miss yours due to a scheduling conflict. In a tightly knit community, it might also help you avoid the nasty business of "competing" for members.

Meeting less frequently than once a month undermines continuity and often prevents the group from cohering into a salon. The meeting may instead resemble an irregular party. An exception to the rule is a group that already exists in another context, such as a business or church group that wants to add salon conversations to its other activities. The *Utne Reader* Alternative Press Reading and Dining Salon is an example of such a group. This breakfast salon, which has met every other month for over a decade, works because it includes a core group of magazine editors who are dedicated to attending, and who have already developed strong working relationships. The salon also benefits from having a defined purpose. It is designed to bring together the community members whose ideas have some impact on the *Utne Reader*.

If your group seems intent on building a circle of friends and developing a sense of community, you may decide to meet weekly. Weekly salons reinforce continuity and intimacy in a group. At the same time, they are generally rather informal, less concerned about sending out invitations, deciding on topics, being prompt, and so on. While you might expect fewer people to show up weekly, the opposite is often true, because people more readily remember to come to frequent gatherings.

Many weekly salons taper off after a year or two, deciding at that point to hold monthly gatherings. People who have established friendships find themselves getting together outside of the salon, so they no longer need frequent meetings to support their connections. Other salons start out holding monthly meetings, then increase the frequency as they grow more involved in their conversations. One Connecticut group found that the salon was split between people who wanted to see each other often and others who didn't have the time to meet more than once a month. They responded by scheduling one constant, "official" meeting for the last Monday of each month, and another informal session arranged by those who wanted to get together more frequently.

What Time? How Long?

Most contemporary salons must accommodate the nine-to-five work schedule and consider people's eating habits. Getting together at around seven or eight in the evening on a weeknight often works best. You can assume that most people have fed themselves before coming, but providing light snacks can help keep those who have not eaten focused on the conversation.

I have visited a few salons that meet for breakfast. My favorite is the Jesse James Salon in Northfield, Minnesota, which meets twice a month. Members hold an evening

"The late [Friday] afternoon time works in fact because it is unlikely: the week is winding down, and the Coffee Hour is a pleasantly interesting place to spend an hour or two before going out to drink beer or simply going home. 99

—Pierce Lewis and Wilbur Zelinsky, "The Coffee Hour at Penn State" meeting every second Friday at a member's home, but they also meet at 6:45 A.M. every fourth Thursday in a local coffeehouse for breakfast and conversation. The group's motto: "Talk first, shoot later."

You may wish to consider variables such as weather and daylight. At least one salon varies its schedule seasonally, meeting early all winter and late evenings in the summer, to avoid spending too much time indoors when the weather is pleasant. In general, you can expect your membership to fall off during the summer months. Some salons opt to shut down altogether during July and August, while others plan a single weekend trip or hold daytime barbecues instead of their usual evening meetings.

Whatever time you decide to get together, I encourage you to avoid setting limits on how long you'll stay. Allow at least two hours for conversation, but be willing to go for as long as three or four if the rhythm of the conversation demands it, and if the hosts and the other salonists are agreeable. Having said that, I must add that the first rule of entertaining is to leave them wanting more. It's always better to call a halt while the salon is still bubbling with ideas and excitement than it is to end on a deflated note. If every last word wasn't said, then revisit the same subject at your next salon.

I regularly attended a highly successful salon that ran only sixty to ninety minutes on Saturday mornings. Such short salons encourage brevity and sticking to the point. They can produce fast-moving, stimulating conversations. But because they don't allow time for socializing, they also reduce the likelihood of forming friendships. They are often run in a rather businesslike, controlled fashion. Some people may not get a chance to speak, and rarely will the conversations probe as deeply into a topic as those in more relaxed salons.

If your salon lasts for more than a couple of hours, you may encounter problems such as topic drift and physical restlessness. It can be helpful to break up long conversations with snacks or other activities. Conversations that seem exhausted often pick up after a break. During the first half of a conversation, people tend to air their preconceived opinions and theories, feeling that they've now said all there is to be said. However, if they have time to think over the comments of others, they often return to the conversation with new insights, greater willingness to reveal themselves, and an eagerness to deal with the subject at a more complex and subtle level. Longer conversations allow more time for frivolity, too. People with a little time on their hands are more likely to joke around, swap movie and book reviews, or listen to a new CD that someone has brought along.

Setting a regular meeting time, one that rarely if ever varies, is almost imperative. Start-up salons should select a fixed day and time, at least until the membership

PROMPTNESS

Attitudes towards latecomers can be a real sticking point in some salons. It is important to realize that expectations about promptness are cultural and personal, not global. Even in the clock-conscious culture of the United States many people consider it appropriate and even polite to be fashionably late, feeling that tardiness allows the hosts more time to prepare. Some people make clear distinctions between formal occasions that require promptness (business and school) and casual get-togethers that do not (family and friends). Mandatory promptness means there's a power dynamic in operation—someone in authority demands your timely presence. Not requiring promptness means the group members are all equals, and each life is as important as the next.

Some people take personal offense when people are late to their gatherings. In part this is because the hosts may feel uncomfortable if everyone has not heard everyone else's name at least once. Some newcomers expect to be welcomed and introduced; latecomers sometimes feel ashamed or chastised as all eyes turn on them. I have attended many salons where the conversation was proceeding smashingly, only to be interrupted by a newcomer, then halted by the host for another round of introductions. The thread of the discussion can be lost for ten awkward minutes, and sometimes the original momentum is never regained. I have been guilty of blaming the latecomers for the interruption and condemning them for their lack of commitment to the group. But over time, I have concluded that structuring the salon flexibly to allow for latecomers is the best approach.

If you assume that some people will arrive late, you can simply set aside the first fifteen minutes to an hour for socializing. This period also affords your host more leeway in setting things up. By the time the "official" discussion begins, everyone will generally have arrived, and the preceding small talk will ensure that everyone feels at ease. This strategy can be especially useful for groups that are having trouble attracting enough members to meetings. More people will come if they aren't ashamed to arrive late, and if the salon feels more like a pleasurable outing than an obligation.

A break midway through the meeting is also recommended, as it gives late arrivals a chance to mingle and introduce themselves. I don't halt the conversation or activity to introduce those who arrive after the session is underway, although I will sometimes take them aside to bring them up to speed on the topic. Curiously, once I changed my attitude about promptness, many more people began arriving on time—and they were more eager than ever to get involved in the evening's activities.

stabilizes and communications are in place. If you vary your meeting schedule in an effort to accommodate everyone, many members will be unable to remember the day and time you settled upon. I'm aware of a few salons that tried setting the next meeting date each time. Unfortunately, they came to a grinding halt. Scheduling also wastes precious talking minutes.

The drawback of a fixed, invariable meeting time is that some people who would like to attend your salon may never be able to make it. One solution is to alternate days regularly, as the Jesse James salon does. This can work, but only if you maintain regular contact with all members through a newsletter or similar device, and if the meetings are fairly frequent—at least biweekly, so people who can't attend on a particular day don't have to wait two months to resume their participation.

I wholeheartedly suggest spending an entire day or weekend together at least once a year, so you'll have the opportunity to participate in extended, virtually limitless conversation. Talking retreats allow conversations to continue far into the night. They draw a group closer together, so that the regular meetings are likely to become friendlier, more heartfelt, and more deeply truthful.

Food and Drink

Probably there had never been such a mingling of art, sex, politics, spiritualism, cold meats, and lettuce sandwiches.
        —Oscar Carghill, describing Dodge's salon

Historically, food has played a major role in the salon world. Guests sometimes visited salons just to be assured of free meals. However, many salons rarely served food, due either to poverty or a feeling that food detracts from conversation. I am of the latter opinion, mostly because I tend to get sleepy and stupid when my stomach is full. But many people liven up after eating. For them, eating together signifies a switch to informality, giving them permission to relax.

Modern salons that provide food usually serve snacks and beverages or potluck meals. The Salon Realité in Vashon Island, Washington, whose motto is "Eat dessert, then speak from the heart," begins a meeting with snacks or desserts and 20 to 30 minutes of informal socializing. "This gets everyone there and all the yak-yak out," observed one member. But they don't eat full meals. The group has found that desserts, tea, and coffee stimulate discussion, but heavier foods seem to suppress it.

In certain cases, food can underscore the salon's theme, as it has for the WOWEE (Women of the World Eating Everything) group in New York. These women have

> "Those who choose to wear a watch
> with a chain are trying to convince themselves
> that they are closer to time, and so to life. **"**
>
> —Ramón de Gómez de la Serna, Spanish tertuliano

been meeting since 1990 in monthly gatherings organized around a country or geographical area. A book may be assigned as a focal point for discussion; members then prepare and share foods associated with the chosen region. When the subject was Cuba, for example, members listened to Afro-Cuban jazz, ate rice and beans, smoked Cuban cigars, and discussed *The Mambo Kings Play Songs of Love*.

Eating together is an age-old way to build intimacy in a group. It is the simplest and most comfortable way to socialize. It gives people something to do with their hands, and something to concentrate on as they ponder a subject. Of course, bringing and preparing food means you must invest more money and time in your salon. Potluck meals are a means of sharing expenses, but they work best in a group that is already quite friendly. Near-strangers are often reluctant to cook for one another, but are usually willing to pitch in for expenses if the host provides refreshments.

Timing may determine whether food helps or hinders the flow of conversation. A full meal at the beginning of a salon can make people too sluggish for lively conversation; on the other hand, they may get impatient or restless if they are too hungry. Food can provide a gratifying break in the middle of a meeting, and it may ease the transition to a different activity or conversational mode.

A red hot Louisiana salon: Les Salonnards in New Orleans

The serving of alcohol (and other drugs) gets mixed reviews. Many think alcohol helps people become less inhibited, making the conversation more interesting.

The Deadbeat Club Salon in Alta, Utah, is fueled by java.

Salonist Susan M. Neulist-Coelho considers alcohol a more appropriate drug than caffeine. Her group "drank wine and Italian sodas, but not coffee."

However, in our current social climate, relatively few people are comfortable drinking with strangers, and alcohol, besides being expensive, is not considered conducive to serious discussion. In my own sad experience, the worst part of mixing alcohol with conversation comes when, after solving the problems of the universe and leaving my listeners spellbound, I wake up the next morning unable to recall my brilliance. For this reason, I rarely serve alcohol at my salons.

Money

Our living room became a gathering place where liberals, anarchists, socialists, and I.W.W.'s [radical workers] could meet. These vehement individualists had to have an audience, preferably a small, intimate one. . . . When throats grew dry and the flood of oratory waned, someone went out for hamburger sandwiches, hot dogs, and beer, paid for by all. . . . These considerate friends never imposed a burden either of extra work or extra expense. In the kitchen everyone sliced, buttered, opened cans. As soon as all were refreshed, the conversation was resumed practically where it had left off.

—Margaret Sanger, social reformer and salonist

Salons are meant to be nearly free. They are not clubs or workshops. In my judgment, there should be no expensive dues or fees; if there are, someone is running a business and calling it a salon.

But salons do incur some expenses. The most common of these are for providing refreshments and mailing notices or newsletters. Refreshment costs can be shared by asking everyone to bring something, as in a potluck. Postage is generally covered if each person contributes a dollar per meeting to the member who is handling the flyers or newsletters. If you are planning a more elaborate project, add up the cost of supplies and divide by the number of people who show up. I've never had to ask for more than a five-dollar donation at my creativity salons, and then only for exceptionally expensive projects.

Federal funding and private grants may eventually be forthcoming for salons whose goals are compatible with federal adult education programs or community service projects. Some library associations are already sponsoring salons, mostly by providing space, use of a copy machine, and information. Issue-oriented study circles are sometimes funded through umbrella organizations such as foundations or government agencies. However, the vast majority of salons are self-supporting.

A few salons ask for five- or ten-dollar donations at each meeting, saving the money to finance a big annual party or a weekend retreat, or to hire a lecturer. I would not expect the cost of any salon to exceed that amount. I have heard about businesses that pose as salons, charging twenty to fifty dollars for the privilege of attending. I consider this antithetical to the spirit of the salon.

The Rule of Three

Whatever format and practices you initially adopt, give your salon at least three sessions before you make significant changes. People need to become comfortable with a process before they can make good use of it. Even the most exciting salons flop occasionally, so one dull evening in your new salon doesn't mean that you should toss out the whole structure. The Rule of Three gives people a chance to gain perspective, to relax, to experience the salon as participants rather than critics. After a number of sessions, you can meet specifically to discuss what has been working and consider whether

"There is nothing served about there, neither tea, nor coffee, nor lemonade, nor anything whatever, and depend upon it, Sir, a man does not love to go to a place from whence he comes out exactly as he went in. "

—Dr. Samuel Johnson

changes might benefit the salon.

In everything your salon attempts, trust your own inclinations. I have been to salons that completely contradict some of the guidelines I suggest, yet are exciting, vital, and important gatherings. They work because they evolved directly out of the values, commitment, and imagination of the people who created them.

The Salon Site:
Choosing a Meeting Place

To every man alive, one must hope, it has in some manner happened that he has talked with his more fascinating friends round a table on some night when all the numerous personalities unfolded themselves like great tropical flowers.
    —G. K. Chesterton, author and journalist

Salons were named after a "conversation chamber" in the home, and meeting in a private home can reinforce your salon's distinctive identity. A room that is familiar, comfortable, and influenced by the people who live there encourages intimacy and informality.

However, salons in public places such as cafés, coffeehouses, and libraries have also played a colorful role in the history of salons. The open, freely mixing ambience of a public meeting place can add a steady stream of newcomers with new ideas to your meetings.

Be it public or private, your choice of venue is one of the most significant decisions your group will make. A thoughtful choice can do much to ensure your salon's success. Once you've settled in, you may even find ways to enhance your salon environment.

Meeting at a regular location is also important. Site consistency helps the salon maintain its sense of continuity. Members can easily find their way to the salon month after month, and those who have been absent for a while can effortlessly return. A regular meeting place also helps people relax, as they learn which cupboard holds the glasses and where the bathroom is located. At a fundamental level, people develop feelings of affection for a familiar place.

However, you may choose to change the meeting place occasionally if you're meeting at someone's home. Your members may enjoy variety, or your customary host may need a break. Rotating the meeting place works best with a close-knit group of people who feel comfortable in any member's home. Some groups rotate locations regularly. This is generally done because the group doesn't want to burden any individual with the task of perpetual hosting—or because members believe that a regular host will be perceived as the leader of the salon. Salons in remote areas, which often draw members from many miles apart, sometimes rotate so that people can take turns driving long distances. But there are many practical difficulties associated with rotating locations. You must keep everyone informed about the location, provide directions, and coordinate transportation. If you change locations, you will need an excellent system of communications, including flyers with directions or maps.

The In-home Salon

You needn't be inhibited about throwing your home open to a salon. Few of us can afford to reserve one room exclusively for conversation, so there's certainly no obligation to replicate this ideal situation. What matters most is comfort and a personalized setting. The artifacts of past salons—doodles and poems taped to the refrigerator, swapped books and photocopied articles left on coffee tables, flyers advertising previous meetings—signify shared experiences. They become evidence that a sense of community is developing. Further, they imbue your salon with a sense of place.

Many people hesitate to host a salon in a smallish house or apartment, because they feel there won't be enough space. But crowding is not necessarily a concern. Guests can sit on the floor if necessary. When their elbows and knees are bumping their neighbors, people often begin to open up, feeling that they have entered a friendly and informal environment.

By contrast, talking becomes difficult or unpleasant for people who are spread out in a big, echoing room. Studies indicate that when people are farther apart than eight feet, they cannot see or hear one another clearly enough to feel fully engaged. If there is significant background noise in the room, they must be even closer together. Many people feel lost or insignificant in a large room; they can't establish a cozy territory or find a place to retreat.

It's preferable to have just enough space for everyone, so the arrival of a few latecomers provides an opportunity for some amiable squeezing together. Close quarters only occasionally have a negative effect, and then primarily among strangers. An individual who feels that his or her personal space has been violated may become argumentative. A few others, hesitant to offend people who are sitting inches away, might clam up or simply repeat popular opinions. If you stay alert to these potential difficulties, offering anyone who appears uncomfortable repeated assurances that they are welcome, your salon members will soon feel at ease with one another.

Decor and Seating
A hostess should never apologize for any failure in her household arrangements.
  —Gertrude Stein

Although any comfortable room suffices, thinking about decor can help you maximize your conversational space. Ideally, the lighting should emanate from different heights and directions in the room. Areas of shadow allow people to retreat and relax, while the brighter areas help people see and focus upon each other. Pools of warm light create a "stage" of sorts, adding emphasis when someone leans into the light to make a point. The best lights are those that soothe with their warmth: sunlight, firelight, and low-watt incandescent bulbs. If only blue fluorescents are available, you can compensate with furnishings (including rugs, slipcovers, and wall hangings) that are warm brown, red, yellow-toned green, or gray to make the environment more hospitable. Some people prefer bright overhead lights, but in my experience high wattage, a single light source, or a bulb that is too blue can make conversations feel anxious and forced.

The placement of furniture can serve much the same function as light, drawing attention to certain parts of the room and allowing some people to listen comfortably while others speak. I recommend sitting in that friendliest of arrangements, a circle. In a small circle, all participants can see each other, and no two people are so far apart that they can't easily talk with one another. This consideration is especially important in helping newcomers feel welcome and included.

Circles are inherently egalitarian. They make it difficult for one or two people to

"The fate of conversation depends on three things: the quality of the speakers, the harmony of minds, and the material arrangement of the salon. By material arrangement we mean the complete disarrangement of all the furniture. **"**
  —Madame de Girardin, salon-keeper

control the conversation. By contrast, a person sitting at the head of a rectangular table will almost always assume a dominant role in the group. This happens because everyone can see the person at the head of a rectangle, but those sitting side by side have a hard time communicating. For good reason, we associate long, rectangular tables with board meetings and big family dinners—occasions often designed to reflect hierarchy.

However, a perfectly symmetrical circle is not needed or recommended. A rough amoeba of chairs, pillows, and couches seems to work best. You can place one side against a wall, but be sure to leave plenty of room to move around the remaining perimeter. Let your members rearrange the sofas, chairs, and cushions as they see fit, so they can face different people as the evening progresses. Asymmetry allows people to choose the spot in the room that best matches their mood. Introverts or newcomers may choose a chair further from the center, while extroverts and old-timers may crowd together on a couch. It's nice to offer chairs of various sizes and shapes, to ensure that different bodies can find comfortable seats. Uneven spacing, varied pieces of furniture, and a path around (rather than through) the group all help make your circle work.

You may choose to experiment by shifting the furniture around from time to time. In static arrangements, people tend to sit in the same spots, establishing "territories" and perhaps places in the social pecking order. If you move the chairs, members will sit in new places. The change may stimulate new perspectives and interactions; members who have rarely spoken may suddenly feel encouraged to hold forth, without knowing exactly why.

Shifting the salon seating arrangement is not without precedent. Gertrude Stein once played a trick on her guests, who were artists. Hanging their paintings beforehand, she placed each arriving artist in a chair opposite his own painting. "They were so happy that we had to send out twice for more bread," she reported. "Nobody noticed my little arrangement except Matisse, and he did not until just as he left, and now he says it is a proof that I am very wicked."

Public Spaces

Many people feel more comfortable meeting strangers outside of their homes, but unless the meeting site is chosen carefully the noise, cost, and sterility of modern public settings can be inhibiting. One salon in the Dallas-Ft. Worth area stopped meeting at the local library, in part because the vinyl-covered folding chairs and steel tables there were so unattractive. When the salon began meeting at a member's home, the group relaxed almost immediately, and members were more open in their conversation.

Nevertheless, it is possible and sometimes preferable to hold a salon in a public place.

Many salons do so out of concern for safety, for convenience, or because no one wants the hassle of hosting. Groups that hope to encourage diversity in their salons can often draw a wider array of people by being visible to the public. Public places are more likely to be wheelchair accessible and easy to reach via public transport. Community centers, libraries, and churches may also offer child-care facilities or a play room for salonists who bring their kids.

"It's so noisy here! I knew we'd be happier in a library."

There are three kinds of public spaces you might first consider: eating establishments (cafés, restaurants, pubs); public meeting rooms (libraries, community centers, churches, schools); and the outdoors (parks, pools, campgrounds, lakesides). I attended one salon that meets Thursday nights in a YWCA jacuzzi. The salon was dubbed "A Heated Discussion" by its founder.

If you'd like to meet in a public place, visit it beforehand and evaluate its suitability. Few public places were designed for conversation—in fact, the opposite is often true. Libraries are built to encourage silence; coffee shop owners may purposely install uncomfortable seats to ensure rapid turnover. Some places play loud music or offer bright, echoing rooms, rendering conversation difficult. Other places forbid noisy laughter, beverages, or messy art supplies—all of which can come into play in your salons. Hours in most public places are inflexible. "We found ourselves continuing the conversation in the parking lot after the library closed at 9 P.M.," lamented Dallas-Ft. Worth salonist Mike McCauley. "It was funny for a while, but it got to be an irritant."

Another potential problem is cost. Businesses such as bookstores and cafes are increasingly offering use of space without charge to salons—partly to bring in customers and partly to become more involved in the community. However, many places charge a hefty rental fee. Louise Davida discovered this while searching for a meeting place for her Westport, Connecticut, salon: "When I first looked for places to hold our salon, I tried the public library. There was a space, but it wasn't available till after Labor Day. I contacted the 'Y' and was told the charge is $30 per hour. I called the churches and temples, and they all charge various amounts." Even a restaurant will probably expect your group to order food and drink, a process that interrupts the flow of conversation.

Meeting outdoors is often free, and the setting can be a plus to people who spend too much time indoors. At least one woman, Plum Johnson of Toronto, Canada, has taken the outdoor salon concept with her on a vacation to the beaches of Antigua. There, she approached other vacationers around the hotel pool

Toronto salon-keeper Plum Johnson organized a seaside salon while vacationing in Antigua.

and asked if they'd like to participate in a discussion. They agreeably dragged their lounge chairs into the shallows of the sparkling blue ocean. "Using the six *Utne Readers* I had brought down in my suitcase for just such an experiment, [we] got to know each other," she reported. "The truth of the matter is that most vacationers are starved for reading material in places like this after about the fifth day. They're also extremely malleable. Their defenses are down. Sun, surf, and rum punches do that."

The biggest problem associated with meeting outdoors is noise. This is especially true in urban settings, where most public parks are lined on all sides by roads and traffic. Changes in the weather, insect attacks, and staring passersby can also become annoying. On the whole, outdoor meetings often suffer from a lack of comfort and privacy.

You might also look into "semipublic" meeting places—rooms that require an inside contact in order to gain access. Semipublic places include conference rooms in business centers (often available at night for employees); common or party rooms in

"Aldous [Huxley] had a habit of his own of squatting down by the fire, and of searching about for little bits of stick, which he poked into the embers . . . I don't remember anything very definite that we talked about, but those fire-light talks wove a web of intimacy and understanding between us. **99**

—Ottoline, from *Ottoline at Garsington*

condominiums and big apartment buildings (for use by residents); studios, galleries, and back rooms of small businesses and nonprofit organizations. Semipublic places combine some of the advantages of a home with some of those offered by public meeting places. They are often free and relatively private, yet roomier and more accessible than many apartments. On the other hand, semipublic places almost universally lack personality. They can be even less attractive and more uncomfortable than truly public meeting rooms. They are most suitable for a salon that is nervous about meeting in someone's home but wants to ensure a closed membership.

Next we'll take a closer look at the kinds of public venues inhabited by salons—and at a few "success stories."

Cafés and Coffeehouses

The Turks called them 'schools of the wise.' In Britain they were known as 'penny universities.' In nations from Europe to the Middle East to our own U.S. of A., cafes have always been centers of intellectual and artistic activity, birthplaces of new ideas, foundries of revolution.
        —Camille M. Stupar, café salonist

The coffeehouse or café salon is the most natural outgrowth of the living room salon. At times, it has been the preferred venue for public conversation. Dominant leaders rarely emerge in café society, because meeting in a café requires little planning or organizing. Food and drink are readily available, which may encourage longer talks. People come and go as they please, without invitation or the need to make an extended commitment. Because they are completely available to the public, these groups can be the most egalitarian of salons. Holding a gathering in a café is certainly a good way to make your group visible to the local community.

The biggest drawback to meeting in most modern American cafés is that they are seldom designed for the purpose of leisurely discourse. The management may actively discourage patrons from taking up seats and tables for very long. The comfortable

European tradition of stopping by the local pub or café after work to talk with the neighbors is for the most part lacking in the United States.

If you want to convene regularly in a café, notify management ahead of time and get consent. Find out what the least busy hours are; whether it will be okay if some people abstain from refreshments; and whether you can move tables and chairs around to accommodate a crowd of a dozen or more. Many owners will respond positively to the requests of people who are part of their neighborhood. They may recognize that encouraging a regular clientele is good for business, and that salonists are likely to recommend and frequent a friendly café, even when they're not saloning. If the space is appropriate, you might suggest that the café owner set aside one large, round table for general conversation. This is common in Germany, where every local tavern and café has its *Stammtisch* or 'root table' reserved for groups of friends who get together on a regular basis.

Salon-keeper Erika Sukstorf was remarkably successful in starting what she called "guerilla coffeehouse salons" in Los Angeles. She visited neighborhood cafés, asking the owners if she could designate certain nights of the week as salon nights. She then posted flyers explaining which night an open group discussion would be held in each coffeehouse, defining each salon as "a gathering of individuals who chew on topics of their choice." Erika was present to get each of the first discussions started, but the salons then took off without her, generating more salons in other cafés. She found that people who initially just wanted to get out of their houses soon became very involved. "Every salon has a different character to it," Erika explained. "Coffeehouses are brilliant that way—very open, always changing, always new people."

Sometimes a salon can turn the café into a booming business. This happened to the White Dog Cafe in Philadelphia, which went from being a small muffin shop to becoming a well-known restaurant, thanks in good part to the café's Table Talks. Proprietor Judy Wicks began by hosting lectures at her café. The lectures now accompany Monday night dinners and weekend brunches. Topics have included the role of universities in American cities, conspiracy theories, and the importance of humor in healing physical illness, to name just a few. A Table Talk session sparked the Philadelphia Swing Project, which raised money to supply swings for children's playgrounds.

❝ We don't stay longer in a cafe because the little coffee spoons become nervous."

—Ramón Gómez de la Serna

Judy Wicks went further in demonstrating her community concern by establishing relationships with "sister" restaurants in the city, encouraging her customers to eat in African-American, Latino, and Korean neighborhoods. Theatrical and children's events often accompanied the dinners planned at these restaurants. Employees of the

Erika Sukstorf (right): Guerrilla salon-keeper in West Hollywood

White Dog Cafe also worked with West Philadelphia High School students as mentors, and the restaurant awarded a culinary scholarship to a graduating high school student each year. Judy set up the "Table for Five Billion, Please!" project, through which she invited patrons to accompany her on visits to countries that are diplomatically distant, eating in "sister" restaurants within each country. "It's person-to-person diplomacy," she said. "We call it 'eating with the enemy.'" All of these local and international activities originated with the postlecture conversations. They have garnered much acclaim and a highly supportive patronage for the restaurant.

On occasion, café owners who agreed to host salons have become *too* popular. The proprieter of the Golden Fountain Cafe in Spain became famous thanks to his salon clientele. The cafe scene was immortalized by Benito Pérez Galdós in the novel entitled *La Fontana de Oro* (The Golden Fountain). But Galdos recounted some of the problems this poor man had in trying to control his enthusiastic tertulianos—many of whom spent hours arguing loudly but didn't have the money to pay for drinks. In the words of the novelist: "One of the matters which most concerned the owner was harmonizing (in the best possible way) politics and business, the club sessions and the paying customers. He directed a conciliatory warning that they not make noise; but this, it seems, was interpreted as a first step toward servility. The noise increased, and so the paying customers fled."

Bookstores

Many bookstores host author readings followed by question and answer periods. Some stores invite several local writers to sit in a circle with store patrons and discuss a topic chosen for the evening. Other bookstores dispense with the author focus altogether and simply make their space available to community members for regular discussions. This sort of gathering is identical to a salon.

The Women's Press Bookstore is situated on the border between Minneapolis and Saint Paul, in Minnesota. The bookstore is also home to a newspaper and library. Reading groups and salons usually take place here after hours, either at a large table in the center of the store or downstairs in the basement library, where sofas and folding chairs can accommodate over fifty people. The bookstore actually came about as a result of reading groups.

In 1984 Glenda Martin and Mollie Hoben founded the *Minnesota's Women's Press* newspaper. Two years later they began to hold book groups, intending to bring women together to read and discuss women's writing. The fee for joining the book groups helps support publication of the free, biweekly newspaper. The store started because a number of books were left over at the conclusion of each book group. The duplicates were sold upstairs as used merchandise, and this space eventually became the small bookstore, which now sells both new and used titles. The book groups continue to this day.

By encouraging people to seek out a variety of views and opinions on topics, Glenda conducts her book groups much like salons. In fact, about six months after starting the book groups, she also began holding a salon, printing the time and topic in the newspaper. Unlike those who join the book group, salon participants need make no commitment to return; there is no charge, and no reading materials are involved. As few as ten and as many as sixty-five have turned up for a meeting. Glenda attributed the success of her salon to consistency, as it met every other Friday for over six years at the same time and place, running from six to eight P.M. (although the women were welcome to stay and talk afterward).

As with any potential meeting place, visit a bookstore you're considering to ensure that it's suitable. Noise and jostling can be a problem in some large bookstores. Smaller bookstores—or larger ones that cram every available nook with shelving—may simply lack the space necessary to accommodate your salon.

Libraries

Salons and books also come together naturally in libraries. Dorothy Puryear, a special services librarian, and Ron Gross, a freelance editor, have been hosting successful monthly roundtables at branch libraries in Long Island for about a decade. Like coffee shops, library salons can be explicitly open to the public. As Ron Gross wrote, "The participants are, quite simply, whoever wants to come. A core of 'regulars' soon emerges at each site, but newcomers turn up constantly, drawn by the special attraction of an evening's topic."

Libraries are generally chosen by groups that prefer a more studious, formal approach. They are safe public places in which to meet, and they often attract a diverse crowd. Libraries can also provide resources that no single person has at his or her fingertips, and the easy access to books and databases often broadens the salon discussion. Librarians and volunteers are frequently willing to sponsor the group; they may also lend their time and office facilities in the effort to inform the community about your salon.

Please don't be quiet: A salon meeting at a library

Again, check out the facility before you decide to meet there. Find out if it's appropriate to bring snacks and beverages into the library; be certain it's okay to get a little raucous on occasion. You may need to book the space several months in advance, and you may be required to quit relatively early if you meet in the evening. According to experienced library salonists, it's a good idea to approach the head librarian before going to the library board, so you are not seen as aggressive and threatening. NSA salon-keeper Griff Wigley suggests that you present your group as "citizens who'd like to team up with [the librarians] to foster and promote an idea that's both educational and civic in nature."

Salons and Businesses

As we've seen, salons can help businesses—especially retailers—forge a positive connection with the community. When a business makes its resources and facilities available, it stands to gain loyal, trusting customers who will recommend the business to others. This can be especially useful to a business that is located off the beaten track, or one that is highly specialized. In addition, customers who meet business owners on an equal footing will let the owners know what their needs are, helping the business serve its clientele.

In many cases, the benefits are mutual. Business sites such as retreat centers, conference halls, and hotels can provide excellent, quiet meeting rooms. A successful hotel exists in Amsterdam, Netherlands, called *De Filosoof*. Each room is decorated in the theme of a different philosopher, and quotes are displayed above the beds. As the owner put it, "We want to get philosophy onto the market." In addition, members of the 140-strong Association of Practical Philosophy, formed over a decade ago, meet each month in the hotel's cozy salon to smoke cigarettes, drink martinis and *jenever* (Dutch gin), and discuss the meaning of life. These are teachers, writers, business managers, organizers of cultural events, and journalists. They share a desire to apply abstract philosophy to everyday situations. Municipal officials from six major cities have asked these practical philosophers for help in solving social problems.

Retirement communities and nursing homes offer opportunities to foster intergenerational communication, which benefits both the young and the elderly. One retirement community in Stockton, California, hosts a salon that meets for one hour every week. The facilitator, Mabel D. Balen, reports that the conversations are "drawn from broad experiences in the lives of our members, ranging [in age] from the late sixties to the nineties."

The news and entertainment industries have in a number of cases sponsored salons. Sponsorship offers magazines, newspapers, and radio and television stations new avenues of communication with their public. For the salonists, the arrangement can provide a means of publicizing the group's opinions, suggestions, and activities, leading in some cases to guaranteed media access. This is particularly useful for salons that are addressing—and attempting to resolve—community and social problems.

If you're participating in such sponsored salons, take care to ensure that educational materials provided by your sponsors are fair, objective, and comprehensive. The emphasis should remain on free and open consideration of all alternatives within the specified topics. Salon members may be asked to fill out ballots or questionnaires at the end of their discussions—a situation that can work for or against the salon. On the one hand, members may enjoy seeing their discussions and responses used as a basis for subsequent articles or news reports. On the other hand, the ballots or questionnaires may be constructed in a biased or simplistic manner, limiting the salon members' ability to supply meaningful feedback.

Even salons can hold salons. Beauty parlors and barber shops have been traditionally splendid sites for community conversation. Minneapolis beauty parlor owner Lynn Baskerfield provided her customers with a new version of old-fashioned community involvement. In her beauty salon newsletter, *The Conscious Body*, she let her customers know about monthly council meetings that took place after business hours and tackled a wide range of topics. She also set up retreats for her customers and decided to donate five percent of the income from her business to peace, justice, or environmental groups. In these ways, Lynn showed her customers that she was an active, positive part of society. In return, her customers became loyal and supportive.

Several corporations have allowed salons to meet in their conference facilities after hours. This usually resulted from an employee request, but in the future corporations may find it useful to host salons as a way of improving employee relations. Companies could wisely adapt salon and study circle techniques to provide adult education, build leadership skills, and provide nonhierarchical forums for communication. Conversational groups instill in their members the ability to present complex ideas effectively, and broad conversations beget broad perspectives. Salonists are often good at suspending judgment while seeking creative solutions, collaborating with others, and resolving interpersonal conflicts. These are invaluable assets in employees and managers.

From the salonists' perspective, there are some potential disadvantages to meeting at a business facility. If the salon is held after hours, employees of the company may be reluctant to return to the workplace in the evening. If all salon members are drawn from the corporate culture, diversity may be lacking. And employees may be unable to set aside the customary hierarchy within the business; they may hesitate to speak openly in a salon sponsored by their employers, for fear of future consequences.

For these and other reasons, businesses that sponsor salons should do so out of a genuine desire to serve the community and the employees. If profit or training are the primary goals, the salon will probably fail. Propaganda, sales pitches, and formal training programs have no place in free, egalitarian discussions. A business can provide a place and time to meet and perhaps suggest topics, but it must then allow members to decide how the group is conducted.

As is the case with virtually any salon, your business-based salon will be most successful if it's held in a place where people are allowed to get a little rowdy, and if it's run by someone who genuinely likes people. Frank Case, who managed and later owned the Algonquin Hotel, attributed the abundance of actors and writers who lived there to the fact that he liked them so much. "If a man should stand in Times Square with his heart simply bursting with love for bricklayers," Case said, "I don't doubt that in time the bricklayers would sense it and gather round."

FIVE

Finding People:
Building Your Membership

Give me new faces, new faces.
—Gertrude Stein

Rounding up salon members can be an easy task. Some people simply form a group by inviting their friends, a few coworkers, and family members over for coffee and conversation. But other would-be salon-keepers—especially those settling into a new home—may have great difficulty coming up with enough guests sufficient to launch a salon. In addition, almost all groups experience periods of declining membership, and they may struggle as they try to attract (and keep) new members.

There are at least four ways to draw people into your salon. You can issue personal invitations; you can acquire names from membership lists; you can post announcements in your neighborhood (advertise); or you can attend other gatherings in order to locate people who might be interested in your group.

Invitations

I tend to rely on informal, verbal invitations to friends and casual acquaintances. I also encourage everyone who comes to invite their friends. Salonist Susan M. Neulist-Coelho drew her salon members from women who regularly patronized her espresso stand in Rogue River, Oregon. One man started a salon by inviting everyone he met for a period of time, collecting an extraordinary combination of people. His attendees included members of the South Bay chapter of American Atheists; lesbian prostitutes he met at a picnic; and a number of ministers, ex-priests, and pastors from his religious community.

If your salon is being organized by a small group of people, the simplest approach involves asking each member of the core group to invite five people to the first salon meeting. At that meeting, ask everyone who attends to bring their friends, roommates, out-of-town guests, and interested acquaintances to the next one. This method produces new faces without losing a feeling of connectedness, and any interested newcomer can be added to a mailing or phone list so they'll be aware of future meetings.

You can also underscore verbal invitations by handing out calling cards for the salon. This works best for a salon that meets at one house regularly. The cards can specify the name of the salon, the meeting time and place, and possibly the name and phone number of a contact person. The friends-of-friends method is simple, but it can be a little wearisome. It requires "selling" the salon idea to people who don't know anything about it. In addition, some people would rather not invite friends to the salon. They may be looking for greater diversity than their circle of friends offers, or they may feel that talking to strangers would be more stimulating. Prospective salonists who live in isolated or very conservative areas sometimes believe they are the only ones for miles around who want to talk about wild ideas. They would rather not risk ridicule by inviting their neighbors to the salon. Still others are concerned that factions might develop if salon members bring personal friends. If you share these concerns, if you live in an area where you don't know anybody, or if you participate in a salon that is suffering from membership attrition, you may prefer to recruit through a membership list.

Lists

Membership lists can provide a seed group for a new salon or new members for an established meeting. A big advantage to finding people through membership lists is that you know they're already interested in joining a discussion group. In all likelihood, you won't have to deal with many people who say "Yes!" and then fail to show up. Media organizations are increasingly developing such lists and making them available for a nominal fee.

One of the least directive organizations, which also boasts an exceptionally wide membership base, is the Neighborhood Salon Association. Founded by the *Utne Reader*, NSA was specifically set up to help people find other salon candidates in their vicinities. Those on the list have already expressed interest in forming or joining a salon. The NSA maintains updated lists of salon members in every part of the United States and Canada, and increasingly in other countries. For a onetime, lifetime sign-up fee, you receive a list of everyone in your area who has contacted the association. The salon's core group (or an individual founder) can then create a flyer and mail it to everyone on the list. In many areas, the list contains forty or more names and addresses, virtually guaranteeing a turnout sufficient to sustain lively conversation.

The NSA also provides a directory of established salons, intended for people who want to join groups rather than start their own. Registering your new salon in the NSA directory is an excellent way of ensuring a steady flow of new members and visitors. If your group decides to list itself, you will need to choose an official contact person who will field calls from potential salonists and the media, and maintain an up-to-date description of the salon in the directory. The contact person should be someone with a stable lifestyle, so he or she can be reached at home or at work on a consistent basis. The role of contact person is not generally rotated, although it can be shared by listing two or three contact people in the directory. If no individual wants to serve as the sole contact, you can instead set up a contact phone number, paid for by the whole group. Members of the salon can take turns picking up and responding to messages left on the answering machine or voice mail.

The only potential drawback to being listed in the directory is that you may occasionally get visitors—usually from the press or television, but sometimes from other salons—who come to observe rather than participate. The presence of such an observer can make the regular salon members edgy. They may respond by retreating into silence, or they may propound their views extensively in the hope of being quoted by the media person. The normal give and take of conversation may fall apart. If you are going to host media visitors, you might tell them ahead of time that they will be expected to participate. Turn the tables on them by choosing a topic such as "Censorship in the Press." Then draw them into the conversation as you would any newcomer.

Other organizations also provide membership lists. Some assume a particular shared goal or focus in groups associated with their organization. This is true of the Mothering Friends groups, which get together under the auspices of *Mothering* magazine to discuss parenting and child care. Some organizations ask for a degree of involvement or feedback. The Minneapolis *Star Tribune* set topics for its free, monthly Minnesota's Talking Roundtable Discussions. The circle members were asked to send responses and ballots to the newspaper for later publication, which allowed the newspaper to take the public pulse on policy and social issues.

"Our salon has grown from simply a few people interested in discussion to a family of diverse individuals. 99

—Sharon Waidler, salonist from Decatur, Georgia

Advertising

Both membership lists and networking through acquaintances are fairly safe ways of reaching a relatively narrow spectrum of people who are interested in salons. If you want to reach a wider range of people in your community and you don't mind dealing with complete strangers, advertising for salon members is useful. Jaime Guerrero of Philadelphia, Pennsylvania, started his salon with a mass mailing to everyone on a local NSA list, but only five people kept coming. The core members decided to conduct a poster recruiting campaign. They posted announcements at the places they frequented, including markets, cafés, repertoire movie theaters, restaurants, performance spaces, record shops, and college campuses. An announcement at a popular bookstore elicited the greatest response. The group's membership list eventually grew to include about sixty people although, as is typical, only twelve to fifteen people turned up at any given meeting.

If you decide to hand out flyers or put up posters, make them as brief and easy to read as possible. Any graphics should be bold and simple. A vague, wordy announcement that asks for donations or solicits potluck contributions is unlikely to garner much response. If you meet in a public setting, list where and when you meet. If not, it is probably best to give a contact name and number, so you can screen prospective members on the phone.

Some salons have successfully advertised in local newspapers or posted announcements on local computer bulletin boards. Like posters, this kind of advertising attracts a diverse membership and is easy to discontinue once you've reached your ideal size.

If you have a stable membership, you may want to recruit new members on an occasional basis only. You might do this by attending regional salon gatherings (described in a later chapter) or by conducting an annual membership drive. Ron Gross described the procedure that works for Nassau, New York, library salons: "Once or twice a year the groups throw an open house, which is widely publicized to the community by the library, via its newsletter, flyers, posters, a story in the local paper, etc. Some topic of wide interest is presented, or a compelling guest speaker. . . . Attendees at these open houses can sign up to receive notices of the next few meetings of the group, and some become regular members." A short-lived membership drive of this sort is a good way to stir up interest in your salon without having to deal with inquiries from strangers throughout the year.

Meeting Size

Conversation is best conducted in a group of eight to twelve people. If everyone in your group is committed to attending regularly, you may have no problem attracting that number of participants. If not, you can establish a membership pool of about sixty people, many of whom show up irregularly. How you invite people to your salon and which methods you use for keeping in touch can serve either to expand or limit the number of people who are present at any given meeting.

There are several reasons for setting an approximate limit on how many people participate in your salon. The primary one is that the more people there are, the less likely it is that everyone will talk. Anthropologist Edward Hall has found that, on average, one person in a group of twelve remains silent. In a group of twenty-four, six people will clam up. This is due mainly to physical constraints—the farther apart you sit from each other, the harder it is to hear everyone speaking. A group of twelve forms a circle roughly eight feet in diameter. If you add more people, the participants must strain to hear those across from them. Those with quiet voices or retiring personalities often give up on making themselves heard.

In addition, the more people there are, the more complex their interrelationships become. In a larger group, it becomes harder to remember names and make personal contact with everyone. It also becomes difficult to address everyone's concerns, and to remain flexible enough so that everyone has an equal say in how the group operates. Hall and other anthropologists have found that factions begin to develop in almost any human group comprised of more than twenty people. If your group particularly values egalitarian involvement, establishing community, and encouraging friendships, a larger group probably won't work for you.

As always, there are exceptions. Some salons operate quite satisfactorily with more or fewer members than I recommend. A task-oriented group such as a study circle can function well with as few as five people when the primary concern is speaking in depth on a chosen subject. At the other end of the scale, I have attended delightful salons consisting of as many as thirty people. Here, the goal was to garner as many diverse opinions as possible. A few salons run up to ninety people. Usually, however, these large groups break into much smaller groups for the purposes of conversation.

A salon in East San Diego, California, experienced a sudden explosion in membership following media coverage. Rather than trying to limit the number of participants, the group began breaking into small subgroups two or three times during each session, shuffling the people each time and discussing whatever subjects came up. Each half hour, the group reassembled and counted off by fives. After doing this for several meetings, they were familiar enough with each other that they could have open and productive discussions in the full circle without subgrouping as often. However, if a number of new members show up on a particular night, the salon returns to subgrouping for a time.

A long-running salon in San Francisco, called A New American Place, often attracts as many as eighty participants. At a typical meeting, members see a short presentation, break into small groups for about forty-five minutes, then reconvene with all members for general conversation.

My own groups tend to run large rather than small. I like new faces and the new ideas that often accompany them, so I welcome visitors to my salons. In my experience, smaller groups risk becoming insular; members may begin to avoid saying things

> "Let the number of guests not exceed twelve . . .
> so chosen that their occupations are varied, their tastes
> similar . . . the men witty and not pedantic, the women
> amiable and not too coquettish. **"**
>
> —Anthelme Brillat-Savarin

that might seriously contradict, surprise, or upset others. But some groups have found that a closed membership is crucial for establishing intimacy and trust. Richard Rogers, a salonist from Washington, recalled that members of Salon Realité began talking about the need for "new blood" about a year after the salon was formed. "I think we had reached a level of comfort and wanted to add new members to create a fresh outlook," he explained. However, the salonists decided instead to wait. After a time, they discovered that the original members were able to take the conversation deeper and rekindle their sense of spirit.

Having too few members is a more common problem than having too many. If you encounter the former situation, there's no need to waste time bewailing the lack of commitment or the proliferation of no-shows. Instead, concentrate on building up your membership pool, recognizing that not everyone will come to every salon. Paradoxically, a large, rotating group of salonists can foster both diversity and stability.

I have found that between one-fifth and one-third of those on an invitation list will actually materialize. If almost everyone has expressed emphatic interest, the one-third estimate applies. If your group is just starting, the topic is obscure, or the meeting time is near holidays, apply the one-fifth estimate. Therefore, your total membership pool should be at least three times as large as the number of people you hope to attract. If you want five people at every salon, you need at least fifteen people on your list. A creativity salon with twenty to thirty participants at every meeting might maintain a membership list of sixty to a hundred. I recommend limiting your list to no more than 150, however. At that figure, you run the risk that fifty people may show up at a particular session.

Keeping In Touch

Once you've established a membership base, you'll need to decide how best to stay in touch with everyone. Phone trees, flyers, and newsletters are the communication networks of salons. These internal "media" encourage new salonists to attend, remind infrequent visitors that they are still welcome, and let everyone know when and where your meetings take place.

Back in 1990, I didn't realize how important ongoing information is to a salon. I initiated my first salon with an invitation mailed to everyone I knew. I thought if I simply told people at the first meeting that the salon would be held at my house on the second Friday of every month at 8 P.M., they would come. I soon realized that most people couldn't recall a monthly date—although a weekly one might have worked out. For a while, I spent hours on the phone every month, reminding people to come; finally, one of my friends suggested a phone tree. This innovation became the single most important factor in keeping my salon up and running.

Phone Trees and Postcards

Phone trees work as follows: One person calls four or five other people—the first branching of the tree. Each of these people in turn have a list of four or five people to call, and so on. Ultimately, everyone on the membership list has been contacted.

The first caller is generally in charge of tracking all phone numbers, determining who is responsible for calling whom, and assigning new members to callers. Callers who will be out of town must notify the coordinator, who will then ensure that someone else makes their calls. The first caller can also set an example by making the calls as brief and simple as possible, including the time and place of the salon and the activity or topic scheduled for the meeting.

It's best to make calls three or four days before the session, not much earlier or later. If you call too far in advance of the meeting, some members are likely to forget about it; if you call too late, members are likely to have other plans. Sometimes a phone list gets too long or cumbersome. You can prune your tree by asking everyone called to contact the coordinator and confirm that they would like to remain on the list. Anyone who does not place a confirmation call is dropped. You'll find that some people who only make it to the salon once a year are nevertheless enthusiastic about getting their monthly calls.

A phone tree takes very little time. It's easy to add new people to the list and keep track of old members who attend irregularly. The only drawback to a phone tree is that the first caller may be perceived as the head of the salon. You can compensate by enlisting other people to act as hosts and facilitators at your meetings. Some salons use postcards to perform the same function. Either option works nicely as long as the information you need to convey is merely a short, simple reminder. But if your salon rotates homes or meets irregularly, if you need to provide maps, or if you want to include short readings with your topic announcements, you'll probably be better served by a one-page flyer or a newsletter.

Flyers and Newsletters

In the old days, salonists kept their pens perpetually at hand, in order to jot down memorable phrases, tidbits of gossip, or sudden news flashes that they could pass on to others in lengthy letters. These served as contemporary commentary on salon society, and as newspapers of a sort for those who were unable to attend a salon.

Many modern salons are equally eager to keep in touch through newsletters. The Arlington Utnut Salon in Virginia puts out a newsletter called *Slouching Towards Consensus*, while a Maryland/D.C. salon publishes *Salon News*, or "Snooze" for short. One of my favorite salon publications is *The Epigram*, produced by the ARF (Addicted Reader's Forum) salon of Schaumburg, Illinois. These newsletters often include cartoons, quotes, and short passages from articles on the next salon topic. They may offer recaps of previous discussions and questions for members on how the salon should be run. Newsletters may state the meeting times and places of other salons in the region; announce life changes such as marriages or births among members; provide movie and book reviews; and even offer items to swap. When circulated among friends, newsletters double as informal advertising for new members.

Newsletters create a feeling of continuity between salon gatherings. The Kansas City Public Conversation Salon deliberately supports community-building by including a list of all members and their phone numbers in each newsletter. The names of those who attended the most recent salon are marked, allowing other members to "catch up" by contacting them.

Cups a cafe journal

Volume 2, Number 11   November 1992

"All sorts of people come to these coffee houses, without distinction of religion or social position."
– *Jean de Thévenot*, Voyages (1656)

Cafe Salons • The American Dream • More on Journaling • Poetry • More!

Although the benefits of newsletters are considerable, they are time consuming, and they can be expensive if mailed to a large number of people. In some cases, an aspiring writer becomes the salon scribe, and this person is happy to create and mail the newsletter regularly. More often, though, newsletters are reduced to one-page flyers produced by a different person prior to each meeting. In either case, a donation of a dollar or two from those who attend your meeting should cover the costs of copying and mailing.

I generally don't require people to RSVP. I want my salons to be viewed as pleasurable rather than obligatory, and I don't believe that commitment can be forced. As members realize that saloning is a process best enjoyed through regular participation, they begin to turn up on their own. The salon serves different needs for different people. For some, it may become a touchstone and a community. They will attend often, and ultimately they will form the core group that stays together through years of change. But for other people, salons are simply entertaining, thought provoking, *occasional* fun. Watching the clock, counting people, and requiring RSVPs is generally counter productive. When people come, let them do so unapologetically. Let them come not because they're obliged, but because they're intrigued. You'll have more fun, and your salon will thrive.

I realize that hosts may feel anxious if they don't know approximately how many people will attend a meeting. And if you are planning activities that require materials and preparation, it may be imperative to know how many are coming. A Washington, D.C., salon has solved this problem with a voice mail line. The salon asks everyone who receives the group's flyer to call an RSVP number. Within a few days of the session, the salon host knows how many people will show up. If the gathering is getting too big, a message is left on the voice mail, telling late callers that the salon is full and asking them to try again next month.

Diversity
The fundamental thing is not to forget that the salon is a cultural buffet.
—Mariajose de Calvalho, Brazilian salon muse

Throughout history, openness to diversity has been an enduring and nearly universal characteristic of salons. The salon ethos is one of egalitarianism; of accepting individuals based on their ability to make a contribution; of particular respect for the voices of people who live on the social, artistic, or intellectual fringe. This is not to say that salonists have always been capable of transcending the prejudices of the day. Nor would I deny that some salons have been cliquish and pretentious. But in general, salons stand in opposition to secret societies, private clubs, gated communities, and other manifestations of exclusion. They tend to embrace eclecticism and inclusivity.

This remains true. Modern salonists often start or join a salon because they seek exposure to new ideas and contact with a broader range of people. If the salon proves too homogeneous, many seek members with backgrounds or lifestyles different from their own. Other salon members look for new members when their salon becomes so comfortable that people no longer disagree with one another. A more diverse membership can revitalize such a salon.

Diversity is easiest to accomplish if you strive for it from the start. Begin by considering what diversity means to you, and what kinds of diversity you would like within the group. Diversity can occur along many lines, including age, sexual preference, political leanings, religion, ethnic heritage, language, rural versus urban upbringing, class, education, and marital status.

Most modern salons are quite diverse when it comes to employment. A typical example is The Seaside Salon of Ventura, California. As of this writing, its members included a retired banker, a judge, a costumer, a publisher of art books, a psychotherapist, a puppeteer, a warehouse manager, a boutique owner, a

"It seems to ME that bald, short, lefthanded men over 50 are under represented here!"

schoolteacher, a jazz pianist, and a writer. The group varies economically as well, ranging from "painfully unemployed to quite comfortable," according to salonist Mary Embree. Today's salons are often less diverse in terms of age and ethnicity. Some groups prefer to limit diversity in some respects, while promoting it in others. They want to feel certain that members have enough in common to express themselves freely. Perhaps they want to avoid rifts that can occur, as when married participants feel outnumbered by single people.

Class diversity has caused tension in at least one salon, where the self-educated, self-employed, and blue-collar workers felt that the white-collar professionals and academics in the group condescended to them. The NSA has received several letters from people who have experienced strong political differences in their salons—most often when Republicans have been outnumbered by Democrats. On the other hand, the NSA has received many *more* letters from liberals, asking how to find conservative members to spice up their discussions.

Some salons have chosen to maintain a closed membership—not to avoid contact with different perspectives, but because they are trying to create greater intimacy within the existing group. Sometimes it's important to spend time building a group identity before welcoming strangers into your midst. But in most cases, groups that shut themselves off from other people become more of a club than a community, more of a support group than a salon. They never experience the challenge of encountering a wide range of ideas and experiences, a challenge intrinsic to the salon.

If you have decided as a group to welcome diversity, you can essentially follow the same recruiting methods described earlier in this chapter, but with the intention of casting a wider net. If you use the friends-of-friends approach, invite more acquaintances—and even strangers. I've invited taxi drivers from parts of the Middle East and Africa, because their political observations intrigued me during a taxi ride. I've met nihilistic punks and heavy metal musicians at coffee shops and invited them. I've met people in the course of apartment hunting, shopping, eating out, and going to parties who have subsequently become salon members. I assume that everyone I run into is a potentially fascinating conversationalist, but I always spend time talking to them first. I must trust them before I invite them to my home.

If inviting people on the wing seems too risky, you might visit places or become involved in projects that reflect the kind of diversity you're looking for. Music and sports groups commonly attract people of varying classes and ethnic backgrounds, so you might visit ball courts, drumming circles, or jam sessions. Some salonists have decided to visit churches as a group, and have found a few people to invite at each church. Cultural and community centers often hold events that draw a wide range of people, providing an opportunity for exploratory conversation. You might also try holding a single salon meeting in a church or community center as a means of advertising your group.

When you're advertising for new members, it's a good idea to be frank about your desire for diversity, and to avoid limiting yourself to any one demographic group. Instead, you might describe your group as a "multicultural salon interested in conversation on a variety of topics that affect all of us," or something similar. Describe your next topic, and try to frame it so it interests all kinds of people. For example, if you plan to talk about pollution, you could entitle your discussion "Pollution Doesn't Recognize National Borders." Consider placing your ad in a variety of newspapers around town, or even in national and international multicultural newsletters such as *The Drinking Gourd*.

HIDDEN AGENDAS

People join groups for any number of personal reasons, many of which they are reluctant to admit. Some of these are relatively benign, but others may be intrusive if not recognized and brought into the open. Discussion at the beginning on what people hope to get from the salon and occasionally reiterating the common desires of the group can help avoid dissension rooted in hidden agendas.

Sex is usually one of the more benign agendas, most commonly encountered in open-ended salons that focus on developing community. You'll probably be able to spot people who are man- or woman-hunting. They may walk in, refrain from introducing themselves, scan the room, and talk only to one or two people of the sought-after gender. These single-minded people usually will not return to a salon unless they've spotted a prospective partner. If they do return, remind yourself that flirtations, unrequited love, and passionate declarations have been part of the poetry of the salon for centuries.

Such relationships become a problem only if the friends or lovers become a faction of two—retreating from the group, whispering to one another, and making snide comments. It's generally best to ignore this, unless it gets so intrusive that it's worth pointing out to the whole group.
A sly joke can be an effective approach. The worst case is when a couple breaks up so unpleasantly that one or both no longer feel able to attend the salon. There is nothing you can do in such a situation except express your regret at losing their company.

Other social or personal agendas are apparent when people come not for intellectual stimulation, but merely to be seen, get a free meal, and rub shoulders with hip or well-known people. The more popular salons become, the more we can expect people to show up without any real commitment. Their worst influence lies in reducing the salon to a gossip session or a preening gallery—a problem that can be addressed by simply refusing to play along.

Others come to salons with the intention of job hunting or networking. They are often recognizable by their forced smiles, their hearty handshakes, their wholesale distribution of business cards, and their eagerness to corner people who might be of use to them. The direct approach is best. Point out that your salon is not a networking venue and that their behavior is making others uncomfortable.

The leader or founder should not be exempt from scrutiny. Even a salon-keeper can in fact be a self-promoter or a mate seeker. Some entrepreneurial sorts label their businesses "salons" and charge participants a good deal of money for the privilege of attending. Expensive workshops, lectures, and performances, completely devoid of conversation, have been advertised as salons. All members should question and discuss any charges for participation, and should consider whether they want to contribute to a for-profit venture.

> " The discussion group allows us to reinterpret ourselves by contrasting our knowledge, beliefs, and opinions with those of others. It allows us to shatter our old illusions and misconceptions and learn about ourselves and others. It is this awareness that keeps me going back."
>
> —Tom DiLillo, salonist

You can post announcements of your salon in the foreign-student union of the local college or university. Many academic societies have long traditions of structured, regular conversations on social and political issues. Foreign faculty members and international students may be homesick for the profound discussions they once enjoyed, and they may be eager to make personal contact with Americans who are interested in talking about things that matter.

Think about diversifying along the age range, as well. Post announcements for your salon at local community centers and retirement homes. Older people often have a great deal of experience with organized private groups such as book groups or bridge clubs; they almost always have fascinating life experiences and opinions to share.

Paula Boose, a Romanian woman, wrote to the NSA hoping to find a salon interested in hearing her voice. She described herself as: "Seventy years old, a love vegetarian, live around small rural community . . . trouble finding mutually interesting uncommon topics with people . . . I'm a stranger in the strange land, born by different culture, survivor from World War Two holocaust . . . always I think globally, act vocally."

Some knowledgeable, farseeing elderly people are interested in joining salons so they can talk about subjects closer to life than death. Darlene Coffman described herself as an old gal living in a retirement home, complaining that: "All I hear all day is about one's ails or ills . . . I need to be around people, so I can exchange opinions and talk about more serious subjects . . . I am so excited since I learned I may have the opportunity to talk about current events, world problems, instead of someone's gall bladder." Salons can maintain connections between people of all ages.

If you'd like to find people who are living in an entirely different social context, try inviting high school students. Their unabashed observations on global and interpersonal issues are often gut-wrenchingly to the point, and many teens are hungry for meaningful talk. In the salon milieu, these students may discover caring, trustworthy adult mentors who (to their astonishment) take them seriously.

I also suggest allowing younger children in and around salons. In my experience, they learn best how to behave socially and how to use their minds and creative impulses when they are surrounded by adults who model these skills. Welcoming children also makes it easier for young parents to join the salon. I enjoy hearing children play in the general vicinity of the conversation, even if they are occasionally disruptive. But it's also reasonable for the salon to collectively hire a baby-sitter who watches the children in a separate room. The cost is shared, parents can check on their children, and interested children may be allowed to listen or participate in salon activities. When the salon is presented as a privilege, most children behave well in their eagerness to be included. They also contribute to the warmth, informality, and development of new perspectives in the salon.

Another approach to building a diverse group involves setting up specific goals and discussion topics that are meaningful to a wide range of people. Diversity occurs spontaneously if people have a shared purpose and equal access. For this reason study circles (described in a later chapter), which are educational and aimed at specific political or social issues, often attract a wider range of people than generic salons.

You will also gain diversity if your salon is visible to the entire neighborhood or community. Despite the potential drawbacks discussed earlier, you may decide to meet in a public setting for the sake of diversity. The meeting place should be wheelchair accessible and easy to reach via public transport. If possible, try to provide a common baby-sitter. Post notices on the walls of your meeting place, letting other customers or visitors know about the salon and welcoming them to participate.

Whatever method of finding people you employ, don't forget to invite newcomers back. Ask them if they'd like to be included on your phone tree or mailing list, and encourage them to bring their friends to the next meeting. This is particularly important with those from another country, who may not pick up on subtle gestures or signals.

"Grown people know that they do not always know the why of things, and even if they think they know, they do not know where and how they got the proof. Hence the irritation they show when children keep on demanding to know if a thing is so and how the grown folks got the proof of it. It is so troublesome because it is disturbing to the pigeonhole way of life. "

—Zora Neale Hurston, writer and Harlem salon-keeper

Dealing with Diversity

In every salon, some people stay and others drop out. The group eventually settles into a mix of people who are more or less at ease with one another. In a more diverse mix, there are actions and attitudes the group can implement to enhance everyone's comfort level.

A comfortable diversity depends upon recognizing the eccentricities that lie in every individual. To summarize a person with a few characteristics or demographic labels is to diminish that person's wholeness, to deny that he or she is a multidimensional human being. Instead of acting upon preconceived notions, assume that every individual has unique experiences and opinions.

"Success? Hah! You call that success?"

Avoid dismissive stereotyping—not because it's politically correct to do so, but because stereotypes rarely hold up under scrutiny. As an example, consider Marian and Joe Arminger. In a letter to the NSA, the Armingers described themselves as "staunch Republicans with four children, who are not animal rights activists, who are anti-abortion and anti-population growth control . . . and are anti-homosexual, plus we are also advocates of less government." These are stances one might affiliate with stereotypical conservatives. But now consider that the family members eat only "organic food, including organic, ethically raised meat, don't wear plastic shoes . . . fight against the use of chemicals as three of our children are chemically sensitive . . . [are] pro-natural childbirth . . . pro-breast-feeding for extended length of time . . . and we're both educated." Clearly, these are people who have given thought to a variety of issues, and have refused to settle for simplistic or automatic answers. Unfortunately, they dropped out of the first salon they visited. The couple thought the group was great, but the other members seemed "only interested in like-minded individuals. . . . Obviously, we made the liberals uncomfortable." In the end, the Armingers decided to seek a salon comprised primarily of other Republicans.

A diverse salon is unlikely to stay together unless all members not only expect but *want* to have their perspectives and worldviews challenged. Members must be ready to defend their beliefs, yet allow those beliefs to change when appropriate. If your group is drawing members from different cultural backgrounds, you will probably encounter a variety of communication styles, norms for physical and emotional closeness, educational backgrounds, ethical systems, and perhaps languages. To handle these differences, all members must be curious about one another and frank about themselves.

Here's the paradox: It's important to avoid focusing on differences that can create barriers between members of the salon. As a particular example, if you have one or two members who form a minority in the salon, do not expect them to represent "their people." No Democrat should be expected to speak for all Democrats; no African-American for all people of color; no Catholic for all Christians; no high school student for all teenagers. If one person is somehow expected to represent an entire lifestyle, belief system, or ethnicity, he or she becomes a token spokesperson and no longer participates as an undifferentiated equal in the group. In addition, if a person is regarded as the expert on a given race, religion, or lifestyle, the other group members may become afraid to voice their opinions, lest they seem ignorant or prejudiced.

You can avoid tokenism by diversifying the group along a number of different lines. If people from varying backgrounds are not returning or inviting their friends, examine whether the behaviors you expect in the salon are too rigid. Every new member will alter the dynamics of the group. People from non-Western cultures may be more comfortable arguing or exchanging affectionate insults than other salon members; on the other hand, they may be more restrained, speaking only in measured phrases and remaining silent the rest of the time. Let newcomers know which ideals or norms you have established for the salon (e.g., that everyone should have the opportunity to speak, or that all members must take turns facilitating meetings, and so on). Filling them in on the ground rules and expectations is another way of making them welcome.

If people attend who do not speak standard American English as their first or primary language, the rest of the group may need to speak slowly and clearly, and to offer clarification at important junctures. However, the ESL guests also have a responsibility to ask for clarification if they're having trouble understanding. (The same responsibility applies to English-speaking visitors if the salon is conducted in another language.)

There is some risk that your conversation may become stilted, fitful, or overly earnest in this situation, but you can generally circumvent the problem by engaging in normal repartee, argument, or storytelling, pausing to explain only key points or particular jokes. Too much focus on a person using English as a second language often results in discomfort or shyness.

If you discover cultural subjects about which most of the group is ignorant, take the time to educate yourselves. Ask the most knowledgeable person in the group for suggested readings or topic ideas. For a time, you might turn your salon into a book club or study circle, reading and discussing key texts on immigration movements, slavery, feminism, colonialism, world religions, non-Western history, or whatever topic has emerged. An excellent jumping-off place for exploring issues of diversity is a book of essays entitled *Multicultural Literacy* (published by Graywolf), which includes a list of globally significant people and events. If you prefer to read fiction, devote a period of time to reading novels translated from languages around the world. You might also plan outings to museums that showcase art from various parts of the world; visit different centers of worship; or contact cultural centers to learn about upcoming events.

Some salons have asked foreign scholars and other visitors to give lectures on their religion or heritage, then answer questions from salon members. During the Gulf War, for example, several salons invited Middle Eastern Muslims to provide a perspective on the conflict and the cultures involved. The salonists reported that their prejudices and assumptions were completely reversed as a result. They gained greater respect for a religion and a part of the world they had known little about. Remember, though, that a foreign guest can't be expected to speak for all members of a culture, heritage, or system of beliefs.

It's equally important to explore your own histories as individuals. Take the time to find out about group members' backgrounds, ages, economic situations, studies, hobbies, jobs, travels, aspirations, politics, and religious beliefs. When all members have revealed a good deal about their personal backgrounds, no one will be viewed as the representative of a "type" or demographic group.

One way to learn about each other involves playing a short question-and-answer game at your meeting. One of my favorites is the "Two Truths, One Lie" game. Ask all members to come prepared to make two true statements and one false statement about themselves. All three statements must involve things that no one else would know about them. As each person speaks, the others debate among themselves which statement is the lie and which two statements are true. The speaker is then asked to reveal the truth. Through this often humorous and surprising game, people not only

GAMES SALONISTS PLAY

Here are a few games that might help your salon members get to know each other.

Deep Questions. Question rounds at the beginning of a salon may not have anything to do with the planned topic. Try opening your meetings with personal questions, such as:

Who are you?

What order were you born within in your family (eldest, etc.) and how did it affect you?

How did you feel about your name as a kid? Have you ever changed it?

If you could invite three deceased people to dinner, who would you invite and why?

What are three personal commandments you try to obey in leading your life?

Grab Bag. Salonist Cheryl Stoyle from Paterson, New Jersey, invented an open-ended question game for her salon. First she collects questions from literature—usually questions that people are asking one another in books she's read—or she asks each person in the salon to bring a question they'd like the group to ponder. The questions, written on separate pieces of paper, are placed in a bag. The bag is passed in a circle. Each person pulls a question from the bag and reads it silently. He or she then decides whether to answer it, pass (forfeiting turn), or open the question to general discussion.

Identity Switch. Ask each member to bring an object to the meeting that somehow represents his or her life or identity. At the beginning of the session, each object is placed in front of the person who brought it, without discussion or explanation. Later, members shift places. While sitting behind someone else's object, each member attempts to take on that person's opinions and attitudes—in other words, to represent that object/person vocally during the discussion.

Commercial Games. Packaged conversational games such as *The Ungame* or *Lifestories*, available in most game stores, can spur conversations. You may choose to use the question cards that come with the game in your own way. In dealing with overly intimate questions, salonist Karen Sundstrom, a member of the Ax Murderers of South Carolina, suggests: "If you don't want to answer the question, you can always lie."

learn about one another, but also gain insight into their own assumptions.

Another way to encourage greater mutual understanding involves deliberately changing how the group interacts. If you have thus far concentrated on discussing topics in open conversation, you might try asking more personal questions or adopting the council method of discussion, in which each person speaks in turn without interruption.

Finally, don't forget to celebrate your diversity. You might stage an annual "family tree" meeting, at which everyone wears clothes, brings food, plays music, and shows artifacts that represent any branch on their family tree or any country they've lived in for a significant amount of time. The more you explore the diversity within your group, even if that diversity isn't readily apparent, the more you come to accept the uniqueness of each person and value the amazing range of behavior and beliefs that constitutes humanity. This exploration is the essence of the salon.

PART II

Big Talk:
Conversation
and Leadership

Choosing Topics:
Deciding What to Talk About

If the flow of talk is to get anywhere, if it is to reach a conclusion, it must be confined within a rather narrow channel or it is certain to dissipate itself.
—Chauncey Brewster Tinker, *The Salon and English Letters*

Some people feel uncomfortable with the idea of structured conversations. They are happy to organize logistics like when and where to meet, but they feel that the discussion should then occur spontaneously. They shudder, and rightly so, at the prospect of formal, rigid agendas for what should be a friendly social gathering.

Other people react negatively to the idea of *spontaneous* conversation, associating lack of structure with lack of direction, or with emotional risk. In their eagerness to ensure serious conversation, they may impose so many rules on the salon that the conversation becomes stilted and perfunctory.

Getting beyond both sets of assumptions requires a shift in attitude.

All guidelines impose structure. Even agreeing not to choose topics or establish rules for interaction amounts to setting up a structure—one that may work quite well in a group of intimate friends, or among people who share a common cultural background. The approach may not work as well for diverse groups, or indeed for most modern people, who have little experience in skilled but free-flowing conversation. A more defined structure can actually provide a framework that supports spontaneity, and an ambience in which everyone feels comfortable expressing themselves.

The best structure for a salon lies somewhere on a continuum between an unplanned free-for-all and a defined, strictly governed formal meeting. A thoughtful structure provides the opportunity for free expression while underscoring the sharing of responsibility within the group; too much structure, however, deadens interactions.

> 66 Not the autocracy of a single stubborn melody on the one
> hand. Nor the anarchy of unchecked noise on the other. No,
> a delicate balance between the two; an enlightened freedom."
>
> —Johann Sebastian Bach

If your group is not dedicated to solving specific problems or achieving defined goals, your need for structure may be minimal. Simply choosing a topic beforehand or setting aside fifteen minutes at the beginning of each salon for small talk may be structure enough.

If your group shares particular ideals or a long-term purpose, or if there are strikingly different personalities within the group, you may wish to adopt a more complex structure—perhaps including defined leadership roles or conversational guidelines. Whatever structure you adopt should support the group's consensual purpose, yet take individual preferences into account.

Deciding what you are going to talk about is the most basic element of salon structure. You may agree to let topics arise spontaneously, perhaps based on current news events, movies you've seen, or books you've read. If you're planning a weekend retreat, or if your salon meets weekly, you will have plenty of time for digressions. Most modern salons, however, last for only a few hours each month, and are comprised of acquaintances rather than friends. In such situations, members may run out of things to talk about or have a hard time focusing on the topic. Which topics to choose, how to choose them, and how to narrow them so they're manageable are important considerations for most salons.

What to Talk About

We did not talk so much of politics as of Parisian manners, pleasures and wickedness, of love affairs, theatres, restaurants—all delightful subjects, are they not?
—Guest at Rahel Levin's salon

While any and every kind of subject can spark discussion, topics that lend themselves to broad speculation are often the most stimulating. In my experience, a trivial, passing incident or fad is quickly exhausted as a source of conversation, unless it has wider implications for people's lives. It's a good idea to avoid framing topics in a way that suggests a specific end or "answer." Your conversations will be most constructive when they are pleasurable and playful; when all members of the salon are in a state of fluid curiosity, willing to become engaged, changed, and startled by new ideas.

Consider topics that engross, puzzle, challenge, or move your members to tears and anger. When your group is brainstorming suggestions for future topics, note those that change the mood of the room and those that people start talking about immediately,

STRUCTURE AND SPONTANEITY

In the past, salon-goers did not often find it necessary to debate the merits of structure or spontaneity in their salons. The salons were run by individuals with a clear social vision, in a cultural context that carefully defined appropriate behavior. There is no question, however, that salons of the past occasionally suffered from overorganizing. Jean Antoine de Baif hosted a sixteenth-century salon that was highly successful, but he felt it was too much like other salons. He felt that salons in general lacked direction and achievement. In an attempt to rectify this, he persuaded Charles IX and later Henry III to support him in setting up the Academie du Palais. This government-backed "salon" consisted of readings of carefully prepared speeches. While the founders preened over the Academie's great seriousness, everyone else complained of extreme boredom. Salon-goers then, as now, preferred the opportunity for free conversation to stiff, academic readings or lectures.

Almost all salons in the early nineteenth century were inhibited by the social mores of the day and fears of government interference. In fact, these considerations nearly squelched conversation altogether. Men and women were seated on opposite sides of the room, or in separate rooms, and discussions were limited to inoffensive small talk sandwiched between musical and theatrical performances. Those who wanted to discuss politics or have any meaningful conversation whatsoever fled these stuffy social events and began meeting secretly outdoors, sometimes in the Parisian sewers. This period brought an end to the traditional, private salon.

Beginning in the late nineteenth century, a new breed of salon began to appear. These gatherings were run by artists and writers rather than society queens. They met in cafés or apartments rather than mansions. They focused less on entertainment and food, and more on easygoing, wide-ranging conversation. They often led to artistic inspiration or political action. These salons were at the extremely spontaneous end of the structural spectrum. But they sometimes encountered difficulties, as exemplified by the changes Mabel Dodge's salon underwent during the 1910s. Her initial philosophy, expressed in *Movers and Shakers*, was: "Let It Happen. Let It decide. Let the great force behind the scenes direct the action. Have faith in life and do not hamper it or try to shape it." However, this led to Evenings that were "really getting out of hand ... were too confused and too crowded. I had left it to people I knew and believed in to come as freely as they liked and to feel they might tell their friends to come; but alas! this was a privilege and grew to be abused. Too many hangers-on came only to eat the good supper."

Her solution was to reschedule her Evenings for a different day of the week, implementing "a more definite direction. There will be standards of ability, parliamentary rule, invitations!" While her Evenings retained their rambunctious spirit, the conversations became more focused, based on topics she selected and announced ahead of time. As rigid as it might sound, this structure was in large part responsible for the provocative, memorable gatherings for which Mabel Dodge became famous.

too fascinated to wait for the next salon. Ignore topics you think you "should" talk about if you truthfully find them uninteresting. Salons arise from the need to make sense of the world. Trust that what feels important to your members is truly important. Face even the most controversial or scholarly topics fearlessly.

Almost any subject is fit for discussion if it is presented in an accessible way. Even politics can be reframed as a pleasant gossip session. I have been engrossed by salons that discussed first encounters with racism, defining ethics in a secular society, theories of brain functions, and the implications of bioengineered foods. Modern salon groups such as the Mind Spa, which meets in the Nassau County Library in New Jersey, have happily discussed such eclectic subjects as biofeedback, children's literature, the causes of suicide, the origin of zero in mathematics, and four kinds of luck. A 1992 survey of topics favored by salons around the country (as reported to the NSA) indicated that the most common concerns were topics connected with gender, death, and the quality of life.

I'm convinced that no political, scientific, or scholarly subject is too abstruse for general discussion. If someone in the group suggests an intriguing topic that other members don't know much about, ask the individual to provide a short written synopsis (no more than two pages) or a verbal presentation (no more than ten minutes) at the next meeting, addressing the challenging subject in straightforward language. Try to avoid discussing unusual topics until everyone is given some background material; otherwise, the individual who knows something about the subject is likely to dominate the discussion, leaving everyone else bored, confused, or resentful.

66 I propose that in a dialogue we are not going to have any agenda. As soon as we try to accomplish a useful purpose or goal, we will have an assumption behind it as to what is useful, and that assumption is going to limit us. We are not going to decide what to do about anything. This is crucial: Otherwise we are not free. We must have an empty space where we are not obliged to do anything, nor to come to any conclusions, nor to say anything or not say anything."

—David Bohm, *On Dialogue*

Once your group understands the fundamentals of the topic, members can draw upon their general knowledge and personal experiences in discussing its implications. If salon members feel the need for more in-depth information, you can form a study circle and explore the topic for a number of meetings. You might invite guest speakers or choose relevant readings to obtain more information. The translation of

"Our guest speaker will now introduce our subject: The Reptilian Mind."

difficult topics into everyday language, and the belief that each of us has the necessary wisdom to form conclusions, are fundamental aspects of the salon.

Most salons attempt to strike a balance between "hard" subjects (those related to the natural sciences, politics, economics, and modern technology) and "soft" ones (topics related to philosophy, relationships, sociology, and culture). Whether the subject is hard or soft, you will discover that discussion can range from the anecdotal to the scholarly, depending on the mood of the group and the way the topic is presented.

Judy Bell, a Minneapolis salonist, considers variety the most important aspect of choosing topics. The café salon she attends mixes the political and the cultural with "topics you'll think about in conjunction with your work or your whole life." The salon considers subjects like personal well-being, food, the environment, health care, and prominent issues, spicing them occasionally with unconventional topics like "The Reptilian Mind" or "Non-Ordinary Reality."

Ways of Choosing Topics

Discussion often begins with a check-in round. Each person speaks without feedback. This always seems to put everyone "in the room" and focused. If a topic was predetermined, the opening round gets that topic started, along with other related or tangential ideas. If no specific topic is to be discussed, the opening round always generates several topics. I like this more organic approach, as it gets right to the heart/mind of what we are all thinking. However, predetermined topics do seem to stimulate deeper thought, because we have more time to ponder the topic before salon night.

  —Richard Rogers, Salon Realité

As I mentioned in Chapter Three, I recommend brainstorming a list of potential topics at your first organizational meeting. Allow people to vote for as many topics as they like, then tally the votes and rank the topics. In most cases, two or three will emerge as the top contenders. Evaluate these as a group to decide which topic would best launch your first salon, but keep the list. Expand upon it through regular brainstorming and voting sessions at future salons. The process draws upon the experience and knowledge of everyone in the salon. It's probably the simplest way to ensure a continual flow of new topics, and it's certainly the easiest way to decide what to talk about.

The brainstorming process may not be familiar to everyone in the group, and the technique may take some practice. It's worth learning, in part because it can be used when you're making other decisions or plans.

First, remind the group that brainstorming is a creative process that permits all members to let their ideas range wildly, without fear of judgment or critique. Then pose your problem as an open-ended question—in this case, "What topics would you like to talk about in the salon?" Set a time limit (fifteen minutes is generally enough), and encourage people to make suggestions freely during that period. Ideally, they should feel comfortable saying anything that comes to mind—without hesitation, without expecting a response, and without defending or explaining their suggestions. During the brainstorming period, no one is allowed to criticize ideas; however, a suggestion can be taken further, so it becomes more specific or more elaborate. No judgments should be expressed during this time period, whether positive or negative—not even a shake or nod of the head. If people run out of ideas before the fifteen minutes is up, repeat the question or pose it differently: "What subjects keep coming up with you and your friends?" or "What concerns you or occupies your mind lately?"

One person who is good at summarizing and writing things down quickly should take notes on all topic suggestions. The note taker may ask for clarification as needed, and can ask people to slow down if the suggestions are coming too fast. The "scribe" may also make suggestions, but he or she must say them out loud before writing them down. It may be wise to have two people take notes, in case one unconsciously edits out suggestions that seem unappealing. Some groups prefer to have one note taker who writes the question on a big sheet of paper at the front of the room, then records all suggestions. I don't generally recommend this, because when people are reading, they

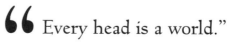

66 Every head is a world."

—Cuban proverb

aren't creating. Some may even be inhibited at the prospect of seeing their ideas on paper.

When the time limit is up, or when members have exhausted their ideas, the scribe reads back all suggestions, again without discussion. Suggestions can be rephrased if the people who forwarded them feel the scribe did not accurately capture their intent. Finally, the list is

Brainstorming Session

read once again, this time allowing some discussion of the suggestions. You may want to evaluate them with a series of questions, such as: "Which ones make you think?" "Are you eager to talk about this one immediately?" "Is it important to you right now?" "Is it something you have not thought much about?" If your group is made up entirely of strangers, the members may initially feel uncomfortable about brainstorming aloud. If necessary, you can ask each person to write three to five ideas on a piece of paper. Pass the sheets in to be collated, then hold a brief discussion and vote on the list of suggestions.

One way to ensure variety is to brainstorm about several broad categories. Put each category, such as technology, religion, pop culture, relationships, and politics, on a separate piece of paper. After brainstorming five times (with five-minute time limits on each category), you will have five different lists of topics. Vote and rank them as already described, then rotate between the lists each time you meet. This not only helps you think up topics, it also broadens the *range* of topics.

At one of my salons, we skip the vote and instead let the person who has volunteered to create the flyer and facilitate the next salon choose the topic. He or she can choose one from the brainstormed list or come up with an entirely different idea.

Commonly shared activities can also become the basis for discussions. Some salons select their topics from lead articles in a magazine read by all members. Others choose books to read or movies to see before their next meeting, brainstorming about the choice of book or movie as you would a list of topics. The same can apply to choosing projects in creativity salons.

WHAT ARE THEY TALKING ABOUT?

The following is a list of topics gathered from salons around the country. It is intended to help stimulate your imagination as you begin thinking about topics for your salon.

Technology and Science
The Impact of Media Images
The Holographic Mind: Does It Explain Psychic Phenomena?
Environmental Illnesses
The Future of Virtual Reality
Extraterrestrial Influence on the Origin of Humans
Defining Intelligence
Twin Studies: Nature vs. Nurture
Biological Destiny
The Future of Nanotechnology
Fundamental Changes in Thought/Technology That Have Most Affected the World
What to Do with Waste Products and Garbage
Getting Off the Grid: Developing Ecologically Sound Energy Sources
Chaos and Order

Politics and Economics
Politicians and Actors: Hollywood Hand-in-Hand with Government
Local Politics
On Creating a Third Political Party
Strategies for Social Change
The Latest Invasion of the Middle East
Who and What are the Progressives Today?
Why Public and Social Leaders Neglect the Environment
Social Activism on a Tight Schedule
The Fall of the U.S.S.R. and the Decline of the U.S.A.
Technological Development and Education in a Viable Nation
Reappraising Marxism
Changing Volunteerism
Buying Locally
How Government Protects People from Themselves
Health Care Payment Systems
The Marginalization of the Masses

Our Modern World
Information Overload
Living Simpler in a Complex World
Urban Happiness
Insurance and Society
The Funeral Business
Live to Work or Work to Live?
The Manipulation of the Collective Consciousness by the Media
On the Elimination of TV
Slave to Possessions (What Could You Live Without?)
What Comprises Quality of Life?
Building Alternative Community
The Psychology of Advertising
Handling Panhandling and Direct Mail Solicitations
Drugs: Why Do We Use Them?

Entertainment and Pop Culture
Tattooing, Piercing, Plastic Surgery, and Other Permanent Alterations
Deconstructing *Cosmopolitan* Magazine
Facing Death: The Joys of Physical Risk
The Taboo Against Humor about Death
Political Correctness vs. Having a Sense of Humor
Your Most Passionate Concerns
Foods We Are Embarrassed to Enjoy
The Greatest Movies of All Time
What Is Art?
The Most Thought-Provoking Movie

Society and Relationships
Community vs. Individualism
Racism (Why Don't They Join Us or Why Don't We Join Them?)
Global Nomadism vs. Village Culture
Universal Human Rights vs. Cultural Relativism
Making Intimate Relationships Last
Is Family Only a Woman's Issue?
Solitude
How Women's Acculturation Affects Men's Mental Health
Who Are Our Heroes?
Team Approach to Management
Textbook Censorship and Propaganda
When Men Get Approached Sexually
Are Pro-Choice and Pro-Life Agendas Mutually Exclusive?
Intergenerational Relationships
Differences between the Women's Movement and the Men's Movement
Career Plateaus
The Effects of Single-Parent Families on Children and Society
The Rise in Hate Crimes
Public vs. Private School Education
The Ins and Outs of Pornography
Growing Older

Spirituality and Philosophy
Personal Rituals
Who Is God?
Childhood Dreams
Coincidences Are Spiritual Hints
Life after Death
Hallucinatory Drugs and Spirituality
Religious Influence on Human History
Do Ends Justify the Means?
Defining Evil
Integrating Spirituality in Family and Work Relationships
Changes in Public Morality
Your Life-Changing Events and Wake-Up Calls
Non-Ordinary Reality

How often you hold brainstorming sessions is up to the group. At most of my salons, we hold a short one at the end of every salon meeting, setting the topic for next time. In this way we are responsive to interests that may change in the space of a few weeks or months. Some salons decide on topics every three to six months, to avoid the need for decision making at every salon. Several salons I'm aware of meet annually, often throwing a potluck party, and decide their topics for the entire coming year.

"No, you're not too late. Cathy's just beginning to put calcium into perspective."

When Judy Bell's Minneapolis salon first started, the members chose topics just two months in advance. This changed, she said, when it became obvious that people didn't want to think about topics that often. The group began selecting its topics every six months, then just once a year. The process of choosing topics is conducted differently in Judy's salon. Topic brainstorming is not involved. Instead, she matches people to months, then the volunteers choose their own topics for those months. "January!" she might announce. "Who wants to take it, and what do you want to talk about?" After each such session, she types up the list of dates, facilitators, and topics, then mails it to all members.

So far, I have recommended choosing a topic before a salon meeting and letting everyone know ahead of time what will be discussed. However, if your salon has been meeting for some time, is comprised of friends with significant common history, or is interested in talking about current events, you may not want or need predetermined topics. Instead, you might start each salon with a round, posing a specific question that stimulates people to reflect on their current concerns. You might ask: "Have you seen anything in the news lately that really intrigued or bothered you?" or "What significant events or encounters have happened to you recently?" Or you could try the question Eric Utne asks to "tap into the zeitgeist" at *Utne Reader* salons: "What have you been thinking and obsessing about lately?"

Pose the question several times during the round. You'll know you've hit the evening's topic when a comment sparks immediate response from the group. Finish the round, take a short break, then return to the most stimulating topic in open discussion. Some groups use these topic rounds at the *end* of salon meetings in order to garner ideas for the next salon. This can be frustrating, though, if people want to start talking about a subject immediately but have to wait until the next meeting to do so.

A more playful approach leaves the choice of topic entirely up to chance. To try this approach, ask each person to write one topic suggestion on a piece of paper, put the whole lot in a bag, and draw. You can also roll dice, use a spinner, or otherwise randomize your topic choice.

Lindsay Dyson of Los Angeles once sent everyone in her salon a small brown paper bag with the following note attached: "this is a GRAB BAG and so is the next salon so GRAB whatever's been 'BAGGIN' or 'BUGGIN' you lately and put it in this BAG and bring it with you . . . then whatever's in the BAG will be let out of the BAG and everyone will know what's in your BAG so maybe it should be something fun or something to eat or something impersonal or political or intellectual but it doesn't have to be it could be something very intimate that you want everyone to know anyway. It's up to you. It's your BAG so fill it up animal, vegetable, or mineral or maybe yours is mainly an air BAG it's okay it's your BAG so have fun with/in your BAG and we'll see you and your BAG next week. BAGISM LIVES."

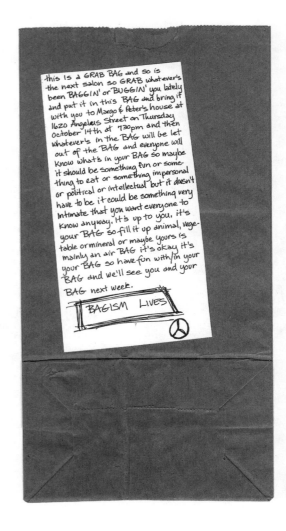

A SIXTIES SALON

The word *salon* was not often heard in the 1960s, but salon-style conversations on a wide range of topics were happening nonetheless. From a letter received by the Neighborhood Salon Association:

"Saloning is a new word to me, but the concept is one dear to my heart. In the early 1960s I was a prime mover in the organization of a Friday Morning Conversation Group in Hollywood, California, which rapidly grew from four to twenty-six, the majority of whom might be present at any particular session. We were a vastly diverse group, including a Ph.D. psychologist, a film editor, a book publisher, teachers, activists, and homemakers. We met for three hours every Friday morning, rotating from home to home among the members who had domiciles large enough to accommodate the group and their children, for whom we hired two on-scene baby-sitters to keep them safely occupied nearby but out of the range of the conversations.

"Our conversations ranged widely from homosexuality, prayer in public schools, local issues confronting candidates for city offices, bodies of work by an author, the historical, biological, and social roles of women, etc., etc. We had no by-laws or officers except for the one rule that if a participant stated something as fact, it should be provable, or if opinion, labeled as opinion. We rotated two roles: that of a facilitator to arrange for and disseminate word of the next meeting place, and a moderator to assure that no one speaker dominated the group. Occasionally those interested would stay on for lunch in order to explore new topics for discussion, which would then be announced for a three-month period, during which participants could read up and prepare for our freewheeling discussions.

"We steered away from 'guest speakers,' except for an occasional representative from a group such as the Matachine Society (male homosexuals seeking to achieve legislatively their human rights) or all of the candidates for Los Angeles City Council (who all came eagerly, and who participated fully). We never discussed a book, but always the body of work by an author, seeking to discover commonalities, style, and growth from book to book.

"That Friday Morning Conversation Group was the most memorable ongoing experience of my life, and some of my lifelong friendships were made in it."

—Carolyn Wardner Buck, 1992

Narrowing Topics

There are no uninteresting things, there are only uninterested people.

—G. K. Chesterton, English author

After a year or two, some salonists complain that they have exhausted the range of discussion topics. This is most likely to happen when one person has dominated the salon and has run out of ideas. The problem in this case is easily solved by having the whole group brainstorm and vote. But an entire group may sometimes feel at a loss for things to talk about, or feel that their conversations are getting stale and repetitive.

The simplest way to be certain you have plenty to talk about involves narrowing or personalizing your topics. When a subject is too broad, people have a hard time knowing where to begin; they stutter around the topic until they manage to latch onto one particular aspect of it. When that aspect is explored, they feel they've covered the entire topic. A general subject with a host of emotional overtones and social implications is even more likely to stop conversation dead in its tracks. Few people can talk about racism, for example, without getting lost in the sheer enormity of the problem. But if you break it down into more specific terms that relate to people's lives, you'll suddenly have a proliferation of topics to

"Anybody have anything to add about root canal therapy?"

choose from, and your conversations are likely to become lively, imaginative, and provocative.

You can narrow the subject by recasting it as a debate or a question with a specific title. The umbrella topic of racism could become: "The Rise of Hate Crimes," "Race Prejudice versus Class Prejudice," "Racism in Schools: Does Integration Work?," "Media Portrayal of Ethnic Minorities," "Ethnic Humor: Catharsis, Acceptance, or

> 66 In the most blissful hours, clocks cease to exist at all."
>
> —Ramón Gómez de la Serna, Spanish salon-keeper

Prejudice?" and so on.

Another way to focus your topic and stimulate discussion is by posing specific questions to the group. Open the salon with a question related to the larger topic: "When did you first become aware of racism?" "How does racism affect you in your daily life?" "How have you been harmed by racism?" "Do you think racism is a natural or learned response?" Some salons formalize this process by asking a specific question in a round, during which no interruption is allowed. Then the topic is opened to general conversation. The initial questions often elicit thoughtful and sensitive responses, building a foundation of trust and honesty that prevails throughout the conversation.

Salonist Judy Bell

It's not only weighty, difficult topics that can benefit from good questions. One of the most enjoyable salons I ever attended was on the subject of solitude. Judy Bell started it off by reading a few quotes on the joys of solitude, then explained briefly why the subject had meaning for her. She opened the discussion by posing the question: "What is the most special place that you go to be alone?" She then began jotting down the places mentioned so she could visit them later. I had been expecting a more philosophical discussion, but the unexpected personal tack elicited more concrete and interesting responses. As others began relating their solitary experiences, I was imaginatively transported into their lives. At the same time (and much to my surprise) I began recalling my own joyful, solitary times.

As the answers wound down, Judy shot out her next question: "What do you do when you're alone?" Again, more personal experiences came pouring out, and we discovered that we held many of them in common. Then she asked: "What things do you reserve only for yourself?," which sent the conversation off in a more philosophical direction. Later, the group discussed related issues, such as how to maintain a sense of independence in a romantic relationship. The conversation continued throughout the evening, never flagging, and everyone had a chance to speak from personal experience. Judy brought the salon to a close by reading back the list of places where people had gone to experience solitude, then reading a final quote gleaned from a book.

Short readings (not more than half a page) and questions related to the topic can help narrow the topic to a manageable size. "Why" questions will usually lead to philosophical discussions. Questions beginning with "describe" or "what" will encourage personal stories. "How" queries will engender practical outcomes and problem solving. I suggest using questions judiciously. Don't ask questions just because you went to the trouble of thinking them up. The best questions are often those posed spontaneously by others in the salon. Questions should stimulate, not direct. With the exception of the initial query, they should be derived from the conversation.

Most salons expect to cover each topic in a two- or three-hour session. Members may consider digressions disruptive—and most salons do run smoothly when everyone adheres to the chosen subject. But your salon can take a more radical approach to conversation by endorsing digression. In a sense, a digression is a spontaneously generated new topic—one that may grab people's attention more forcefully than the original topic. You may choose to let digressions take you on new paths, then return to the original topic later in the evening or at another session. Permitting conversations to take their own course works best if your salon meets fairly frequently, but it can benefit any salon. The anarchy of digression forces members to pay close attention to the flow of conversation.

Salons that meet less frequently but would like to try the free-flowing approach to conversation can open each salon by discussing any new thoughts that have arisen about the last session's topic before broaching the next subject. This provides continuity, gives those who were absent from the last meeting a chance to comment, and lets those who don't think quickly in the heat of discussion articulate ideas they've come

"That Evening was not successful. There had been no form to it. Of course that was the risk one took when one let things be and did not try to shape events or direct people there. Sometimes there would be a sudden quickening of the vibration in the place and men would surprise themselves by their own eloquence—things would happen of their own accord. And then again it would be quite flat as on this occasion. "

—Mabel Dodge, *Movers and Shakers*

up with since the last session. The conversation may become more animated the second time around; you may even need to abandon your planned topic.

Indirectly, I am encouraging you to practice ignoring the clock. You may have to break up a meeting at a particular time because people need to go home, but that doesn't mean the conversation must end. Conversations have their own lifetimes; some are brief and bright, while others last many hours over the course of months or years. Any new point of view, discovery, or event can resurrect discussion of an old topic. If your group is willing to return to a subject again and again, each time with deeper insight, you will never run out of conversation.

SEVEN

Conversational Skills:
The Art of Successful Conversation

You go to see each other; you talk about the good weather and the bad; everyone says, unaffectedly, what passes through his head; some are grave, others extravagant; some are old, and others are young; some are profound, and several are innocent. Madame asks a malicious question; Monsieur makes a biting answer. An enthusiast eagerly tells a story, a frondeur makes a harsh criticism; a gossip interrupts the conversation, an epigram wakes it up, a passionate tribute sets it afire. . . . A wild joke brings it to an end, and puts everyone into agreement. Time passes, people separate; everyone is happy, everyone has had his say, a happy word that he did not think he was destined to utter. Ideas have circulated; people have learned a story that they did not know, an interesting detail; they are still laughing about someone's mad idea, the charming innocence of that young girl, the witty persistence of that old scholar, and it happens that, without premeditation, and without a plan for conversation, they have talked.
—Madame de Girardin, salon-keeper known as "the Tenth Muse"

We all grow up using language, but few in modern times have been raised with an appreciation and understanding of *conversation*. If we receive any education in verbal interaction, it is often through that metaphor of war called "debate." We are taught how to use words strategically to attack an opponent's weak points; to defend our opinions; to cut our opponent to shreds with a few sharp words; to shoot down someone else's ideas; and to demolish their arguments. At best, we learn to negotiate an occasional compromise; more commonly we are expected to win or lose the discussion, to bring the opponent around to our way of thinking or concede defeat.

This is not the only way—or the most productive way—to converse. In other countries and other times, talk has been revered and consciously practiced. There are cultures today, particularly in Africa and the Pacific Islands, where oratorical skills are the key to political power, where humorous play with language is the same as social brilliance, and where achieving consensus through conversation is the foundation of community harmony.

Salons offer us the opportunity to practice new ways of interacting. Salonist Ted Harris expressed the possibilities when he wrote a letter to his salon members, saying he wanted "to *know* each of you. To study and appreciate your character, to learn from what has happened in your life, or in things that you have heard that have mattered to you. I want your Passion, not your debating ability, nor your conversation-dominating/stopping ability. I want your conversation-*inspiring* ability."

Suppose, as Harris suggests, we entered conversations not to persuade others, but to learn about them? Imagine how different life would be if, instead of competing in conversation, we were taught to value speaking itself. Suppose we approached conversation aesthetically? What if we began to look for elegance, beauty, and simplicity; to appreciate charismatic and creative delivery; to become engaged and transported by words? Suppose we listened to discover the whole, complex beauty of others' ideas, instead of listening with the intent of picking out flaws? We might become wiser and more eloquent. Indeed, all of us might come to know more about the world and humanity.

Of course, such a transformation does not happen easily or quickly. Conversation is a fluid, ephemeral art form. It cannot be readily analyzed. We can learn debate and rhetoric, for the rules are clear and relatively rigid. But reading about a conversation, for instance, does not allow us to grasp the elusive emotions that swept through the group; to hear the tone of voice that sparked a seemingly illogical digression; to witness the eye and hand signals that halted a monologue or applauded an observation; or to feel the sudden excitement as an insight charged into the thoughts of a quiet person in the back of the room. Even those present during the conversation may not comprehend all of its nuances.

> **"** When you fall into a man's conversation, the first thing you should consider is, whether he has a greater inclination to hear you, or that you should hear him."
>
> —Sir Richard Steele, British essayist

Seven Suggestions

Because there are no hard and clear rules, the practice of conversation is somewhat subjective. However, there are concrete things you can do to help sustain the quality of conversation in your salon.

First of all, show up. You can't converse if you're not around.

Second, take risks. Reveal a little more of yourself than you normally would. Share your observations, even when they don't fit snugly within with your sense of reality or your political beliefs. Don't shy away from contradictions, ambiguities, or unpredictable reactions. These are what keep the conversation from dying. They are the meat of conversational creativity.

Third, pay attention to the conversation and assume some responsibility for making it work. Intervene subtly when it appears to be going awry. Stop talking when you've been holding forth for too long. If a person hasn't spoken, ask that individual a question. Suggest a ten-minute break, point out a digression, ask for clarification.

Fourth, vary the process. Explore different ways of conversing and interacting. Try taking turns speaking if your group is often stuck in the intellectual or argumentative mode; let the conversation slide into a free-for-all argument if everyone is usually polite. Try breaking into smaller groups. Try communicating by drawing pictures or reading poetry to one another. Play board games together, eat together, move the salon outside. Willingness to experiment brings vitality to conversation.

Fifth, practice speaking. At the great salons, guests gave thought to the act of speaking and the words chosen. They appreciated one another's wit and intelligence, and freely applauded and critiqued each other's skills. Conversation is a talent that can be brought to the level of genius in some people; for the rest of us, it is a skill that improves with practice. Don't be afraid to think up and save bon mots for the right moment. Sprinkle in quotes and proverbs. Tell an apt joke or an anecdote.

Sixth, listen. Savor the witticisms and insights of others. Write them down, and include them in your newsletter. Repeat someone's pet phrase or a newly coined word. If you aren't confident on the fly, keep a pen in hand during the salon and write down things you'd like to say when there's an appropriate opening. If you believe you are a dull speaker, start studying language. Pay attention to the dialogue in movies, go to plays, listen to books on tape, read epic poetry aloud to yourself. As you become more alert to the nuances of the spoken word, your own words will gain elegance and impact.

Seventh, reflect. The day after a salon meeting, take the time to think over what really worked for you during the salon. Go back over the actions or words that influenced the group. Those who seek community in the salon hope for a feeling of trust and intimacy, cooperation, inclusiveness, and overall peacefulness. Who and what contributed to these qualities? Others might seek creative interactions marked by exploration, play, fun, and risk. Were these present? Still others aim for intellectual stimulation. They want to learn and teach in the salon; to share information within a diverse group; to brainstorm solutions to world problems; and to analyze systems and philosophies. Did any of these things happen? Who furthered which kinds of interactions? How was this meeting different from the last one, or from conversations a year ago? What did you most enjoy, and what triggered your enjoyment?

As you can see, there are a number of qualities that you and your salon members may want to develop as conversationalists. However, no one person can be expected to embody all of them. To do so would be nearly impossible. Rather, each individual should be allowed to thrive in the way that best reflects his or her talents. As everyone in the salon learns to appreciate different qualities in one another, the group as a whole will encompass all aspects of skillful conversation.

Knowing the characteristics of successful conversation can be helpful. You can cultivate these characteristics, use them to evaluate the conversations that take place in your salon or, if you wish, design your salon so that it emphasizes certain characteristics while minimizing others.

Brevity
Brevity is the soul of lingerie.
    —Dorothy Parker

Brevity virtually guarantees inspired, exciting conversation. In the past, salon habitués derided those who would not relinquish the floor to others. "The noise of those who speak too much is just as bothersome as the silence of those who hardly speak," cautioned Mademoiselle de Scudéry. The time constraints of modern schedules make brevity compulsory in many situations; in the salon, if everyone is to have a say, then everyone must be as concise as possible. Those who are not brief must at least be entertaining.

If the members of your salon have trouble being succinct, you might try imposing a time limit on each contribution for a few sessions. Although this may initially seem

❝ He can compress the most words into the smallest idea of any man I ever met."

    —Abraham Lincoln, commenting on an associate

> "The most valuable of all talents is that of never using two words when one will do. **"**
>
> —Thomas Jefferson

harsh or artificial, keeping track of time forces people to condense their ideas into fewer (and more powerful) words. Three- to five-minute limits generally work best. The speaker can flip a small, hourglass egg timer as he or she begins speaking. You might lengthen your time limit to ten minutes if you prefer unhurried conversations, or if you are discussing subjects that require a great deal of background information.

If you prefer a fluid conversation and don't want speakers to be watching the timer, you can nominate someone to serve as timekeeper. Asking your most loquacious member to take the job can enhance his or her awareness of time. The timekeeper can signal any speaker whose time limit is approaching with a visual gesture. After a few sessions of rigorous timekeeping, most people begin to trim and focus their contributions.

Another way to cultivate brevity is by condoning vigorous interruptions. Though interruption is not the accepted standard in the United States, it can be a natural and energetic way of improving speech habits. It is also more discriminating than other methods, in that skillful storytellers are generally allowed to finish their tales, while those who drone on without direction are quickly challenged.

Interruptions are standard behavior in the West Indies, where conversation serves as a form of entertainment as well as a means of swapping information. In Antigua, for example, people are allowed to speak all at once. A person who comes late into a conversation is neither filled in nor paid any attention. The newcomer simply stands by, listening until ready to speak, then jumps in full throttle as if he or she had been there all along.

Most modern Western salons are reluctant or unwilling to try the interruption method. The only potential drawback—aside from the possibility of fistfights—is that the process may favor those with strong, domineering personalities, leaving quieter

ANNER-ISMS

These excerpts from a manual on manners might well have been written to advise contemporary salonists. Although expressions and attitudes change with the times, it appears that certain fundamentals of good manners and pleasant conversation may remain constant. The manual was written for men in 1891 by Richard A. Wells.

- Manners constitute the language in which the biography of every individual is written.

- Be swift to hear, but be cautious of your tongue, lest you betray your ignorance, and perhaps offend some of those present too. Acquaint yourself therefore sometimes with persons and parties which are far distant from your common life and customs. This is the way whereby you may form a wiser opinion of men and things. Be not frightened or provoked at opinions differing from your own.

- We are all short-sighted creatures; our views are also narrow and limited; we often see but one side of a matter, and do not extend our sight far and wide enough to reach everything that has a connection with the thing we talk of. We see but in part; therefore it is no wonder we form incorrect conclusions, because we don't survey the whole of any subject.

- It is the practice and delight of a candid hearer to make it appear how unwilling he is to differ from him that speaks. Let the speaker know that it is nothing but the truth [that] constrains you to oppose him; and let that difference be always expressed in few, and civil, and chosen words, such as may give the least offence. And be always careful to take Solomon's rule with you, and let your companion fairly finish his speech before you reply; "for he that answereth a matter before he heareth it, it is folly and shame unto him."

- Never talk upon subjects of which you know nothing, unless it be for the purpose of acquiring information. Many young men imagine that because they frequent exhibitions and operas they are qualified judges of art. No mistake is more egregious or universal.

- Remember that people take more interest in their own affairs than in anything else which you can name. If you wish your conversation to be thoroughly agreeable, lead a mother to talk of her children, a young lady of her last ball, an author of his forthcoming book, or an artist of his exhibition picture. Having furnished the topic, you need only listen; and you are sure to be thought not only agreeable, but thoroughly sensible and well-informed.

- There is a certain distinct but subdued tone of voice which is peculiar to only well-bred persons. A loud voice is both disagreeable and vulgar. It is better to err by the use of too low than too loud a tone.

- Long arguments in general company, however entertaining to the disputants, are tiresome to the last degree to all others. You should always endeavor to prevent the conversation from dwelling too long upon one topic.

- Do not be always witty, even though you should be so happily gifted as to need the caution. To outshine others on every occasion is the surest road to unpopularity.

types behind. On the other hand, it may compel quieter members to become more skilled and assertive, much as a child learns to compete successfully for attention in a large, talkative family.

Brevity cannot easily be taken to an extreme, although you may occasionally encounter a person who makes abbreviated, obscure statements, then refuses to explain. The absolute of brevity is silence—itself often a positive, reflective element of conversation.

Clarity and Specificity

Don't, Sir, accustom yourself to use big words for little matters.
        —Dr. Samuel Johnson

At its best, speaking is not only brief and to the point, but straightforward, without the need for decorative words that serve only to dress up common thoughts. Clarity—the plain, simple use of language, ensuring that everyone can follow your thinking—requires avoiding multisyllabic, specialized jargon, convoluted grammar, and obscure references.

Simple language should not be confused with simplistic thought. Clarity and specificity go hand in hand. Vague, broad statements lead to thoughtless agreement or antagonism. Salonist Ted Harris has found that, when salon members are unwilling to accept specific suggestions or make specific personal observations, the discussion inevitably deteriorates into general arguments, in which "every statement is loaded with unshared assumptions and methods."

Exacting language—clear, specific, and to the point—leads to meaningful conversation and mutual understanding. In the words of author Mark Twain, "The difference between the right word and the nearly right word is the difference between lightning and the lightning bug." Whenever possible, avoid vague or sweeping statements that confound the thought process. Use examples to illustrate your meaning. Tell stories, relate events, give details, make analogies, tangle with paradoxes. Strive for specifics and keep your language jargon free. Remember that you speak so that you may be understood.

"Do not use a hatchet to remove a fly from your friend's forehead. **99**
        —Chinese proverb

Originality

Originality consists in thinking for yourself, not in thinking unlike other people.
—J. Fitzjames Stephen, English jurist

The more specific you are, the more original you will become. Anyone can proffer a generalization, but rarely do such statements contain significant insight. Being specific, on the other hand, forces you to think for yourself; simplistic attitudes and habitual responses are cast aside. When you value, reflect upon, and draw conclusions from your own life experiences; when you allow others to challenge you; when you aim for the "transfiguring reality" treasured by tertulia host Ramón Gómez de la Serna, you enter the realm of original thought.

The best salons encourage the expression of original ideas. Members learn to recognize the assumptions and reflexive reactions that stifle conversation. Your salon can deliberately choose topics that encourage the expression of unusual ideas and experiences. For example, you might hold a salon devoted to "Pet Theories." Virtually everyone has developed unorthodox notions or ideas, beliefs that may or may not be supported by facts. Some of these theories may seem superstitious, while others draw conclusions about human nature. In any case, these original thoughts about the nature of reality are gems. You can turn them into in-jokes or shared history by keeping a list of them or publishing them in your newsletter. They can epitomize your salon's commitment to originality.

Another topic that elicits original responses is "Great Business Ideas." The discussion allows members to describe business concepts or inventions they believe would be enormously successful if only someone with the proper resources were willing to take the risk. Or the group might discuss "Childhood Revelations and Experiments," sharing youthful insights and the results of testing these insights. As long as they're not overly obscure, creative or adventurous topics lead to original thoughts.

A session devoted to brainstorming on absolutely *any* subject can also trigger innovation. You might invite people to suggest unusual solutions to a particular world problem, then brainstorm about how to actually implement these solutions. You could find yourselves at the forefront of a new social movement. This has been known to happen in salons.

Tolerance

Evenings dedicated to the art of conversation, where we can meet our neighbors and hear what moves the people we rub shoulders with on the X bus, where—for a couple of hours, at least—all judgment is suspended, and we are free to speak without fear of being rated or told we are wrong, without needing to convince . . .
      —Salonist Camille Stupar, describing the café salons in San Francisco

Salon conversation presents the opportunity to practice at least three kinds of tolerance: tolerance of different ideas, tolerance of how others treat you, and tolerance of idiosyncratic personalities. The first of these, tolerance of different ideas, is indispensable to the salon. Exploring new ideas requires a willingness to deal with statements and beliefs that may make you feel uncomfortable.

San Franciscan Ruthe Stein learned to appreciate this kind of tolerance in her book club. "My fellow book club members happen to think highly of their opinions. More often than I would have thought, those opinions are not the same as mine. So we have a situation in which a group of people who have always gotten along suddenly find themselves having words once a month. . . . We have had to learn it is okay to have divergent points of view—that, in fact, the best discussions are the ones in which we differ the most."

A tolerant group allows everyone to say what they really think and feel, comfortable in the assurance that they will be respected even in the face of disagreement. Tolerance includes enjoying the give and take of conversation, and trusting that others

"The art of conversation consists of two fine qualities; you must originate and you must sympathise; you must possess at the same time the habit of communicating and the habit of listening. The union is rather rare, but irresistible. **"**
—Benjamin Disraeli

will not be personally offended by your statements but will cheerfully argue if you get too outrageous.

You can practice tolerance on an individual level by thinking before you speak. Set aside your spontaneous, possibly defensive reaction to a speaker. Wait for a deeper response to emerge. Put yourself in the speaker's place, and allow your imagination free rein. If you find yourself unusually irritable, ask yourself why trivial comments are affecting you so intensely. When someone's words make you angry, ask yourself if the remarks are addressing a subject you are reluctant to face. If an idea upsets you, consider the consequences of adopting the idea for a time. Enjoy the novelty value of impossible notions.

However, you needn't become so easygoing that you no longer have opinions. Tolerance taken to an extreme is apathy. Trust your own ideas and feelings, and demand respect for them if necessary.

Salons afford us the opportunity to become less sensitive to slights, more open to tactful criticism of our behavior, and better able to accept casual scrutiny of our offbeat opinions. It's easy to be tolerant of others when you feel confident and secure, but individual security is partly a group responsibility. All members must work to ensure that no one is cast aside and that all are included. A warm, friendly group that welcomes and accepts each member can get away with teasing, jokes, and honest feedback that might devastate an individual if he or she were in a different environment. Even if your group is not so intimate, you can practice tolerance of how others treat you. Try changing your attitude about words that are directed at you. If you are being teased, consider it a form of observation. Incisive commentary about what you've said is ultimately a compliment: Others are listening to you closely. If you have been the victim of a particularly sharp tongue, consider the possibility that the wound was not intentionally inflicted. Those who shoot barbs are often insensitive rather than wicked. If necessary, you might take such individuals aside privately. Let them know that their comments bothered you, and ask if they would pay a little more attention to the implications of their words. Most offenders are surprised and apologetic.

66 Do not fear to be eccentric in opinion, for every opinion now accepted was once eccentric."

—Margaret Anderson, *The Strange Necessity*

Of course, there are those who enjoy making others squirm. It may be necessary to take a different tack with these individuals. A cool response to a hurtful phrase can be an indication of your superior maturity. You might respond with a raised eyebrow and a haughty tilt of the head, or issue a witty retort. You needn't react to every little comment, but neither should you allow yourself to be bullied.

The third kind of tolerance, that of accepting idiosyncratic personalities, is perhaps the most difficult. I habitually judge myself by the company I keep; as a result, I may feel uneasy when I'm with a group of people whose style and values do not bolster my self-image. If I find myself tensing up or wondering what I'm doing with such people, I remind myself why I joined the salon. I recall that salons are not singles clubs, and I'm not there looking for a sexual partner—or even a best friend. I remember that I'm seeking community, and that healthy community includes diversity. The salon is a place designed to encourage new perspectives, not an enclave of like-minded homogeneity. From previous experience, I also know that the more I appreciate the eccentricities of others, the more accepted and relaxed I feel.

Changing the conversational process can affect how salon members view one another. Intolerant reactions frequently occur when people are dealing with each other on a superficial level. The more general the conversation, the more likely that people will form superficial judgments. If the group as a whole seems stuck at this level, try using a talking stick (described in a later chapter) for a few sessions, concentrating on narrowly defined topics that all members feel strongly about.

What happens if you really can't stand someone—if an apparently unresolvable personality conflict makes attending the salon an agonizing experience? First, ask yourself if the person you dislike may personify a part of yourself that you deny or detest. If so, you'll acknowledge that you are part of the problem. Then imagine how you'd like to be treated if you were that person. If you force yourself to respond to that person in a kindly manner, he or she may do a complete about-face.

If the problem persists, it should be aired in the salon. Given wise, neutral facilitation, sufficient honesty, and the essential respect for others, the group can probably get at the root of the problem and negotiate some kind of reconciliation—though the two of you may never become friends. The solution of last resort involves asking one of you to leave the salon. This is an extreme measure. It often creates a rift in the salon and a feeling of fear or distrust that lingers for some time. It could even signal the demise of the group. It's far preferable to practice tolerance and honesty.

Tact

Tact is a beautiful quality because it is based on kindness.
—Margaret Anderson, *The Strange Necessity*

Tact is hard to describe, much less study. You may notice that someone has been tactful without knowing how or when to exercise tact yourself. Tact involves an unexaggerated sensitivity to the interpersonal dynamic, combined with genuine appreciation of other people's talents and experiences. It requires a degree of detachment—the ability to see a situation as it is without needing to impose a solution upon it. According to Alabama salonist D. S. Lodge Peters, the essence of tactfulness is "knowing when to shut your mouth instead of hollering about your Great-I-Am."

In practice, tact involves finding ways to resolve difficulties between people without putting anyone on the spot. It is often conveyed through nonverbal signals and indirect comments. Although tactfulness is not my strong suit, I've noticed that I can often effect a change simply by looking away from someone, looking toward them, or nodding in their direction. I seldom attempt to influence people directly or point out flaws—the things I'm noticing may not, after all, turn out to be flaws. For example, perhaps someone in your group has indicated a desire to say something, but has not found an opportunity to break into the conversation. Perhaps the person shifted impatiently in his or her seat, raised a hand unconsciously, nodded, or demonstrated eagerness to speak with some other gesture. You might look at this person directly and say, "I'd really like to hear from people who haven't spoken yet." In this way, you avoid putting the person on the spot (he or she can still remain silent), and you have not criticized anyone for monopolizing the conversation. You have simply stated your desire to hear from others. It is now the responsibility of the person who wanted to speak to seize the opening.

I suggest waiting, taking a few breaths, and evaluating your own motives before you tactfully intervene. Be certain that the salon isn't about to shift on its own. If you suggest a change, do so as unobtrusively as possible, preferably without causing a break in the conversation. Frame your concerns as your own, without attempting to speak for everyone else. If you hear a sigh of consensus or a murmur of agreement pass

> **❝** Lettuce is like conversation: it must be fresh and crisp, so sparkling that you scarcely notice the bitter in it."
>
> —Charles Dudley Warner, American essayist

through the group, you may decide to press your point a little more firmly. Be aware that even tactful suggestions can incite conflict.

In my opinion, too many people these days insist that they have a right to be rude—it is labeled "being honest." Tact, of course, should not be used as an excuse for dishonesty, but neither should honesty be used as an excuse to disdain others. A few remarkably insensitive people claim that rudeness is actually preferable to kindness—that basic politeness is inhibiting, and that any intervention is a form of censorship. It's wise to avoid confronting these people, because you'll never dissuade them from their aggressive stance. Instead, you might appease them by sincerely agreeing with them on some small point, then asking another person for an opinion. It should be said that a rude person who has something to contribute—who is funny or smart in a unique way—can add spice and dimension to the salon. It's important to ensure, however, that such a person doesn't dominate the group.

Excessive tactfulness can become a lack of engagement. Tact can be used as an excuse to sidestep confrontations that could actually lead to deeper mutual understanding. It can also become a form of one-upmanship, in which people try to "out-polite" one another. Taken to a distorted extreme, tact is covert manipulation coupled with disdain; in the name of tact, people can become arrogant if they assume the attitude of a parent handling a temperamental child. In general, people who have grown up in inhibited, emotionally cool, or ultrapolite environments should practice sincerity and outspoken passion, worrying less about tact. Learning tactfulness is most important for those who have had the misfortune of inheriting foot-in-mouth disease.

Sincerity

Mme de Staël is sincere in innumerable contrary ways in succession, but as in each moment of speaking she is really sincere, one is overcome by the accent of truth that echoes in her words.
        —Benjamin Constant, salonist

Sincerity stands almost in opposition to tact, for sincerity is the spontaneous outpouring of genuine emotion. Yet sincerity alone can compensate for a lack of all other conversational skills. An earnest willingness to express one's emotions honestly invites others to discard their masks and conventions, so that real concerns and raw feelings can be revealed.

Because it opens the way to greater honesty about complex issues, sincerity is a radical act. Curiously, it can set people at ease and energize them simultaneously. In a letter to the NSA, salonist Marco Ermacora described an electrifying session at which most people had no problem talking sincerely and honestly. "[It] created some critical mass, and all this energy was released," he wrote. "I hadn't felt so relaxed in a long time."

Coolness undoubtedly has its place, especially in the exchange of witticisms. But the salon comes most alive when each person's essence and charisma shine forth. Those who are afraid to be seen as fools or idealists stifle themselves and others in the group. Sincerity means taking risks.

Ask your questions, then, because you may elicit answers that someone else desperately needs. Reveal the truth of your life, because you may reveal to others their own truths. Discuss your doubts, because in doing so you may allow others to share theirs. Tackle taboo subjects. Allow your passions to guide you. Let your voice ring with energy and excitement.

If there is a downside to sincerity, it is exemplified by people who bring up the same subjects repeatedly, no matter what everyone else is talking about. The worst form of sincerity happens when passion and singleminded righteousness combine to create fanaticism. A fanatic constantly turns the conversation to the particular topic with which he or she is obsessed, boring and frustrating everyone else in the group. Tact is unlikely to inhibit a fanatic, and tolerance exacts a heavy toll. You will probably have to tackle the problem head-on, perhaps asking the person not to mention the overworked subject for at least three meetings. Fanatics are sincere, and their sincerity should be acknowledged, but the point must be made that the world can be viewed through other lenses. Remind fanatics that all salon members have agreed to explore many perspectives and many issues. Most will recognize that they've overdone it, and will back off. The others will probably leave the salon and look for a more submissive venue.

Lightheartedness

But beyond all that I have said, I also want a certain joyful spirit to reign there, that . . . inspires in the heart of each member of the group a disposition to enjoy everything and not to be bored by anything; and I want great and small things said, provided they are always well said.
    —Mademoiselle de Scudéry

Come to your salon with a light heart, prepared to engage with others, to laugh, to be entertained. Sincerity is crucial, but unrelenting earnestness can lead to a draining, exhausting level of intensity that simply wears people out. It can even allow an atmosphere of depression or despair to pervade your salon, or make your members feel prohibited from expressing their "lighter side."

A playful spirit does not necessarily imply a failure to take the problems of the world seriously. In fact, problem solving of any sort requires enthusiasm, energy, and open-mindedness. When salon conversations come to an uncomfortable and perhaps painful halt, it may mean that your group is focused too intensely on one perspective or one approach to your topic. A lighthearted remark made at an appropriate moment can remind members that other perspectives exist, allowing the conversation to proceed in a new direction.

Lightheartedness is conducive to originality and tolerance. Your interactions will benefit from a playful spirit, even if you are discussing the gravest social issues. Further, joy is often what keeps us engaged and moves us to protect what we love. On a fundamental level, lightheartedness can ensure that your salon remains a pleasure to attend.

Wit and Humor

To be wildly enthusiastic, or deadly serious—both are wrong. Both pass. One must keep ever present a sense of humor.
        —Katherine Mansfield, salon guest at Garsington

Lightheartedness goes hand in hand with an unforced sense of humor, skillful use of language, and witticisms. Throughout time, laughter has pervaded salons; throughout time, a ready epigram has been the calling card of the salon guest.

Humor is indicative of creative, flexible minds at play. Wit springs forth when unusual connections are made between words and concepts. Humor turns reality around, making normality seem more malleable and fundamental beliefs less rigid. Humor facilitates a change of perspective.

In some tribal cultures, humor is so important that it is considered sacred. Clowns or "contraries" ceremonially poke fun at accepted, habitual ways of doing things. They help prevent stagnation in the community and temper the excesses of people in authority. Humor can have a similar effect on salons, supporting egalitarianism and preventing self-appointed leaders from taking themselves too seriously.

Pinpointing the contradictions and absurdities inherent in virtually any subject helps people determine what they really think. Caricatures and easily remembered jokes reduce authority figures to fallible people, allowing those who may lack power in society the opportunity to express their chagrin and envision changing the status quo. A good belly laugh implies disregard for proprieties. When we hate someone or something, it has power over us; when we laugh about it, its influence is diminished.

The political and social influence of salons has frequently come through the use of humor, and laughter is the social glue that cements community. It reduces boredom and tension within a group, while increasing solidarity. The bonds of familiarity are forged and reinforced by joking with one another. Nicknames, so prevalent in the early salons, spring from relaxed, shared intimacy. Assuming a tone of humorous informality with newcomers quickly brings them into the group, and teasing lets them know what the social rules are. Laughter breaks down the differences and boundaries between people. When all members are laughing, all are momentarily in agreement.

Language Play

I have nothing to declare except my genius.
   —Oscar Wilde, speaking to a U.S. Customs official

Salon humor traditionally consists of language play. Salonists enjoy every kind of word game, including puns, rhymes, anagrams, and charades. A favorite form of humor has been epigrams—short, witty remarks or verses improvised on the spot in order to add flavor to the conversation. In the past, composing perfectly apt, clever epigrams on the spur of the moment could make a person's social reputation. In a sense, epigrams were the sound-bites of their day. They were spread by word of mouth or in letters, and many of them infected entire countries with new ideas.

Oscar Wilde

Verbal play can be a wonderful way of extracting yourself from a sticky social situation. In the sixteenth century French lawyer Etienne Pasquier, a salon guest of the Madames des Roches, found himself unequal to the group's repartee. As he was about to lose an argument, he noticed a flea perched on Catherine des Roches' breast. Pasquier immediately began to "salute the uninvited guest with wit and boldness," suggesting that he would feel lucky to be in the flea's position. The mother and daughter des Roches were delighted with his extravagant praise of the flea; from that moment on, writing about the flea became all the rage among salon habitués in the area. The resulting humorous poetry, complete with puns on the name des Roches ("roaches"), was later collected in small, hand-bound books. The flea incident became famous in salon history, while the original argument was, of course, forgotten.

Verbal play reached its height—or perhaps its

> ## "People show their character by what they laugh at. "
>
> —German Proverb

nadir, depending on your point of view—among members of the Vicious Circle. Most of those who frequented the Algonquin Round Table were writers, editors, or actors with a shared love of language. As remembered by Margaret Case Harriman, daughter of the Algonquin Hotel's
manager, their favorite game was an elaborate form of punning called "I-Can-Give-You-a-Sentence." According to Harriman, the game "consisted of saying to someone [for instance], 'I can give you a sentence with the word *burlesque*.' Courteous attention was required of your opponent as you added, 'I had two soft-burlesque for breakfast.'"

Not all salon humor has been friendly and lighthearted. Salonists have gotten downright nasty on occasion—sometimes with each other, but more often by desecrating some important person's reputation. Irony has been a favorite, sharp-edged tool. The use of irony implies a great deal of shared understanding within the group, for an ironic statement says one thing while meaning something else altogether. The true meaning may be suggested with only the slightest inflection or change in expression. Because it is so subtle, irony is one of the more intellectual forms of humor. Sometimes verging on satire, it is a critique of all beliefs, an undermining of all authority, a challenge to all premises.

A game of ironic comments and smart retorts can be great fun. On a riskier level, so can an aggressive game of slinging insults—one in which an aggressor may become a victim at the turn of a phrase. A classic eighteenth-century verbal battle took place at London's Beef Steak Club between John Wilkes, a journalist and politician, and rival politician Lord Sandwich. According to accounts, Lord Sandwich initiated the exchange by predicting that Wilkes would die "either of the pox or on the gallows."

"That," Wilkes retorted, "will depend on whether I embrace your lordship's mistress or your lordship's principles."

The Tempering and Practice of Humor

Wit lies in recognising the resemblance among things which differ and the difference between things which are alike.
> —Madame de Staël

Being humorous requires practice. For many of us, it seems almost as if the brain needs training and permission to be funny. But it takes just one ready wit in your salon to encourage the latent humor in everyone else. Punsters beget punsters—like a plague, some would say.

Even if there is no stellar comic in your salon, you can instigate humor. First of all,

66 Hanging is too good for a man who makes puns:
he should be drawn and quoted."

—Fred Allen

laugh. Trust your personal sense of the absurd. When something strikes you as funny, let loose with a chuckle, giggle, or guffaw. Don't wait to see if anyone else thought it was funny. If you're asked to explain, go ahead, and don't stifle your mirth. As you express what tickles your fancy, the others will come to understand you, and will feel comfortable revealing their own private amusements.

When a witticism springs to mind, speak it quickly, then let it go. If your remark passes unnoticed, there's no need to explain or repeat yourself. Humor generally works best when it's delivered off-the-cuff and doesn't insist upon attention. A non stop wit can even become intrusive. Benjamin Constant once praised a guest at Germaine de Staël's salon for refraining from the perpetual insertion of bon mots. "However clever in themselves," Constant observed, "[they] have the disadvantage of killing the conversation; they are, so to say, shots that are fired at other people's ideas, and which slay them."

Opportunities to try out many kinds of humor—physical as well as verbal—can be created in your salon. Silly faces, impersonations, parody, and prepared jokes can become salon activities, and can be just as amusing as impromptu humor. If you want to repeat a joke you've heard, you can wait until it relates to the conversation or try it out during a break. Entire salon evenings can be devoted to reading aloud funny passages from books, sharing favorite cartoons, or telling funny anecdotes. You might also try games that encourage unusual associations. My friends and I once pulled out a book on dogs, then tried to decide which breed each of us resembled. In a similar fashion, salonist Margaret Anderson and her friends asked a member to walk across the room two or three times. "Then we would all try to evaluate that person's essence," she recalled. "Was it a dry, thin essence? Was it like a fruit with much juice?"

Be careful if you try making a game of insults. Nowadays, people seem more easily wounded or offended than they were in days gone by. Even in the past, a sharp remark sometimes led to ill feelings and caused people to leave a salon, never to return. Being too protective of salon members' feelings can be smothering, but don't hesitate to call things to a halt if the laughter becomes too mean-spirited. Wit that wounds, that tries to establish unequal relationships, or that leads to accusations of "You can't take a joke" generally contains elements of abuse.

Wit can be used as a tool to reflect on reality and the nature of life; to point out absurdities in the grand scheme; to bring people together in camaraderie, rather than isolating individuals. If you decide to insult one another, do so playfully. If members react to your comments with dead silence and averted eyes, realize that you are on the way to ostracizing yourself. Beware of wit that is racist, sexist, classist, or otherwise derides any identified subset of people. Women or members of ethnic minorities may choose to make fun of themselves, but even this kind of self-deprecation is risky, for those who make fun of themselves may be believed. Humor is best used to criticize those in power, to tease out paradoxes in an argument, and to gently puncture pride and posturing.

Despite these cautions, the practice of wit is important. I have heard many people complain about organizations, clubs, and activist circles that have become dour and humorless. I have noted a decline in joke telling and lively wit within my own circles of friends and acquaintances. Salons would do the world a great service if they succeeded in banishing apathy with laughter. As the author Aldous Huxley once said, "People are much too solemn about things— I'm all for sticking pins into episcopal behinds."

Argument

Gatherings at which feelings are never hurt are not salons, they're tea parties.
        —John Berendt, "The Salon"

Argument is a form of verbal sparring that can enrich your salon. Typically, one person presents a hypothesis; others in the group poke at it, bring up exceptions, identify faulty premises, and otherwise test the idea, making it stronger or perhaps knocking it down altogether. Salonist Alan Chamberlain (known as "<axon>" to his on-line acquaintances) has explained his involvement in computer conferences, which often tend to be argumentative: "i come here for the free, frank exchange of differing viewpoints . . . there are places on the WELL [computer network] where stiffly formal courtesy is observed, and others where no holds are barred. i like all of those areas, but i am most intellectually stimulated by those places where participants are not afraid to get rowdy."

Allowing argument is closely aligned with allowing originality. Without a willingness to debate, salons become dull occasions. One of the commonest complaints I've heard from members of long-running salons is that the participants have all come to think alike and agree with each other, so they have nothing left to talk about. In many cases, fear that discussions may erupt into arguments is what's inhibiting them. When people are afraid that the group can't handle differences of opinion, none will be offered.

The concern can be a reasonable one. Few people are skilled debaters. Some consider argument a matter of being loud enough long enough to wear everyone else down. Others refuse to listen to other people's ideas, lest they lose a point in their favor. And still others resort to name-calling and derision.

66 A man never tells you anything until you contradict him."

—George Bernard Shaw

Learning to relax and enjoy a good debate may require practice and a shift in attitude about argument. Arguing should not be a means of proving that you are right. It can instead be an educational process in which you willingly consider contrary notions. Ideally, it's another verbal game—one that improves your mental agility and informs your opinions. In his autobiography, journalist Lincoln Steffens illustrates this when describing the debate game he and a friend often played at salons and social gatherings: "Twachtman would whisper to me as he passed on to his place, 'I'll say there can be no art except under a monarchy.' Waiting for a lull in the conversation, he would declare aloud his assertion, which was my cue to declare the opposite. 'You are wrong, Twachtman. Art is a flower of liberty and blossoms only in republics.' Others would break in on his side or mine and, marking our followers, he and I led the debate, heating it up, arousing anger—any passion, till, having everybody pledged and bitter on a side, we would gradually change around till he was arguing for the republic, I for the monarchy. Our goal was to carry, each of us, all our party around the circle without losing a partisan. The next night Twachtman would whisper and later declare that 'Foreign women are not beautiful; only American women have real beauty,' and again we would try to lead our heelers around to the opposite view. It was amazing how often we could do it."

Fighting Fair

I'm willing to explain, but not justify; I'm willing to answer a question, but not a challenge; I treat every request as honest, even if it is tinged with sarcasm. I'm finding the responses I'm eliciting are rising in general quality.
  —Carol Anne Ogdin, on-line salonist

Enjoyable argument often requires adherence to standards. In general, a good argument should be conducted within the conversational guidelines I've already discussed. It's far better to express disagreement through wit than rudeness; far more effective to argue with sincerity and tolerance than with rancor and disdain; far more clever to debate with precision than with rambling generalizations.

When arguing, confine yourself to a specific, debatable topic. Nothing will come of an argument that boils down to insistence on one absolutist viewpoint. Salonist Ted Harris explained what can happen when an argument is reduced to two opposing generalizations: "You often get two paralyzing situations: one is that the conversation becomes ever more abstract until we reach pure metaphysics, at which point all of the shared meanings of terms are lost. The other is a retreat to divisive pontification: e.g.

someone saying, 'Men and women are intrinsically different, and you must accept this!'"

If your salon stumbles down this path, Harris suggests looking for "common ground from which to begin." Once your group has found a place of agreement, however narrow, you can return to the original topic, focusing on specifics rather than generalizations.

Although specificity spurs healthy debate, I discourage the "prove it" game. Members shouldn't demand a citation or source from a speaker unless they are genuinely interested in the article or reference and intend to track it down. Nor should they deride someone who supports an idea because he or she read something, but can't tell you who wrote it, when it appeared, or the title of the relevant book or magazine. It's imperative to deal with the substance of what someone is expressing; whether the person has a good memory for names, titles, or peripheral facts is virtually irrelevant.

When others argue with you, they're paying you a compliment. People rarely bother to contradict someone whose views seem inconsequential or stupid. Be playful, humorous, and respectful. Unless you have made a deliberate decision to allow teasing and insults, vitriol should be avoided. As on-line salonist Carol Anne Ogdin puts it, "What you gain with sarcasm and insinuation, etc., is to win the battle and lose the war."

Arguments can proceed without a plan and end without a declared winner. Over time, the subject can be examined again and again in your salon, each time from a new perspective. To avoid taking arguments too seriously, play devil's advocate from time to time, or try arguing from a point of view opposed to what you really believe. The entire salon can do this on occasion. If an argument has grown too polarized, suggest that everyone reverse their positions and argue the opposite view just as vehemently. This exercise inevitably results in broader thinking about the subject and warmer mutual understanding within the group. Members quickly realize that their original position is not the only defensible perspective.

What should you do if things simply get out of hand? What if everyone refuses to consider a different viewpoint? What if the argument has become a shouting match?

"The result of our differences was—argument. At last I could argue as long as I wanted. . . . I had always been confronted with people who . . . lost interest in any subject the moment it became controversial. . . . I had never been able to understand why people dislike to be challenged. For me challenge has always been the great impulse, the only liberation. "

—Margaret Anderson, *My Thirty Years' War*

Try to break the tension. Do something sudden and completely distracting. You may or may not wish to follow the advice of tertulia host Ramón Gómez de la Serna: "If you pour a glass of water over the table, you abate the anger of the conversation."

Leadership and Rules:
Facilitating the Process

A community is like a ship; everyone ought to be prepared to take the helm.
—Henrik Ibsen, *An Enemy of the People*

I once regarded salons as informal, egalitarian social gatherings where the tangled problems of responsibility and group dynamics would never emerge. It *is* possible for a salon to carry on for years without conflicts around leadership, provided all members share similar expectations, the various personalities complement each other, and some members enjoy running things while others remain contented guests. But most groups are not so ideal.

When all tasks are left to the self-appointed, the salon runs several risks. The most common is that the person who has maintained the salon will begin to resent all the unacknowledged work and drop out, leaving the salon in shambles. Alternatively, one person may exert so much control over the group that other members drop out because they have no say in the direction the salon is taking. The most extreme situation arises when the individual running things is perceived as far more dynamic and impressive than the other group members. This can transform the salon into a personality cult, in which diverse opinions are rarely tolerated and the needs of the group are ignored. All of these problems can be avoided by clearly defining the tasks involved in leading the group, and by deciding up front how you will choose people to carry out these tasks.

For starters, leadership should not be covert or assumed. If just one person runs the salon, he or she should be acknowledged openly and held accountable when the salon succeeds or fails. This allows each member to choose on an informed basis whether he or she wants to be part of the salon as it is structured.

Although there are exceptions, it's usually best for several or all members to share leadership responsibilities, and for the salon as a whole to develop consensus guidelines

> **❝** It's the height of folly to want to be the only wise one."
>
> —Francois La Rochefoucauld

for appropriate behavior. If salons are to maintain their commitment to egalitarian participation, leaders must be defined not as authorities, but as performers of a service.

Salon leadership requires a series of skills. Particularly skillful people may serve as models for others in the group, but ideally they should not be the only leaders. Through regular group interaction, everyone in the salon can practice the skills of effective, democratic leadership. These include, for example, organizing group activities, recruiting members, maintaining communications, listening respectfully to others, seeking creative solutions, motivating group action, reconciling conflict, and gauging when to intervene and when to let things run their course.

Shared Leadership

In several of the successful groups the "leader" was more of a presence than a person . . . a role that was taken up only when the group seemed to need it and usually by one person in particular, but occasionally by someone else. The nominal leaders of these groups often spoke of some identifiable CHEMISTRY being the bottom line for "what works": They spoke of groups that were able to bond around a core of members who were committed and persistent in their intent to make it work, open-minded enough to let things happen, and respectful of people even if their opinions were contrary to their own. In turn, these qualities often emanated from a group because the "leader" projected them.
—Lorraine Suzuki, Southern California salonist

The leaders within a salon fall into two broad categories: those who handle organizational details (*hosts*); and those who handle group dynamics (*facilitators* or *mediators*). By sharing and rotating these roles, and by breaking them down further, everyone in the group can assume a leadership role.

In some salons, one person acts as both host and facilitator. In others, these roles are distinct—the host provides a place to meet, while the facilitator initiates the conversation, asks questions to keep it going, interrupts if someone talks too long or digresses too much, and so on. The host may remain constant, while the facilitator changes with each meeting.

However, your group may decide to split the host's responsibilities. One person could still serve strictly as the host, holding meetings in his or her home. Another person could fill the role of the *convenor*, who is sometimes called the *organizer* or the *coordinator*. The convenor's tasks involve finding new members, sending out invitations, and keeping track of the mailing or phone list. These tasks can be further broken down. You might designate a *contact person* who keeps track of visitors and newcomers to the salon; a *recruiter* who advertises for new members; and a *scribe* who creates and mails your salon newsletter or flyers. Other people might assist the host by cleaning up after meetings, bringing food, arranging for child care, or buying supplies for activities. One member may act as *treasurer*, recording donations used for postage, food, and other expenses.

In most salons, a topic is chosen for each meeting and one member volunteers to facilitate that particular discussion. By default, this person usually ends up acting as the ad hoc leader during the meeting. The facilitator is generally the person most interested in the topic, but a few salons prefer to choose disinterested facilitators who are free to concentrate fully on group dynamics.

Most salons change facilitators every time the salon meets. However, some groups find that allowing a member to facilitate two or three consecutive meetings provides practice and time for reflection. One Connecticut salon that meets monthly rotates its facilitators and cofacilitators. One month's cofacilitator becomes the next month's facilitator, and the new cofacilitator is chosen on an alphabetical basis. Everyone thus plays a facilitating role for two consecutive months. If your salon meets more frequently, you may want to let each facilitator serve three times in a row—once to observe and try things out; a second time to refine his or her abilities and take greater risks; and a third time to see how the refinement has affected group dynamics.

The facilitator's duties can also be divided into more limited roles. For example, one person might serve as the *timekeeper*, keeping track of how long people are talking or when it's time to move on if there is an agenda for the meeting. If your salon has problems with group process, you may want to create several processing roles: a designated *includer* might call on people to ensure that everyone has a chance to speak; a *summarizer* might restate and list ideas as they are presented; and a *checker* could clarify statements, remind people of agreed upon rules of behavior, and ask questions. When you're dealing with particularly difficult topics or problems, some groups nominate a *supporter* or *acceptor*, whose tasks involve giving sincere, positive feedback and restating things in an affirmative manner. As defined by one group, a *vibeswatcher* deflects tension in the salon by objectively pointing out what people are doing, and by reminding them to breathe deeply and acknowledge each other's feelings.

"It may be useful to have a facilitator, whose function is to work him- or herself out of a job. **99**

—David Bohm, *On Dialogue*

No matter how you decide to structure the leadership roles in your salon, try to rotate the tasks among members, in order to prevent hierarchies and factions from forming within the group. Regular rotation also prepares members for keeping the salon going even if key people leave. New Jersey salonist Terri Schiesser noted that a problem can emerge when newer members don't feel comfortable volunteering as hosts or facilitators while, simultaneously, core members are experiencing crises, new developments in their lives, or overcommitment. If old-timers actively welcome newcomers, encourage them to assume leadership roles, and reassure them that leadership isn't all that difficult or time consuming, the problem can be averted. If you let new people know what to expect and offer some guidance, they are usually eager to help out.

Facilitator Glenda Martin

Facilitation Skills

Leadership is something you do to a group; facilitation is something you do with a group.
—The Center for Conflict Resolution

A salon facilitator is not usually a professional in the field; he or she may not even be a gifted mediator. The egalitarian principle often means that all members take turns acting as facilitators. Even if one person is considered the leader of a group, everyone should be encouraged to step in when problems arise. As facilitator Glenda Martin says at her book groups, "All have the responsibility, not just me, to say 'I don't like the way things are going' or 'Can we move on?'"

Being a facilitator means agreeing to pay extra attention to group dynamics and attempting to keep the conversation flowing. From an egotistical perspective, facilitating may not seem terribly rewarding. You'll have fewer opportunities to contribute brilliant observations, because you are trying to monitor the moods of participants. As you attempt to assess what's going on with each individual, you're also trying to move the group steadily toward any stated goals. People may blame you if you intervene often; they may be unhappy if you intervene infrequently. Being a good facilitator is not the world's easiest job.

The first rule of facilitating is to *do* as little as possible. You may often choose to do nothing when the conversation falters or disputes arise, instead allowing others to find their way. Good facilitators trust themselves, but they also place great trust in the group.

The facilitator should primarily be a presence, rather than an actor. While facilitating, you should be alert, focused, and injecting energy into the group, but otherwise mostly passive. If you spot a potential problem, wait and see if anyone else notices it, or whether it will resolve itself without intervention. If you do intervene, professional facilitators at Rapid Change Technologies, Inc. suggest that you "take a hundred deep breaths before making another intervention, especially if you tend to be quick and articulate. Long before the hundred breaths are taken, someone will have understood that you really mean to hear them, that you will listen. Be prepared for a flood of new energy." In other words, listening can itself be a solution to the problem.

As part of the practice of minimal intervention, professional mediators and facilitators may use body language, sounds, colors, conscious breathing, musical rhythms, and poetic images to affect group dynamics without having to interrupt the verbal process. Two simple tools that everyone can learn are the use of body language and compliments.

Eye contact is one kind of nonverbal signal. Notice when you find yourself watching someone speak, and when your eyes drift around the room. Notice whether others look at you when you're talking, or if they glance at their watches instead. A determined monologist will often fall silent if you turn away, and he or she might let others know it's their turn to speak by deliberately glancing in their direction. Likewise, a speaker can be acknowledged and encouraged through steady, alert eye contact. But there must be real attention behind the gaze. Glazed eyes belie boredom or self-absorption.

Any group member can call the group back to the subject of the discussion, interrupt patterns of conflict or misunderstanding between other parties, offer clarifying comments, summarize activities, or give evaluative feedback. **"**

—The Center for Conflict Resolution

MILT:

On the verge of saying something kind of interesting.

You can also employ more obvious body signals. A wink, a squint, a raised eyebrow—these shared signals, intercepted by the group, can lighten the mood of the salon and bring the group into closer intimacy. Leaning forward or backward, sitting with crossed arms, and nodding or shaking your head sends messages. Try one or two such physical signals during each salon meeting, and notice the effect. I rely increasingly upon these tactful hints when I facilitate salons.

If your salon feels too formal and inhibited, or if people complain that they aren't becoming friends, you might remind yourselves to touch each other more often. Touch encourages a feeling of inclusiveness. Shaking hands, patting each other in greeting or farewell, or nudging one another gently in the ribs can help create an atmosphere of closeness. It is not necessary to promote ritualized hugs, as many people feel that hugging represents too much contact among acquaintances. In some cases, it can seem forced or invasive. However, small gestures of warmth and welcome are rarely taken amiss.

The facilitator should not impose anything upon the group. This is especially important if your salon includes people from diverse ethnic or family backgrounds. Some people regard eye contact as friendly; others may feel it is intrusive or domineering. A man who touches female members of the salon too often or in a manner that's too familiar may be misconstrued. Interpretations of gestures and tone of voice vary widely throughout the country and the world. Experiment by increasing your use of nonverbal tools in subtle increments, remaining alert to reactions that indicate discomfort.

Offering praise or compliments is another good means of bringing people into greater intimacy and trust. The compliments I have received as a salon muse have done a great deal to encourage my continued effort and involvement. More specifically, they have helped me feel sufficiently at ease to let my personality shine forth in the group setting.

Praise must not be faked, automatic, effusive, or trivial. It should be person- and incident-specific rather than generalized: "That was fun, Bob," is virtually meaningless, but "You really have a knack for expressing complicated ideas simply" is a remark that targets a person's real abilities. A powerful compliment is a simple, direct, and sincere recognition of something about another person.

If your salon has a penchant for literary creativity and you'd like to formally encourage the practice of complimenting one another, you might adopt the old salon tradition of pen portraits. Set an evening or two aside to write complimentary essays about one another. A slightly more intimidating experiment can be tried by groups in which the members know each other fairly well. Place one person in the middle of the room (perhaps the evening's host), then ask each member in the salon circle to give that person a compliment. Each insight should be distinct, brief, straightforward, and honest, beginning with such phrases as: "I like the way you . . .," "I really admire you because . . .," "Our salon is more enjoyable because you . . ." and so on. Avoid sideways, left-handed, or insincere compliments, which may start with phrases like: "You'd be just perfect if only you . . ."or "Most people wouldn't appreciate this, but I think it's great when you . . ." and the like. The person on the receiving end should remain silent, but may jot down the praises for future reflection.

My experience of being the center of such a circle is that the initial, awkward embarrassment quickly gives way to a luxurious sense of being stroked. The exercise should not be repeated too often, lest it become routine and superficial, but the occasional circle of praise confirms to the less secure members of the group that their wonderful qualities are being noticed. Perhaps more importantly, it emphasizes for everyone which kinds of behavior and characteristics are most appreciated in the salon. However, these formalized exercises should not displace compliments offered spontaneously and in a heartfelt manner during regular discussions.

Conflict
It wasn't for me to reconcile different points of view.
        —Mabel Dodge

A problem that every community or committed group grapples with is how to allow healthy conflict without letting it destroy the group. In the salon context, some people feel that any conflict whatsoever indicates that the facilitator isn't doing a good job. When people are angry, when their feelings are bruised, or when they violently disagree with someone else, they may not be able to appreciate the value of conflict. But a willingness to deal with differences and even yell at one another may be the only

> **66** If you shut your door to all errors, truth will be shut out."
>
> —Rabindranath Tagore, *Stray Birds*

way to move beyond ideas about ideas—and into the feelings and values behind them.

When people truly reveal themselves, even while disagreeing, they discover commonalities that bring them together in a powerful way. They become more attentive and creative when they are challenged by unexpected and different views. If they are afraid to say what they really think, the result is boredom—a far more common cause of group breakup than conflict.

Of course, some groups have no desire to become intimate. Straightforward, intellectual conversation is all the participants want, and they prefer to maintain a polite demeanor under all circumstances. Such a group provides a pleasant social outlet without the risk inherent in emotionally charged discussions. But for others, conflict can be viewed as part of the participants' commitment to reaching deeper levels of mutual understanding.

Conflict arises from any number of sources. It can come from arguing about the topic, arguing about the process, or arguing about how to run the group. It may emerge from differing needs and goals, attempts to prove ourselves and attract others, or power struggles and personality clashes. Sometimes the facilitator's main job involves trying to figure out what the conflict is really about, for the expressed problem may be quite different from the underlying tensions.

If a conflict arises, you (as facilitator) can first describe your observations and feelings as clearly and nonjudgmentally as possible. Avoid singling people out; instead, point out changes in group behavior and mood. It's generally not a good idea to apply the more coercive techniques practiced in therapeutic, self-help, or spiritual groups. You are not there to provide therapy, only to encourage others to work together, listen to one another, and find their own solutions. Ask the others to describe their feelings and responses to what's going on. The more honest you are initially, the more likely it is that others will openly voice their concerns. In most cases, this allows you to get at the root of the conflict. Asking for other perspectives also serves as a reality check— sometimes what you interpret as a potentially dangerous confrontation just feels like a fun, heated argument to everyone else.

As a group, you may want to establish specific rules for dealing with healthy conflict and preventing needless damage to the group. For example, you might wisely decide to prohibit insults and personal attacks, thereby minimizing conflict born of name-calling. The facilitator might also be empowered to call "time-out" during heated discussions. You can agree to return to the touchy subject after a break or at another meeting. In addition, you might allow the facilitator to change the discussion method, perhaps switching from open conversation to taking turns.

Asking pertinent questions is also a useful way to get people thinking about the dynamics of the conflict rather than their positions in the argument. Questions and statements by the facilitator should be accurate and well timed, deepening the focus of the conversation. The best questions are open ended, and are aimed at the group rather than any individual. Examples of questions commonly posed by facilitators include:

- Does anyone have a really different idea about that?
- Have you had any personal experiences that influenced your feelings?
- Does anyone want to play devil's advocate and argue a different view?
- I don't quite understand what you mean. Can you give an example or rephrase that?
- I'd like to hear from someone who hasn't talked yet. What do *you* think?
- I'm confused. Does anyone know what's really going on here?

Sometimes it's enough to repeat what someone has said, thinking it over and letting the person know you've heard the comment. Deliberately simplifying and rephrasing what someone has said may bring out a more specific, detailed response. At other times, it's helpful to summarize what everyone has been saying, then ask for confirmation or clarification.

If you come up with a question that evokes a stronger or deeper response, rephrase it slightly and try it again. This gives participants time to think and rethink about the same idea, each time going deeper. On the other hand, don't badger people with questions. If a thoughtful pause occurs, don't rush to fill the silence. Each shift into

"Use your intuition. This does not always mean taking the easy way out or pursuing the most comfortable direction. As you gain experience in facilitation, you will learn to trust an inner sense of direction in determining the best behavior in a particular situation based on humane values and an understanding of humans as individuals and in groups, whether this behavior is comfortable or awkward, pleasant or unpleasant, easy or difficult. **"**

—The Center for Conflict Resolution

greater understanding and mutual trust requires a transition, a short "time-out," as people take a breath before plunging deeper.

Finally, don't stifle your own natural reactions. When something is funny, laugh. If something brings tears to your eyes, let them glisten. As long as you are not running roughshod over people, allow yourself to have a personality. Take a deep breath and expose your feelings. Each time you do so, you are giving others permission to be whole and present. The risks you take as facilitator stimulate the courage and honesty that other members need to face each other. When each person in the group is seen as a whole, complex human being, the group will abandon simplistic and fixed opinions. Therein lies the key to conflict resolution.

Dropping Members

Mrs Montagu has dropt me. Now, Sir, there are people whom one should like very well to drop, but would not wish to be dropt by.
    —Dr. Samuel Johnson

In a salon, extreme and unresolved conflict can lead to the exclusion or departure of members. Every departure, other than those due to circumstances outside of the salon, is a symptom of underlying problems that must be dealt with. Departure indicates that the tolerance level of the group has been stretched to the breaking point, raising the possibility that others will feel inhibited about expressing themselves. Even if a dropped person is regarded as the intolerant member of the group, you should examine the circumstances that made his or her presence so difficult.

A disruption can also occur when new people join a close-knit group. If your group rarely recruits new members, you may not be sure how to accommodate someone who doesn't understand the tacit behavioral rules, shares no history or intimacy with other members, and perhaps holds opinions the rest of the group finds offensive. One or more of the longtime members could end up leaving the group as a result. Again, the group should look closely at what has happened, and should work to reestablish intimacy and safety in the salon.

At times, a salon may have to deal with a major breakdown in communications, a violent antipathy between two people, or a person who simply cannot function in a community setting. Groups that are open to the public or frequently include new members are especially prone to crossing paths with someone they can't handle, who may even represent a threat to the existence of the salon. Perhaps a man attends who persists in hassling women, or someone is a virulent racist, or someone else is chronically inebriated. But more often, major problems arise because a member refuses to give others a chance to talk, argues off the topic all the time, or holds views that are anathema to everyone else.

While people who might be considered mentally ill can offer some contribution, it may be that no one in the group has the training to deal with them. If your group is devoted to building a community comprised of all comers, you may choose to obtain help by hiring a mediator. Professional facilitators can transform even long-standing personal feuds into cooperative relationships. On the other hand, if the person is truly out of control or the group is not willing to do that much work, you may need to bar someone from membership.

Such a decision should never be made lightly; nor should the decision rest on just one person. As a group, examine your motivations carefully. Is that person really going to tear the group apart? Are you sure that you aren't simply reacting to differences? Do you need to work on expanding your tolerance limits instead? Are people aligning along friendship or belief lines to exclude someone? Would explaining the rules of your salon clearly help a particular person behave more appropriately? Or is that person really dangerous to the group—in other words, is he or she vicious, intimidating, manipulative, or determined to create factions?

Author Kristin Anundsen

If the exclusion must be performed, everyone in the group should be involved in asking the person to leave. Likewise, all must take responsibility for the aftermath. Kristin Anundsen, coauthor of *Creating Community Anywhere*, reflected on the implications of the situation when six members of her salon asked another member to stop coming: "This issue, then, is not that '[So and so] is disruptive,' but that the group does not know how to deal with a disruptive member. Plucking out a member who offends is clearly not an effective tactic. Even assuming that the member is intrinsically offensive, this is like surgically removing a cancerous tumor. If the patient never deals with the conditions that gave rise to the tumor, chances are that other tumors will appear in its place, or the disease will express itself through different symptoms. . . . If one member can give rise to so much anger—and I heard fear, too—it would seem to me that this is a signal of an imbalance or disease in the system."

M. Scott Peck

Author M. Scott Peck, who has written extensively on building healthy community, suggests exclusion on an interim basis. In this scenario, a group asks the disruptive member to leave for a specific period of time, after which he or she becomes eligible to return.

Alternatively, the group can allow the person to return whenever he or she feels able to cooperate and participate equally in the salon. The remaining members should plan on dealing with the issues that arise after the departure, whether it's temporary or permanent. Exclusion means that the salon process has in some way ceased to be effective. Others may now feel that their own position within the group is jeopardized, especially if they act or express themselves differently from others.

In essence, shunning someone violates the spirit of community. Trust must be rebuilt, sometimes from the ground up. But if you are willing to deal with it rather than pretending that nothing significant has happened, exclusion actually becomes an opportunity for enhancing intimacy among the remaining members. Again, whether people leave voluntarily (but angrily) or are asked to leave, it may be wise to hire an outside facilitator for at least one meeting, so that everyone can freely express their concerns.

The Problem of Ego

He who puts himself above others, whatever talent he may possess, puts himself below his talent.
—Comtesse de La Fayette, from *Women of the French Salons*

The main danger a strong leader or facilitator faces is his or her own ego. The longer you lead a group, the more sure of yourself you will become. Knowing what to do and when to do it will become easier. But beware of self-congratulation, for it probably indicates that you are missing things. You may find that others have come to rely upon you and admire you to an excessive degree. Becoming a charismatic figure means that you are diminishing the scope of everyone else's involvement and responsibility. It also means they'll become angry if they decide you've let them down.

To prevent this, always remain open to challenge. Look for and welcome all kinds of feedback on your behavior as a leader. When a member takes the risk of criticizing the group, the process, or your leadership, listen carefully. Those who seem most opposed to you may be providing just the balance you need in the group.

No matter how well things are going, keep asking yourself questions. How can I be sure everyone is as involved as they would like to be? Has everyone expressed what they want to get from the group? How might the salon be changed so it more closely meets the needs and expectations of members? Are people's eyes focused on me too much of the time? Am I serving them or my ego? How can I be more at ease when things don't go the way I planned? Are other people involved in cofacilitating? Why or why not? How can I do a better job of modeling respect for people's feelings, sensitivities, and beliefs? Are people dropping out because of problems in the salon? How can I encourage more trust and support? Does each meeting end on an upbeat note, leaving people eager to return? If not, why not? How can I make the salon more fun?

Participate in groups where you are not the leader, teacher, or facilitator. Notice how others handle the same dynamics you deal with in your group. Notice how you feel when you are not the leader. When you think you aren't having enough opportunity to participate or being accorded respect in these groups, ask yourself what you would do if the situation were reversed. Discuss it with the other facilitator.

A large part of your leadership role lies in encouraging others to develop their leadership skills. Allow others to take over for you, or divide up the tasks so that no one person is the obvious head of the group. The salon should be able to survive without you—if it can't, something is amiss.

Make mistakes, admit them, and keep going. I have not attempted to offer every possible solution to any problem that could arise in a salon. To do so would not only overwhelm this book, it would be unnecessarily negative. The whole point of gatherings like salons is to develop your own ways of handling things, to trust yourselves to resolve problems, and to learn from each other—and, of course, to enjoy meaningful conversation.

"This isn't exactly what I meant by shared leadership."

Social Intelligence

Social talent is distinct, and implies a happy poise of character and intellect; the delicate blending of many gifts, not the supremacy of one.

—Amelia Gere Mason, from *Women of the French Salons*

Facilitation literally means "to make facile," or easy. Logically, then, a salon facilitator's work involves making communication easier. The subtleties of facilitation require the exercise of what is called social or interpersonal intelligence—an aptitude for getting along with and understanding other people. In modern times, social intelligence is seldom taught. Few of us consciously understand what makes people tick; even fewer are sensitive to the nuances of group interaction. True social intelligence is closely related to a gift for listening; it is not so closely related to a gift for talking. Mabel Dodge admitted that she generally sat quietly at her salons, smiling in the background. Yet journalist Lincoln Steffens told her: "You attract, stimulate, and soothe people, and men like to sit with you and talk to themselves! You make them think more fluently, and they feel enhanced." That doesn't mean facilitators should simply nod, listen, and smile, but the ability to do so when appropriate is a valuable social and leadership skill.

Journalist Lincoln Steffens

Social intelligence is developed through trial and error, observation, and reflection in social settings. By definition, it's an interactive skill. On a personal level, you can begin enhancing this form of intelligence by paying close, nonjudgmental attention to the moods you experience and witness in your salon. Notice when you begin to think in new ways; when you feel suddenly friendly or empathetic toward another person; and whether, at the end of a salon session, you find yourself looking forward to the next one. Notice specific words, events, or tones of voice that make you feel alert and interested. Notice times of heightened camaraderie or animation in the group. Notice when you're bored, frustrated, angry, or repelled. Examine how you feel about the salon later that evening, the next day, or a week later.

Ultimately, though, working toward shared leadership means cultivating social intelligence among all members. You might begin by playfully altering minor aspects of the salon. You could serve food at one meeting but not the next, then talk later about how the change affected your conversation. You might decide to change seats halfway through your discussion, turn the lights up or down, or move outdoors. You might meet at a different time of day, invite children and pets to wander through, or come to the meeting dressed more formally or informally than usual. Whatever parameters you choose to change, avoid analyzing the consequences during that particular salon. Instead, hold a special meeting afterward and share your observations. You may even decide to make some of the changes permanent.

Discussion Modes

Social intelligence includes the ability to recognize different kinds of discussion and determine which discussion mode your group favors. Sensitize yourself by taking a reading on the overall personality of your salon. Some groups like to debate and compare factual, scientific, and technical information gleaned from newspapers, magazines, and books. Others are interested in exploring the causes of various social problems and brainstorming possible solutions. Others generally fall into philosophic discussions, focusing on questions of ethics and the meaning of life—the favored mode of the historic salons. Still others prefer telling stories and illustrating their points with incidents drawn from their personal lives.

Virtually any topic can be discussed by employing any of these approaches. Generally, a group will range through different modes, unless one has been ruled out. Deliberately changing the discussion style can deepen and broaden the conversation, but if it's done too rapidly, people may get confused. For example, speakers sometimes shift modes from one sentence to the next. Unfortunately, they seldom let their listeners know when they jump from facts to assessments or beliefs. On occasion, I find myself in the midst of describing a problem; then I suddenly revert to the brainstorming mode, tossing out wild possibilities and fanciful solutions. If I forget to tell others that I'm

"Necessary waiting (which often appears to be weak leadership) is possible only when designated leaders are willing to empty themselves of their need to be in control. 〞

—M. Scott Peck

A LEADERSHIP SALON

In lieu of formal training, those who serve as facilitators in your salon will benefit from a discussion of leadership styles, qualities, and experiences. At a separate session, you might consider questions such as the following:

- What was your earliest experience of participating in a group? What did it teach you?

- What experiences influenced you the most as you were learning to get along with others?

- What have you learned, formally or through life experience, about group dynamics?

- Which lessons have been the most useful?

- What would you like to change in your interactions with other people?

- Have you led groups in the past? If so, what insights resulted from the experience?

- Which behaviors have led you to trust or distrust teachers, bosses, therapists, religious leaders, parents, and other authority figures in your life?

- How would leaders function in an ideal society?

just testing ideas, I may be taken as far more extreme than I actually am— perhaps regarded as frivolous or out of touch with reality. I may get into trouble trying to defend things I haven't even begun to think through.

One way the whole group can learn to recognize such shifts is by consciously practicing each discussion mode. You might choose to discuss one subject over the course of several meetings, adopting a different approach each time. What are the factual dimensions of the subject? What are its philosophical implications? Are social problems relevant to the subject? What ramifications does the subject have for your personal lives? This can be an excellent way of dealing with emotionally charged or highly complex subjects.

Suppose you've decided to look deeply at racism. You might start with the *investigative* approach, sharing facts, statistics, and academic studies of hate crimes, immigration, historical genocide motivated by racism, and so on. During this session, read and discuss materials critically, looking for hidden assumptions, errors in experimental setups and conclusions, statistical biases, and social contexts that influence the opinions of the writers. The facilitator can point out generalizations and ask people to return to specifics.

At your next meeting, shift to a *personal* approach. In this mode, group members can relate incidents of racism they have witnessed or experienced, and explain how they dealt with these incidents. Note that the personal approach is not a license to talk about personal problems in a general sense. The stories your members tell should be pertinent to the topic. The facilitator might help focus the conversation by posing such questions as: "When was the first time you experienced racism?" "How have you been harmed by racism?" "How have you benefited from racism?" "Which incidents have helped you overcome racism?" Members can answer in a round, with a time limit imposed on how long any individual talks if that's desirable. Notice that, as people tell the true stories of their lives, your discussion becomes both more human and more ambiguous. People who were previously at political and philosophical odds are often able to find common ground via this discussion mode.

Some people may find the personal approach very threatening. Do not press anyone to reveal themselves. Be aware that some people may not be ready to test their theories or beliefs by acknowledging the ambiguities and paradoxes implied in real experiences. There may be times when a person's worldview is so threatened that he or she simply cannot bear to hear what others are saying. Recognize that this can happen to any of us at any time, especially if we find ourselves in the minority opinion. Be gentle with those who are unwilling to acknowledge the validity of other people's experiences or reveal their own. As a facilitator, don't let others attack the person's views. Instead, find some aspect of their viewpoint that seems congruent with the larger group's opinion and emphasize it. Then continue the storytelling session. The threatened person will probably be able to relax and join in after a time.

Personal reality can also be shaken if your group tries the *philosophical/theoretical* approach. This is different from investigating, in that you attempt to make connections between many different experiences and fields of knowledge. A group in this mode might end up discussing what racism implies about human nature; whether children can be taught to grow up without racist tendencies; or whether racism is a product of nationalism. This sort of conversation can be marvelously creative, as long as the discussion remains open ended and people do not attempt to reach definitive conclusions. If creativity and rigorous thinking are lacking, the discussion might even devolve into collective despair over the enormity of the world's problems or the group may polarize into two philosophical camps, simply restating old prejudices and habitual opinions. If this happens, the facilitator should again encourage everyone to focus on specifics rather than generalizations.

As an alternative, you could shift into brainstorming possible solutions and outcomes, taking the *social activist* approach. The group may concentrate on examining ways of combating racism. What has and has not worked in the past? What is being done now? What can your members, as a small group or as individuals, hope to accomplish? This is a practical approach in which people are mostly interested in tinkering with things, even if there are no assurances that such changes will ultimately work. This mode is also a form of closure. It can help prevent an emotional letdown at the end of your discussion.

Once the group is aware of these approaches, you can use objects to signal which tack you're taking in the discussion. You might keep balls of different colors or other symbolic objects on a table in the center of the room, allowing people to reach out and hold up the appropriate prop as they shift into a particular mode of communication. Picking up a small doll might mean "I'm moving from analysis into storytelling"; holding a rainbow-colored question mark could indicate a switch from fact to speculation. Different people might be assigned to tackle a question or topic from specific viewpoints, as symbolized by these objects.

Edward de Bono, a Maltese author and academic who studies logic and rhetoric, uses "Six Thinking Hats" to represent different thinking modes. Using his method, speakers wear the appropriate hat when they want to express themselves from a specific mode. The White Hat represents the objective, neutral computer mind, which offers factual information and statistics; the Red Hat suggests the emotional mind, expressing feelings, hunches, intuition; the Black Hat is used for troubleshooting, playing devil's advocate, pointing out risks, and analyzing both past and potential outcomes; the Yellow Hat represents optimistic thinking, fantasies, opportunities, benefits, and ways of making things work; the Green Hat represents fertility, creativity, movement, brainstorming without judging, change, and heading into the unknown; and the Blue Hat is the facilitator's hat, donned for thinking about process and communications, defining problems, focusing on the agenda at hand, providing overviews and summaries, and asking questions. The wearer of the Blue Hat can suggest to others which hats they might try on.

The "Six Thinking Hats" approach may be too complicated for most groups to use on a regular basis, but you might try them for a session or two. You can change colors or add more hats to customize the process. For example, you could add a Purple Hat to indicate mystical, spiritual, or dreamlike communication; a Dark Red Hat to represent physical reactions and instincts; or a Rainbow Hat to represent the multicultural or global view. Even if you don't use the hats often, they can serve as visible reminders of the many directions your discussion can take.

Flawed Logic

Where logic and emotion freely mingle and the difference is poorly understood, you'll discover logical flaws. These stumbling blocks are likely to cause misunderstanding and tension during your discussions unless the entire group can distinguish between sound logic and potentially incorrect assumptions. The ability to identify flawed logic is yet another aspect of shared leadership.

Many people create illogical or unproven links between two ideas by using the "if this, then that" construct, often backing up their *cause and effect assumptions* with statistics. They might place two trends next to one another—for example, increased teenage pregnancies and rising drug use—then assume that these are related, or that one causes the other. However, what they've really done is to reduce complex sociological systems to simple statements, in order to support their previously held beliefs.

Another kind of flawed logic is the *problem of opposites*. This arises when someone ascribes a positive or negative value to a phenomenon, then assumes that its opposite must also be opposite in value. That is, if A is good, then its opposite, B, must be bad. Thinking and speaking in opposites almost guarantees rigidity and narrowness. If salon members are engaging in this, the entire conversation will likely get into trouble. The participants may split into sides on an issue and refuse to consider other, less simplistic approaches. It's useful for the group to realize that there are rarely just two sides to an issue. The habit of putting things into opposites is in fact a kind of mental laziness. It is much easier to argue for or against something than it is to delve into complexities, but your salon will encounter a series of dead ends if you wrap your discussions in black and white.

The inability to distinguish between *value judgments* and facts will also lead to communication breakdowns. Sometimes people simply cannot understand how anyone else would question an idea that seems incontrovertible. I once got into trouble at a salon when I told a woman that her statement, "People who leave their dirty dishes in the office kitchen are inconsiderate and selfish," was only an opinion. The fact: They leave dirty dishes. The value judgment: They are selfish people. I suggested that perhaps people who leave their dirty dishes around are dedicated workers, eager to get back to their projects. But I had touched a sore spot. She became quite angry, insisting that anyone who left dirty dishes was certainly selfish; this was an inarguable fact. Like so many of us, she was not able to separate her feelings from the facts of the matter.

Value judgments often go hand in hand with an assumption of *absolutes*. Salon members should be able to spot simplistic, all-or-nothing principles, which allow no exceptions or deviations. When you encounter one, you might suggest testing the absolute as a working hypothesis. Make a mental game out of it by asking questions

> **❝** The great enemy of the truth is very often not the lie—deliberate, contrived and dishonest—but the myth—persistent, persuasive and unrealistic."
>
> —John F. Kennedy, American president

like: "Could this be true even if there were an exception?" "If this *weren't* true, what would the implications be?" "Can you think of any examples that might be exceptions?" When people begin to examine their absolutism, they begin thinking more creatively about problems and solutions.

Another problem is *labeling*, which happens when people have previously encountered an idea or situation, have determined what they think about it, and have ceased to reexamine it. This is essentially a timesaving device, but it can become a problem when people are attached to or identified with those labels, in which case it again becomes absolutism. Pointing out the use of buzzwords, jargon, and labels, and asking what the terms really mean, helps people kick the habit of labeling.

Edward de Bono has written extensively about some of the preceding logic flaws in his book, *Future Positive*. Your group might benefit by reading and discussing the book. You may want to devote one meeting to a discussion of the errors in logic and false assumptions you have discovered in your conversations. It is especially enlightening to spend time reviewing national news magazines, looking for examples of misleading statistics, value judgments, cause-effect assumptions, and so on. If your group often lapses into particular erroneous zones, you might choose objects to represent these problems and symbolize them during meetings. For example, if you often end up talking about good/bad opposites, a yin-yang symbol on the table could remind you that nothing is absolutely good or bad. You might even nominate someone to serve in the role of logician, asking him or her to point out unwarranted assumptions and faulty logic. Asking for specific examples and personal experiences is also useful in jolting people out of simplistic beliefs.

Standards of Behavior

We've forgotten how to be together. Salons or salon-like gatherings are what humans have done since before recorded history. Our ancestors developed all kinds of rules and signals and etiquette that facilitated being together in groups. We've lost those social skills. We need to rediscover them, partly from other cultures and partly from our own fumbling, awkward experience.

—Eric Utne

Achieving a consensus on standards of behavior is a fundamental exercise in social intelligence—and the process enhances every salon member's facilitation skills. Once established, behavioral standards help people relax their critical or anxious scrutiny of one another, and eliminate some of the friction between diverse personalities. Accepted standards are part of what binds individuals into friendship and community.

As you might expect, agreeing on which behaviors to encourage is a delicate process. Some members may insist that they know the "right" way to behave, while others are more ambivalent. What one person considers simple politeness may be regarded by another as inhibition. Some would never argue for fear of offending; others consider forceful argument a sign of strong character and intellectual stimulation. Some have never learned how to listen to others without framing a contrary opinion; others listen too well, waiting for someone else to speak instead of voicing their own thoughts. Some consider sex, money, age, and appearance taboo subjects; others cringe at the thought of discussing religion or politics. Acceptable behavior comes in many forms, from the shouting, laughing insults of West Indian women at market to the restrained delicacies of formal Japanese speech.

And my 54th point on the subject of diesel fuels emissions is...

"Do you suppose we have a fanatic on our hands?"

Given such varied and even contrary notions of proper behavior, you'll want to be careful about the rules you establish and the ways you put them into practice. Keep in mind that all behavior is both culturally influenced and open to individual interpretation. Be civil, but don't use your standards as an excuse to stifle different ways of talking and behaving. Instead, seek to expand your range of behavior as a group. Establish structures that give everyone the opportunity to practice the values they espouse in respectful relationships with one another.

The first rule of rule making is to have as few as possible. Once your rules are established, be certain that a problem really exists before you attempt to address it with

> **66** Politeness is good nature regulated by good sense."
>
> —Sydney Smith, English writer

new rules. For example, suppose one or two people dominate most of the conversations at your salon. You have become concerned that others in the group are not getting the chance to express themselves. Before you propose a solution, find out whether others agree with you. It's possible that the quieter people prefer to avoid the spotlight, but will speak up when moved to do so. Perhaps the loquacious members are gifted storytellers and original thinkers who stimulate the other members. In this case, there is no need to create rules that might inhibit the group. Instead, when you feel that someone has been speaking for too long or that one of the shyer people would like to say something, you might gently interrupt the talker.

If, however, your group experiences frequent breakdowns in your discussions and all agree that something has to change, hold a meeting (at a different time than your usual gathering) to discuss what might be done. Rather than complaining about one another, brainstorm a list of behaviors you've noticed that aren't working in the group. Often simply voicing the problems will change behavior in the group without naming, punishing, or ostracizing anyone. If that does not seem sufficient, tackle each problem separately, again without blaming anyone.

You can brainstorm approaches to changing the dynamics in the salon, considering not only individual habits, but also the possible effects of time, place, and other external influences. Then lay out explicit rules. It's much easier to recognize and change *what people do* than it is to change their attitudes, although altered behaviors can result in changed attitudes. Alabama salonist D. S. Lodge Peters has found that tolerance is difficult to instill, but "civility was another matter. 'Please,' 'thank you' and sweet silence in the face of scoldings could be taught and learned formally and by example."

Work to make your behavioral standards simple and easily practiced. The more clearly everyone understands the rules, the fewer reminders will be needed. People generally regulate themselves once they know what is expected and appreciated, provided the rules are fair and allow for personal eccentricity. If salon members need to be reminded of the rules on occasion, they will be less defensive because they took part in drafting them. Whatever guidelines you adopt, consider doing so only experimentally—perhaps for three meetings at a time. Then evaluate how well they're working.

I'll refrain from recommending a full set of rules for your salon. Instead, I encourage you to seek many possible solutions to each difficulty. For example, let's revisit the problem I brought up earlier. Suppose that one or two members are dominating the conversation, to the apparent detriment of the group. You might take any number of approaches to this situation. You might decide to take turns talking during the session. You might decide as a group to learn about and practice active listening, or to set time limits for comments.

Here's a simple exercise that can help instill sensitivity to time. Pair people up and ask one person to listen to the other talk about something specific (perhaps a short family history or another form of self-introduction) for a predetermined amount of time. The listener should time the speaker and indicate when the allotted time has expired. Now ask your partners to switch roles. People are often surprised by how quickly the time passes when they are speaking but how long a minute or two seems when they're listening.

You might also implement a rule suggesting that people stay focused on the topic. Some people maintain conversational dominance by continually rerouting the discussion, so it returns time and again to their favorite subject or their personal life stories. Digressions can be a real nuisance when you only meet for a couple of hours a month to talk. If you agree as a group that you want to stay on topic most of the time, establish a rule that anyone can interrupt the speaker to ask how his or her point is relevant to the subject. The facilitator may also interrupt to summarize what someone is saying, to ask if the summary is accurate, and then to indicate that it's time for someone else to speak.

Repetition is a sign of loss of focus. People who are trying too hard to be agreeable sometimes reiterate the same idea, stating it in slightly different words each time. If this occurs, the facilitator may observe that nothing new has been added. Then he or she might reintroduce an earlier point, inject a provocative opinion, or ask a question that will startle people into approaching the subject from a different angle.

Some salons find it necessary to establish the "no side conversations" rule. Side conversations often happen when two or three people get bored with the general discussion and start whispering among themselves. If this goes on for a short time, just a comment or two, it probably isn't worth pointing out. To some degree, side conversations are natural and inevitable, especially between people who like and feel at ease with each other. Comments from the peanut gallery, if shared with the group, can be a source of amusement or take the conversation in an entirely new direction. But if secondary conversations go on too long or take place too often, they are disruptive. At their worst they may involve heckling, or they may simply indicate that the whisperers are not interested in the thoughts of the other members. When the no side conversations rule is established, the facilitator can glance at the disruptive

"The mind, stretched to a new idea, can never return to its original dimension. **"**

—Oliver Wendell Holmes

members or ask one of them a question, or a neighbor can give them a friendly nudge. They will generally resume their participation in the primary discussion.

Formal, effective rules outlive their usefulness. As soon as your members are comfortable with the new standards of behavior, abandon the rules. While I have suggested becoming conscious of your behaviors in order to develop your social intelligence, salon conversation should eventually become a free-flowing, ecstatic, and unselfconscious act.

PART III

Variations on a Theme:
Other Directions for Salons

Book Clubs
and Study Circles:
Education and Involvement

M. de Varillas admitted that out of the ten things he knew, he had learned nine of them in conversation.
—Magendie, from *Politesse*

Education is inherent in the salon process. When you listen, you learn. Contact with a diverse group provides access to a wide range of information. Pooling and discussing information lets you test, expand, and alter your storehouse of knowledge and opinions. The creative, often humorous interplay of ideas yields unexpected insights.

Salonists are sometimes so stimulated by their conversations—or so frustrated by the social or political problem under discussion—that they decide to undertake an in-depth study of the subject. Group members begin to gather, read, and discuss relevant books and articles. If the effort is focused on a particular social issue with an eye toward improving life in the larger community, the group becomes what is known as a study circle. If the emphasis is placed instead on education and literary exploration for its own sake, the group has formed a book club or reading circle.

Book Clubs

As social gatherings and tools for self-education, book clubs have existed for generations, providing much-needed intellectual stimulation for single parents, people in perfunctory jobs, retirees, and anyone else who enjoys learning and discussion. Though they're seldom publicized, thousands of such groups meet throughout the United States.

Many book clubs are organized around themes, perhaps focusing on books written by and about women, developments in science and technology, nineteenth-century poetry, history, the literature of a particular nation, or a specific literary genre. Book club conversations can be as free flowing as those found in general salons, but some book clubs are more structured. Members may give short lectures on the background of an author or other topics. Authors may be invited to give speeches or readings.

Marge Lamb and her husband have attended the Book Group in Madison, Wisconsin, for twenty-five years. The group is structured like many other salons. The four or five participating couples meet monthly, rotate the meeting site, and take summers off. The hosts for each session choose the reading matter ahead of time (usually fiction, but sometimes plays and nonfiction), and act as moderators if the conversation gets too heated. The discussion of the book lasts an hour or two; then talk turns to "solving the problems of the world," a general discussion of politics and current events. The secret to their longevity? According to Marge Lamb, the group works because it has "very little structure and a lot of personal responsibility," combined with a shared desire to read books that members might not find or choose on their own.

Reading circles offer some conversational advantages. Books provide a context for the discussion. When everyone has read the same book, the members benefit from common knowledge. They aren't stifled by the need to bring one another up to speed. In addition, reading material often provides the kind of specific focus that supports diverse opinions. When people can call upon ready examples and details from the book, they're less likely to fall into generalized agreement.

The primary difficulty encountered by book clubs is that everyone must choose and read a book before the next meeting. Discussion may be limited by the choice of books, especially if the group discourages digression. Members may have trouble finding the time to read the book. But at least one participant, then college student Rachel Nesse, considered reading circles such as the Great Books/Great Thoughts seminars the best means of promoting learning. "Information shared across the table, personal and often poignant," she reported, "is a delightful change from the usual college educational fare. We meet twice weekly to discuss the nuances and ideals, interests and ideas, thoughts and metaphors, history and hearsay, truths and standards,

❝ Fitting people with books is about as difficult as fitting them with shoes."

—Sylvia Beach, Shakespeare and Company bookstore

relevancy and subjectivity, of and around that week's reading. Basically, twenty people sit and talk about life in relation to the *Iliad*, or the Bible."

Starting a book club is much like setting up a general salon. You'll need to devise a means of choosing which books to read, perhaps within a selected genre or subject area. Leadership roles can be straightforward. In many groups, the person who chooses or recommends the book also becomes the evening's host and/or facilitator, and the choice of books rotates among the membership. Some book clubs convene in public spaces such as libraries, inviting all interested persons to join the discussion. Others meet in private homes, limiting membership to a group of friends or neighbors. These circles are generally self-contained; the members are more than satisfied with the pleasures of reading and discussion.

Book clubs don't often get involved as a group in political and social activism; however, there are exceptions. Lana Turner, the "keep-everything-all-together person" of the Literary Society of Harlem in New York, was instrumental in producing Silent Read-Ins every February during National Black History Month. Participants in this public service event gathered, usually in a large church, to read in silence from books written by African-American writers. Following the silent reading, authors were invited to read aloud from their works. The first year this event was conducted, over six hundred people came to read together.

In 1993, the organizers of the annual "New York Is Book Country" festival adopted the silent read-ins, asking people to read together on the steps of the main branch of the New York Public Library, the main branch of the Brooklyn Library, and the Queens Village Library. The theme was African-American literature. Festival organizers formed an African-American advisory committee, inviting Turner to organize other events to be held during the festival weekend. One outcome was called "Literary Salons in Historic Harlem Houses." On September 17, 1993, six literary salons/book signings were held simultaneously in private homes throughout the stately Hamilton Heights Historic District. This successful literary consciousness-raising effort thrilled the authors, the participants, and the salon hosts.

Study Circle Origins: Lyceums and the Chautauqua Movement

Study circles can be traced back to the town hall meetings prevalent in America by the early 1600s. These community gatherings were later described by Thomas Jefferson as "the wisest invention ever devised by the wit of man for the perfect exercise of government." But the development of modern study circles begins with the early nineteenth-century Lyceums. These were voluntary associations devised to help working-class men improve their education as they saw fit—a perfect example of democratic participation without the intervention of private interests, profiteering, or hierarchical institutions. There were 3,500 Lyceums in existence by 1835, involving entire families in discussions of public issues. Unfortunately, this pioneering experiment in adult education deteriorated with the onset of the Civil War. After the war the Lyceum became a circuit for paid lecturers who toured the country, bringing uplifting and rarely controversial messages to small towns, particularly in the Midwest.

Meanwhile, a religious educational institution in upstate New York gained popularity for its summer programs in the little town of Chautauqua, where families came to camp out and attend weeks of classes, music, lectures, and preaching. The Chautauqua Literary and Scientific Circles, begun in the 1870s, were initiated as another experiment in adult education. Chautauquan president John Hoyl Vincent intended that each circle would become a combination home reading course and correspondence school. He set up a press to print pamphlets the size of index cards but seventy to one hundred pages long. The tiny paperbacks included poetry, astronomy, philosophy, history, and excerpts from various classics in literature. They were used as the primary basis for study and discussion, and the circles were eventually expanded into four-year correspondence study programs.

This educational model was adopted by young black leaders in decades following the Civil War, as part of an effort to educate freed slaves quickly and effectively. The Chautauqua Literary and Scientific Circles eventually became popular from New Jersey to California. Thirty existed in Des Moines, Iowa, alone. By 1915 there were seven hundred thousand correspondence enrollees and fifteen thousand study circles across the country. The CLSC provided cheap, democratic, self-paced, and cooperative education for women, African-Americans, and working-class people who otherwise had little access to higher education.

In 1904, a showman named Keith Vawter got the bright idea of combining Lyceum lecturers with stage shows and classes similar to those held in Chautauqua. He began putting these educational revues on the road. Before long the brown tents of the traveling Chautauqua had become the most welcome of summertime sights for hundreds and then thousands of communities. The road shows reached their peak in 1924, when over thirty million Americans attended in twelve thousand rural communities nationwide. As a result, while urbanites in New York and Chicago talked in literary salons, the rest of the country was involved deeply in a larger public discussion.

Chautauqua organizers wanted their programs to be instructive and inspiring,

> "There was no shush-shush of public issues in America, no undemocratic fear of speaking out. The ten million people who crowded into the tents during Chautauqua's hey day wanted, and got, the pro and con of a problem. **"**
>
> —Karl Detzer, *Culture Under Canvas*

but they did not shy away from controversy. Their speakers included women as well as men. They employed lecturers who supported abolition, woman's suffrage, temperance, socialism, and other controversial causes. They sent Catholics to Protestant towns, Protestants to Catholic towns, and atheists just about anywhere. When the anti-Catholic Ku Klux Klan tried to take over one New England town, the Chautauqua manager sent a Roman Catholic lecturer to the community. The lecturer effectively blunted the Klan's efforts.

If a mayor or minister complained that a scheduled lecturer was too radical, the Chautauqua manager refunded the town's money, but the lecturers went onstage anyway. Such complaints were rare. For the most part, people around the country were too hungry for learning to be intolerant. They listened because the Chautauqua had won their respect. Following the programs, they might talk for months about the new ideas they had encountered.

The process of selecting and hosting programs was invaluable for many communities. During the winter, each town received a list of the available shows and lecturers, along with prices. If a village was to afford the program, everyone had to pitch in and help raise the money. The hardworking Chautauqua committee in town was often the single organization that crossed ecumenical and ethnic lines, spanned the railroad tracks, and brought rural and town interests together. Townsfolk learned how to organize, how to tolerate different views, and how to reach decisions democratically.

The traveling Chautauqua came to an end in the age of radio and the automobile, but study circles persisted elsewhere. In the late 1800s, Swedish representatives of the temperance movement were inspired by the then hugely popular Chautauqua Circles while visiting the United States. They returned home and started their own program in 1902. As it turns out, they had discovered an avenue of education and adult involvement that would help transform the poverty, illiteracy, low standard of living, and underdevelopment of nineteenth-century Sweden.

Swedish study circles were quickly subsidized and promoted by large organizations, starting with the temperance movement, the church, and unions, but later including local and national governments, corporations, libraries, and cooperatives. Sponsorship has fostered enormous growth. Each year, at least one-fifth of the adult population now takes part in one of roughly three hundred and twenty five thousand Swedish study circles. The original goals of conquering illiteracy and leading citizens into active debate on political issues were reached long ago. The well-organized, highly visible study circles are today considered an integral part of Sweden's democracy.

Sponsorship of Swedish study circles led to a need for stricter definitions, to ensure that unscrupulous individuals wouldn't simply claim to be a study circle and pick up their grants without actually meeting. Eligibility requirements state that "a study circle must have at least five and no more than twenty participants, and must be in session for at least fifteen hours over a minimum of four weeks." Educational associations provide training for study circle leaders, but participation remains voluntary and each circle is shaped according to the group's needs and interests.

Americans eventually rediscovered the form of group participation that had been invented here in the first place. In an updated form, study circles now enjoy renewed popularity among citizens who seek ways to learn about politics and become involved in issues that affect their communities. Two organizations help organize community-wide study circles throughout the United States: the Study Circles Resource Center (SCRC) in Pomfret, Connecticut, funded by the Topsfield Foundation; and National Issues Forums (NIF), sponsored by the Kettering Foundation in Dayton, Ohio.

Tackling Issues

A study circle can be formed by any salon. Some salons adopt aspects of the study circle format while maintaining their usual monthly or bi-weekly meetings. Others might set up a study circle for a specific period of time, advertise it to attract new members who are interested in the chosen topic, then invite newcomers to attend the ongoing salon. However, contemporary study circles are more often formed on a community-wide basis. They have evolved into a forum for small-group deliberation of critical

❝ Greetings to all the Chautauquas . . . a movement based on an idea which has now spread over the whole of our country and, in fact, over the world; an idea which has been and will continue to be of immense educational value to all the people and, therefore, of first importance to their welfare."

—Thomas A. Edison

public issues, and their influence on society is growing. In fact, study circles are chang-ing the communities in which we live.

The first community-wide effort began in 1992 in Lima, Ohio, as a means of easing racial tensions in this city of fifty thousand. As a first step, Mayor David Berger con-vened a multiracial task force of clergy mem-bers. Study circle leaders were then trained by the mayor's office and by faculty members at the Lima campus of Ohio State University. Nearly one thousand community members, drawn pri-marily from church congregations, were recruit-ed for the initial round of study circles, meeting in groups of ten to fifteen people to discuss race relations in the community.

Many of the study circles were extended beyond the prescribed time period. Researchers at the university subsequently reported signifi-cant, positive changes in attitude toward people of other races, and a second round of study cir-cles was in the planning stage at this writing. In the words of Mayor Berger: "Participants come out of the discussions fundamentally changed. This city will never be the same."

In the past four years, study circle programs have been established in many communities. Study circles from Yarmouth, Maine, to Los Angeles, California, are now addressing crime, violence, race relations, education, wel-fare reform, sustainable use of natural resources, and other important issues—and the movement is just beginning to gather steam. This forum for "dynamic democracy" holds great promise for those who feel overwhelmed by the enormity of community problems and locked out of the political system.

Newsletter of the Study Circles Resource Center

Starting Your Own Study Circle

Community-wide study circle programs often develop out of a powerful collective belief that "We've got to do something about this problem." They are typically started by a community institution—a mayor's office, school board, human relations commission, church council, neighborhood association, or civic group. However, any group of citizens (or any capable, determined individual) can set a program in motion. The Study Circles Resource Center offers an excellent step-by-step guide entitled *Planning Community-Wide Study Circle Programs*, available for fifteen dollars.

If you're concerned about an issue or problem and you'd like to tackle it through a study circle, your first step involves identifying and contacting individuals who are concerned about the issue. Suppose you'd like to address air and water pollution in your community. When you're recruiting your core group, try to include knowledgeable professionals who have dealt with pollution, as well as community leaders. These people can offer their knowledge, and they may be able to help you obtain program sponsorship. If the core group members are not familiar with the study circle process, hold a meeting to explain how it works and how it can make a difference in your community. Alternatively, conduct a study circle with this core group, so they can experience the process firsthand.

Your group can then begin working on several fronts: recruiting participants and potential study circle leaders; locating potential meeting sites throughout the community; finding an organization that can train facilitators; obtaining funding for the program; and, in the later stages, attracting the attention of the media and the community at large. You may need a sizeable, active group, perhaps broken into committees.

Next, hold a training session for those who have volunteered to become study circle leaders. The training could be conducted by the continuing education department of a local college, an adult education program, or by professional mediators or group facilitators. Be certain that those who train your facilitators are familiar with the principles of nonhierarchical, democratic group processes. The Study Circles Resource Center can be a valuable source of technical assistance and advice.

66 The study circle is a small-group democracy in action. All viewpoints are taken seriously, and each member has an equal opportunity to participate. The process—democratic discussion among equals—is as important as the content."

—Study Circles Resource Center

When you're ready, stage a "kickoff event" to emphasize the importance of the issue you're addressing and to publicize the opportunity for public involvement. Publicity is the best means of attracting a diverse range of participants, and community visibility is the *only* way to ensure community participation.

Your core group will need to match participants, leaders, meeting sites, and schedules. You may simply be able to assign leaders to specific sites, then advertise the meeting places and times. Now you're ready to examine pollution—and perhaps to come up with meaningful solutions to the problem. The study circles themselves are, of course, the heart of the program. Midway through the sessions, you might call a meeting for circle leaders only, allowing them to compare notes, discuss group interaction problems, and garner new approaches to the subject. When the sessions have been completed, hold a community meeting that includes all circle participants and leaders. This "grand finale" is a celebration of the process, a means of reporting on the process and achieving closure, and an occasion to inform participants about new and existing action groups. You might want to begin planning a second round of study circles, to ensure that the fresh enthusiasm of your participants doesn't dissipate.

Funding

Unlike traditional salons, community-wide study circles often seek outside funding. Your planning group will probably need to purchase or copy study guides and supplementary reading materials. Some advertising may be necessary. Because circles often meet in public places, you may need to pay for use of the facilities. Training your facilitators may necessitate further expenditures. The costs are hardly astronomical— any small group could probably cover them with a donation of ten or twenty dollars per participant—but remember that study circles evolved from a philosophy of free and universally available adult education. The desire to include the poorest members of society ruled out asking for even small donations, and most contemporary study circles retain this egalitarian philosophy.

Fortunately, many organizations and companies have become interested in convening and funding study circles. A sponsoring organization may pay for meeting place rentals, study materials, and facilitator training—particularly if you'll be studying an issue relevant to the organization's activities. Some libraries are willing to cover the costs of copying materials under their educational or outreach funding, and they may be able to help by posting notices for the circles or locating information that the group needs.

In Sweden, study circle associations receive over $100 million annually in governmental grants. However, government aid in the United States is virtually nonexistent,

> 66 Why should we subsidize intellectual curiosity?"
> —Ronald Reagan

so local businesses and community organizations are your most likely funding sources. When you seek funding, keep a few things in mind. Organizations that provide funding may not be acting from purely altruistic motives. At the least, they may hope to glean ideas and opinions from a broader base of people than they ordinarily contact. They may attempt to set your agenda; they may even ask you to use internally developed (and potentially biased) study guides. Before you accept any money, be certain that your sponsor understands the purpose of the study circles and supports the participants' freedom to choose or supplement reading materials. Determine in advance whether the sponsor requires you to present a report, summary, or other information after the circle has ended.

Basic Format

Despite their name and their historic association with adult education, study circles are more like public salons than traditional classrooms. They emphasize analysis, integration of information, and the airing of opinions, rather than passive learning. Like salons, study circles also enable people to practice their communication and group organizing skills.

A study circle is generally comprised of five to fifteen people who meet regularly over a period of weeks or months to address the chosen issue. In most cases, facilitators receive leadership training. The facilitator is there not as an expert, but to keep the discussions focused, to help the group consider a variety of viewpoints, to ask difficult questions, and to help participants find areas of common ground. Because most study circles are organized around a particular issue, participants may discuss the subject more deeply than they would in short-lived, informal salon conversations. The circle typically progresses from shared personal experiences relevant to the issue to informational sessions encouraging a broader perspective, culminating in a final "action session," in which participants determine what they would like to do about the problem at hand. However, attaining a consensus is not always necessary or appropriate. Some groups will remain divided in their opinions; there is no need to attempt to hammer out an agreement.

Study circle participants should be committed to the effort. The program is time-consuming in the short run, because circles usually meet once or twice weekly for two to three hours at a time, for a total of three to five sessions. Attendees are urged to show up for every meeting, as the group's comfort level depends in large part upon familiarity, but the group may disband once the course of study is completed. The commitment, then, is often intense but short term.

Study Guides

Study circles follow a clear course of study, often using study guides designed for the purpose. The guides provide information, but in most cases they also frame the discussion with specific questions and establish an agenda for each meeting. For example, the Bricklayers & Allied Craftsmen union has used guides and other materials intended to: bring all members into the initial discussion (session one); provide content on the topic (sessions two to four); and encourage discussion of next steps, collective action, and the future (session five).

Prepared study materials are available through the Study Circles Resource Center and National Issues Forums (see appendix for addresses). The SCRC also trains facilitators and publishes a newsletter called *FOCUS on Study Circles*. National Issues Forums concentrates on making study circles accessible and widespread, providing both English and Spanish language topic books, videos, audiotapes, moderator guides, and promotional materials. NIF also tries to convey the opinions of study circle participants to policy makers. Study guides provided by the SCRC or NIF are inexpensive or free. They are clearly written, and they span a fairly broad range of viewpoints. Perhaps the most important advantage of using prepared study guides is the knowledge that groups all over the country are discussing the same issue and using the same materials. Your group may find itself invigorated and motivated by being part of a nationwide effort to come to grips with a particular issue.

Use prepared study materials cautiously and critically. Be prepared to supplement them with additional articles, books, or information if you find that the study materials are biased, incomplete, or simplistic. You may also put together your own study guide from copied news reports and book extracts. Some private study circles use rented video documentaries as the basis for study, or discuss a series being aired on public radio or television.

Most study circles ask all participants to read the same materials at the same time. However, members of the Southern California Salon Community Network have used reading materials for short sessions, without requiring

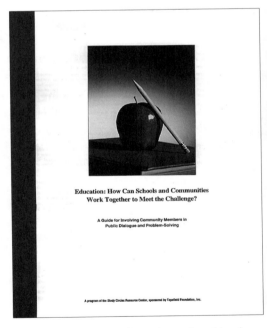

Education: How Can Schools and Communities
Work Together to Meet the Challenge?

A Guide for Involving Community Members in
Public Dialogue and Problem-Solving

A program of the Study Circles Resource Center, sponsored by Topsfield Foundation, Inc.

A study guide produced by the Study Circles Resource Center

people to read them ahead of time. They either read together in the group or cut the proposed article into paragraphs, discussing one paragraph at a time.

Study Circle Leadership

Leadership begins with the study circle *organizer*, who may or may not be the same person as the *facilitator*. The organizer selects reading material, recruits participants, arranges the meeting places and times, and may choose the discussion facilitators. If the organizer does not serve as facilitator, his or her job is over once the study circles begin to meet.

During the initial session, participants develop ground rules and share their personal experiences. This meeting is typically wide ranging and open ended, but study circle facilitators become more directive in later sessions in order to cover the territory within the specified number of meetings. Because time is limited, the leaders are less likely to tolerate digression; however, most are intent on examining underlying values and achieving deep analysis of the issue.

The study circle leader may function primarily as a referee, guiding the discussion but refraining from expressing personal opinions. Facilitators are expected to be more familiar with the study materials than anyone else; to provide supplementary materials; to guide the discussion so that each session follows a clear agenda; to intervene when arguments arise or the discussion gets too far off track; and to conclude the study circle by organizing the participants' opinions and recommendations into some kind of summary.

The leader may be assisted by a *note taker* or *recorder*. This role can be assigned to one person, or it can be shared by several members. Essentially, the recorder takes notes on what people say, thereby tracking the progress of the study circle. He or she may take notes while sitting down and read them back if called upon; or the recorder may take notes while standing at a blackboard or large tablet. Taking private notes is less disruptive to the flow of conversation, but the note taker must be careful to write what is really said, rather than interpreting or eliminating opinions. Writing notes publicly can slow the conversation down, but the process lets people clarify and refine their ideas as they are written. If the recorder has skipped something, deeming it unimportant, the speaker can demand its inclusion. The recorder should write things down in the speaker's own words or get permission to paraphrase, so that the meaning is not unintentionally changed.

Like salon scribes, recorders should be good at asking people to clarify their comments without appearing disagreeable or confrontative. In fact, the recorder's requests for clarification often help keep the discussion focused. A good recorder knows when this kind of question will be helpful and consistent with the group's purpose. The job of taking notes carries with it a substantial amount of power. It can influence which subjects (and people) are regarded as most important, where the discussion is headed, and how the group perceives itself.

The facilitator may also ask one participant to serve as *researcher* or *resource person*, locating extra reading materials, videos, or a guest lecturer when members decide they want to learn more about a topic.

Facilitation training is encouraged in study circles to ensure that leaders understand the intent and spirit of community involvement. It's best if the facilitators are not experts, professional teachers, or lecturers; instead, they should be people devoted to seeking common ground with other participants on a significant issue. In the words of the Study Circles Resource Center, facilitators must ensure that "participants do not attempt to convert each other, express outcomes through voting, or force a consensus."

The focus on a single subject sometimes attracts one or more members who are not interested in learning, but who intend to coerce others into adopting their pre-conceived views. Even study circle leaders must constantly monitor themselves to be certain that they

GUIDELINES FOR STUDY CIRCLE LEADERS

- Establish a friendly and relaxed atmosphere from the start.

- Begin each session with a brief review of the reading material.

- Keep the discussion focused on the topic.

- Do not allow an aggressive, talkative person or faction to dominate.

- Draw out quiet participants.

- Be an active listener.

- Stay neutral and be cautious about expressing your own values.

- Use conflict productively. Don't allow participants to personalize their disagreements.

- Don't be afraid of pauses and silences.

- Don't allow the group to perceive you as the expert or "answer person."

- Don't always be the one to respond to comments or questions.

- Synthesize or summarize the discussion from time to time.

- Ask hard questions.

- Use open-ended questions.

- Don't worry about attaining consensus.

- Close each session with a summary and perhaps an evaluation.

Source: Study Circles Resource Center

are not promoting a personal agenda. One form of insurance involves recruiting as diverse a group as possible. In truly diverse gatherings, biases are quickly pointed out and protested.

You can often recognize proselytizers by their tendency to reduce every discussion to the simplest, broadest dichotomies, and by their intolerance for doubts or gradations. As facilitator, you may be able to handle these speakers by finding a small point of agreement, then inviting others to speak. Some coercers are well intentioned, and can be cajoled or joked out of their insistence on one right answer or viewpoint. Those who will not be swayed, however, may split your circle into two factions—those who are influenced and those who are resentful. If two camps stubbornly polarize, you might set up a separate meeting to focus on their respective positions. Allow each side a chance to present the bases for their beliefs, then open the discussion up to the whole group. In most cases, early agreement upon the values, goals, and ground rules will circumvent sermonizing and conflict. Most true "fanatics" don't want to participate in egalitarian groups that aren't easily manipulated, so they will simply drop out.

Much of the study circle leader's work is performed during the first session. At that time, the facilitator describes the study circle format, briefly reviews the reading materials, and explains any ballots or questionnaires that will be filled out at the conclusion of the process. He or she then guides discussion of the values, ground rules, and goals the group wants to adopt. The leader should remember that some people have no previous experience in a member-run group. Some facilitators lead a brief discussion of the differences between hierarchical and nonhierarchical groups. The core values integral to the functioning of a nonhierarchical group may emerge during this discussion, and may be posted on the wall as reminders.

The Center for Conflict Resolution in Madison, Wisconsin, lists the core values of nonhierarchical groups as follows:

❝❞ Defend democracy not as the most efficient but as the most educational form of government—one that extends the circle of debate as widely as possible and thus forces all citizens to articulate their views, to put their views at risk, and to cultivate the virtues of eloquence, clarity of thought and expression, and sound judgment."

—Christopher Lasch, "Journalism, Publicity, and the Lost Art of Argument"

Democracy. Each person has the opportunity to participate in any group of which he or she is a member without prejudice; the planning of any meeting is open and shared by the facilitator and the participants; the agenda is designed to meet participants' needs and is open to participant changes; and for the period of time during which the facilitator is working with the group, no hierarchical organizational structure is functioning.

Responsibility. All members agree that they are responsible for their own experiences, behavior, and participation.

Cooperation. Everyone in the group works together to achieve the agreed upon goals.

Honesty. Everyone is committed to a straightforward expression of values, feelings, concerns, and priorities, especially the facilitator.

Egalitarianism. Everyone can and will contribute to the group; however, anyone can choose at any time not to participate for a while. The facilitator has as much to learn from group members as they have from the facilitator.

The commitment to egalitarianism means that the facilitator must strive to prevent others from reading too much expertise or authority into what he or she says. Facilitators should regularly explain what they are doing and why. The more they demystify their actions, the more others will learn to act with authority.

Following the discussion of core values (including any other values suggested by the group), the facilitator can help the group establish a list of behavioral ground rules. These rules specify how to go about taking turns, time limits for speakers, and so on. The leader must be certain that everyone understands and agrees upon the rules before writing them down. The rules should not be too inflexible; nor should they be the primary focus of the group. The only universal rule is that everyone must make a good effort to show up for every meeting, as the study circle will not function properly without a strong commitment from participants.

In many cases, the remainder of the first session is devoted to sharing personal experiences relevant to the subject the group is studying. However, if the "groundwork" portion of the meeting has been time consuming, personal experiences can instead become the focus of the group's second session.

It is likely that, at some point, a participant will question the credibility of the group leader or the validity of the group process. If you're the leader, regard it as an opportunity for growth and improvement. Don't get defensive or try too hard to maintain control of the group. Remember that everyone's insights and concerns are valid—and if one person has qualms, so might others in the group. Instead of criticizing or arguing with the participant, take a deep breath and trust your common sense. Refer to the common values and goals the group has outlined. Ask the whole group to

THE PROS AND CONS OF EXPERTISE

In a salon every opinion is, at least initially, accorded equal weight. The insights of non-scholars are treated as seriously as those of academics. Some people balk at this. In a letter to the *Los Angeles Times*, following the publication of an article about salons, one reader wrote: "The proposal to have neighborhood 'salons' or Kaffe-Klatches with neighbors to discuss weighty matters is about as impractical, unrealistic, and certain to be fruitless as any idea since city councils opened chambers to public participants to steer common interest debate. Many people end up squabbling about subjects most of them know nothing about. Do you really want to discuss President Bush's 'new world order' with Frau Housewife from across the street? Are you anxious for input from neighbor Jones about the reunification of Eastern Europe? I am not! ... Let's satisfy our intellectual wants at the hands of acknowledged scholar/experts."

These comments reflect the indoctrination that most of us receive in schools. Implicitly and explicitly, we are taught not to think for ourselves. The Department of Education or the local school board determines what students should learn; teachers are expected to provide all the necessary knowledge. Many of us have been penalized for asking questions or challenging the information presented. Upon graduation, the media becomes our socially approved source of knowledge. News agencies transmit the (often trivial) information that will effectively sell newspapers and television programming, while ignoring or glossing over complex issues. Thus we are dissuaded from investigating issues or discovering the truth for ourselves.

One problem with relying on outside knowledge is that we are left unempowered. In addition, people who are experts on a particular subject may jealously guard their knowledge. In extreme cases, a self-proclaimed genius will insist that his or her ideas are so brilliant that no one could possibly understand them. Such "experts" are reluctant to rephrase their ideas in clear terms that might pave the way for discussion. They may use mysterious jargon and contorted grammar to ensure that their ideas seem profound and extraordinary.

When a pedant's ideas are translated, they are often revealed as illogical or trivial.

I do not mean to imply that anyone who has obtained in-depth knowledge of a subject is a boor and a fake. Many people who have undertaken thorough study of a particular field are eloquent and passionate when discussing it. It makes no more sense to dismiss all experts than it does to rely exclusively on outside expertise.

I also do not wish to imply that salon members should avoid seeking information from experts on subjects about which they are mostly ignorant. But the information provided must be treated critically. It should not overwhelm the group or take the place of independent thought.

If your group decides to investigate a topic more thoroughly, you may decide to invite a guest speaker. Choose the speaker carefully. A good speaker has a lively personality, is at ease talking to groups, can explain information in layperson's terms, and has unusual ideas to present. The speaker should assume that he or she is addressing an intelligent, experienced audience, and should welcome interruptions and questions. I suggest avoiding professional speakers. Their talks are often canned lectures, and they may expect to be paid. However, according to library salonist Ron Gross, distinguished experts who are invited to his salons are often flattered that such a group wants to hear from them. As a result, they are willing to forgo their customary lecture fee.

The habit of turning to experts and authorities for information while discounting personal knowledge is, in the final analysis, detrimental to democracy and conducive to oppressive government. It is therefore critical that every citizen establish his or her intellectual independence. Unfettered group discussions are one way of overcoming reliance on outside expertise and authority. After Minnesotan Sally Shelton attended a local study circle, she realized that "Nobody has the right answer, but we all have our own perspective and experience, and those are equally important to help find the answers. I started to feel that I had not only a right but a responsibility to speak up."

> **66** When everyone listens
> and everyone speaks, everyone learns."
>
> —Rachel Nesse, from a letter to the *Utne Reader*

discuss the problem openly and decide whether changes should be made. Recognize that the group may be fumbling with an unfamiliar subject in an unfamiliar setting. If you do feel attacked or hurt, ask that the problem be dealt with at a later time, after you've had time to reflect and to distance yourself emotionally from the situation. You might choose to turn the meeting over to a cofacilitator, or to someone else in the group who can remain relatively neutral.

When the facilitator demonstrates wholehearted dedication to the group, yet is able to relinquish authority, the study circle will function well. When the leader lets go of his or her plans and allows members to find their own way, even imperfect words and mistakes will ultimately aid the group in its search for knowledge and solutions.

Harvesting the Public Voice

Study circle participants frequently want to convey their opinions and recommendations to local or national policy makers. This is what the NIF calls "harvesting the public voice." In a handout on the subject, the NIF explains that harvesting ideas is primarily a matter of creating a written record: "Depending on the issues you harvest, you may develop: statements that guide policy; statements about the nature of [the] conversation; statements about how the public talks about the issue; and statements about values." The written record can be used to let political representatives know what their constituents are thinking and how they recommend dealing with various problems.

For the study circle, arriving at a summary or interpretation of the process is a form of closure. It ensures that participants are not left feeling empty or dissatisfied after several weeks of intensive discussion. It may also move the group a step closer toward community involvement and activism, especially if members are providing feedback to a sponsoring organization. A case in point is the Minneapolis Board of Education's "Quality Schools Study Circles," a series established by the board in the spring of 1993. Parents throughout Minneapolis were invited to discuss how children should be assigned to schools, bearing in mind the need for integration in the city and its suburbs. Local group leaders were trained in evening sessions before the study circles started. The leaders then recruited participants. Materials were provided by the board, including information on the nature of study circles; maps of the districts, neighborhoods, and schools; sample agendas for meetings; newspaper articles on issues affecting the schools; and research results from surveys of parents. Ballots were also provided, allowing participants to choose among three options. However, parents were encouraged to discuss all aspects of education and talk about their criteria for quality education. As a means of harvesting the participants' input, information was subsequently collected, summarized, and presented to the school board.

Harvesting can take the form of a ballot, in which participants reach a consensus endorsing one of three or four courses of action. A questionnaire can be used in lieu of the ballot to provide more in-depth reflection on the values and issues at stake. Sometimes each participant is simply asked to reflect on the process and provide feedback about what worked or didn't work in the circle. The ballot method is popular because it is easy to fill out, and because it provides participants with several clear choices to debate. Ballots were used in the Minneapolis *Star Tribune*'s abbreviated versions of study circles, which were called "Minnesota's Talking Roundtable Discussions." People from the community met throughout the metropolitan area once or twice a month to discuss an issue chosen by the *Star Tribune*. The newspaper let readers know where groups were forming in their neighborhoods and who to contact. It offered free facilitator training and provided optional reading materials, evaluation forms, and ballots that participants could send to the paper. At the end of each month, the paper printed information from these ballots in the paper, usually to augment a series of articles on the subject.

The problem with the ballot system is similar to the one posed by prepared study guides. Ballots often reduce complex issues to just a few choices, and the choices may represent middle-of-the-road approaches rather than genuine alternatives. The ballot provided by the *Star Tribune* for roundtable discussions of racism made some unwarranted associations between racism and crime. This angered participants of the group I attended, but it also spurred some spirited and creative debate. The participants ended up writing their own choices on the ballots, rather than accepting those provided. One way to avoid focusing a discussion on just a few choices is to hand out ballots at the *end* of the study circle sessions, rather than using them from the beginning.

A study circle in Somerville, Massachusetts

MINNESOTA'S TALKING

Monthly in the **Star Tribune**

The NIF recommends another method of harvesting opinions. Post a large chart with the following four headings: Directions or Courses of Action That Most of Us Can Live With; Areas of Disagreement; Dilemmas or Hard Choices We Are Not Able to Resolve at This Time; and New Thoughts and Insights. At the end of the study circle, ask participants to fill in the chart together, based on what they've discovered during their conversations. This sort of open-ended chart encourages much freer discussion throughout, but it must be summarized clearly if you intend to present it elsewhere.

Of course, reading and discussion don't necessarily lead to social change or political participation. However, studies in Sweden have shown that if a study circle stays together as a group, the subjects explored over time tend to move from cultural studies to increasingly difficult, controversial issues, and eventually toward political and social activism. The "dynamic democracy" reflected in today's study circles offers an avenue of participation for all of us, regardless of race, religion, gender, or economic status. The authors of *Hard Choices*, a publication of National Issues Forums, see a direct connection between discussion and democracy: "The task our democracy faces now is to blend thousands of divergent interests and points of view into a common sense of direction for our country and our communities. The only way to do this is for us to talk with each other. After all, democracy does not begin with elections; it begins with conversations."

Councils:
Friends, Palavers, and Talking Sticks

We should neither be hindered from making experiments by fear or undue caution,
nor prompted by novel suggestions to ill-considered courses.
—Religious Society of Friends' *Book of Discipline* (1960)

In the European conversational tradition, one person offers a remark. The next person picks up where the first left off—by agreeing, adding more detail and clarification, providing a related comment or experience, or arguing a contrary view. By contrast, in the process called "council," one person speaks for a while, then there is a period of silence. The next person's remarks may pertain to the same topic, but they are not necessarily related to the content of the previous speaker's comments. Each participant in a council is expected to hold a piece of the truth; only when each has contributed can the whole truth be discovered. There is, therefore, little debating or weighing of pros and cons in most traditional councils.

Council is essentially a formal, even ritualized, way of taking turns, to ensure that everyone in the group contributes. The council method includes storytelling and oratory intended to persuade and entertain others. As a matter of integrity, it asks people to practice active listening, a way of speaking and listening with generous hearts rather than critical minds.

Conversational groups are increasingly experimenting with council methods when making decisions, resolving interpersonal conflicts, or attempting to add a spiritual dimension to meetings. Participating in the council process can be a transformative experience, particularly in groups that habitually fall into argument and debate. Like study circles, the purpose of council is to discover a common ground, a context that can incorporate everyone's views.

However, council groups are still relatively uncommon. Most aspects of the method are foreign to modern North Americans, just as they were once foreign to me. In creating this chapter, I have drawn from extensive reading on council forms from different parts of the world, as well as my own participation in discussion groups using council processes. From the Christian tradition of the Society of Friends, or Quakers, I learned about the uses of silence in both spiritual and business meetings, and about building consensus through council. From the Hawaiian council method called *ho'oponopono*, I learned about the use of ritual, the role of facilitation, and techniques for promoting group harmony. Primarily through reading, I learned about the power of oratory and storytelling as used in political discussions, or *palavers*, that have taken place in African village councils. In addition, I have studied Native American councils and those conducted by the Maaori, a Polynesian people native to New Zealand. It's my hope that these multicultural precedents will be a source of inspiration as you conduct your own investigation of council methods.

I hasten to point out, however, that the methods and concepts described here are much simplified. Though potentially powerful, they do not carry the weight and complexity of a true cultural practice. Traditional councils are culture-specific; they are deeply rooted in community, politics, and religion. Unless you have been raised in such a culture or accepted into a religious belief system that makes use of council, please do not claim to be following traditional practices as you explore council methods. On the other side of the coin, be particularly suspicious of anyone who charges money for the privilege of attending their "council."

Native American activists have become increasingly unhappy with other people who borrow their spiritual practices without acquiring a deep understanding of what the practices entail or forging a commitment to a specific Native American tribe. On February 28, 1993, Maine Indian activists protested a New Age "talking circle" because they felt the group was exploiting their heritage. "Only Indians can teach or practice Indian spiritual rites such as talking circles," the activists stated. "Indian spirituality can never be sold, bartered, or exchanged for money."

I do believe, however, that the following methods have enormous potential for transforming group interaction. If your group practices them willingly, approaches them with flexibility, and imbues them with a sense of humor, you can create your own context for the use of council. Instead of attempting to co-opt or appropriate the traditions of other cultures, encourage your group members to study their own religious and ethnic heritage for examples of storytelling, oratory, ritual, silence, turn taking, and cooperation. These traditions can enrich and distinguish your council process.

"Not too long ago, before our ears became accustomed to an increasing barrage of stimulation, many people knew how to listen attentively from a state of stillness—for example, while tracking an animal or hearing the approach of rain or sitting in Council with a group of similarly intentioned peers. When we are graced with that kind of listening and devoted to its practice, our ability to be empathic grows. We enter a world of spontaneous self-discovery and ultimately come to recognize our inseparable connection to all forms of life. **"**

—Jack Zimmerman and Virginia Coyle, *Council*

Taking Turns

Traditional councils are strictly structured. Members speak in a predetermined order, and for a specified period of time. However, any group attempting to ensure that everyone gets a chance to speak without interruption is adopting a simplified version of the council process. The Twelve Step groups of Alcoholics Anonymous are among the many support and recovery groups that in effect practice council.

Many salons use the council method as a training device, abandoning it once they have established a habit of truly listening to one another and allowing everyone a chance to speak. By itself, this device can be quite beneficial, especially if a salon tends to be dominated by a few members. Sometimes progress can be made simply by asking everyone to start paying attention to the person speaking. The salon facilitator may suggest that, for one meeting, all members must speak (or decline an opportunity) before anyone can speak a second time. Some salons are dominated by one gender. For one meeting, the facilitator might suggest that men and women take turns speaking.

Another approach involves dividing the room up and asking people to take turns speaking from two long lines, as some Maaori tribes do. In these tribal councils, called *hui*, all local speakers sit along one side of a long hall, while speakers visiting from another village sit along the other wall. The locals may speak in turn until they're finished, followed by the visiting speakers. Or the speakers may alternate from side to side, progressing down each line.

If your group spans a wide age range and the oldest members seem to do all the talking, you might learn from the people of Idoma, Nigeria. There, council participants speak in order by age, and the youngest child is urged to speak first. Alternatively, you can break down hierarchy in any group by assigning turns randomly. You might accomplish this by rolling dice or drawing names from a hat.

The Fishbowl

The fishbowl is another method of taking turns. With slight variations, the fishbowl is used in parts of Africa for conflict resolution. It has also been taught by the Ojai Foundation, headquartered in California, which has been instrumental in popularizing and teaching council methods in the United States. To try this approach, ask two or more people to sit on chairs or cushions in the center of a circle comprised of everyone else in your group. Ask each of the people in the center to speak. As one speaker finishes, he or she should leave the center seat, returning to the outer ring. Anyone from the circle is now free to move to the center and speak. Members can return to the fishbowl a second time, but most wait until everyone in the circle has had a chance to sit in the center.

The fishbowl is an effective turn-taking practice, especially if your group is large or is discussing a complex, emotional issue. The method reduces confrontation by maintaining the group's focus on just one person at a time. It is also useful when two clear sides emerge in a discussion, or when two people are at odds with one another. In the latter case, the two people representing antagonistic viewpoints can sit in the center, facing one another. Each speaker takes turns stating his or her views as clearly and nonjudgmentally as possible. Then each chooses someone from the outer circle to discuss the same problem, relinquishing the center position and returning to the larger group. The process continues until everyone is satisfied that all aspects of the issue have been aired.

In a variant developed by the Ojai Foundation, two individuals who represent antagonistic positions may be joined in the fishbowl by two witnesses. The witnesses may be chosen by the two adversaries or by the

"It does seem to limit the length of his comments..."

larger circle. All four sit facing each other, and the two who have been disagreeing with one another state their positions in turn. Then each one speaks a second time in response to the other, or to clarify the first round of statements. Finally, the two witnesses take turns making comments—not taking sides, but describing what has been said. The witnesses can then leave the center; anyone from the outer circle is free to enter the fishbowl and share ideas or observations. Alternatively, the fishbowl may end, and the larger group can continue the discussion.

These methods help provide emotional distance from the issue at hand. They enable two people who are polarized to hear more evenhanded accounts of the problem. The fishbowl and most other methods of taking turns are not necessary every time a group meets. These techniques should be suggested primarily when the group needs to focus on a particular problem or establish new patterns for interacting.

The Talking Stick

The talking stick is one turn-taking device that can be used regularly. For many people, its use defines the council method. The talking "stick" can in fact be any object signifying that the person holding it is entitled to speak. The custom of using such an object is most often attributed to Native American tribes, but it has been a tradition in many parts of the world, including ancient Greece.

The ritual object reminds the holder to take a deep breath, and to speak on a contemplative, highly personal level. It acts, almost mysteriously in some cases, to facilitate a sincere sharing of ideas and feelings. This may be because, as Jack Zimmerman and Virginia Coyle of the Ojai Foundation have explained, an object gains significance when used repeatedly over months or years by a group. In their words, "[It] becomes a symbol of the group's integrity and capability for spirited communication, and so can help empower the expressiveness of the individual who holds it."

Traditionally, a talking stick is selected from a tree that the group considers meaningful. The stick or wand is then decorated with paint, fabric, and any small items that remind the group of shared experiences. To enhance its symbolic power, the stick is wrapped in a silk cloth or stored in a box when not in use.

The talking stick doesn't have to be a stick, and it doesn't have to last forever. If your group is interested in using a ritual object, you might choose a flower for your first attempt—or a feather, a stone, a shell, or virtually any other object. At salons held in Mad Magda's Russian Tea Room and Café in San Francisco, members have passed around a wooden borscht ladle. Other groups use a small noisemaking device.

Traditionally, the talking stick is handed clockwise around the circle, allowing each person to speak in turn. It is always acceptable to pass if you have nothing to say, but it is wise to hold the stick for a few moments of silence before doing so. Unexpected thoughts may well up from within.

There are other ways of taking turns with the talking stick. Becky Meagher's salon in Nashville, Tennessee, has left an old gourd in the center of the room. Members carry on their conversation as usual until someone feels moved to pick up the gourd. When this happens, the normal flow of talk ceases; the person holding the gourd has the floor until he or she returns it to the center. Other groups use the talking stick throughout, but return it to the center after each speaker finishes. Anyone who wishes to speak next picks it up.

The talking stick can be used in many environments. Bruce Hyde, assistant professor of speech communication at Minnesota's St. Cloud State University, has used it in the classroom. According to Hyde, the method is so powerful that no theory or explanation need accompany its introduction. He described an incident at a departmental retreat: "The person who was facilitating the meeting just grabbed a magic marker off the blackboard and handed it to the first person. It started a round. It really allowed people to express themselves fully.

I think in any environment where there's tension, or where people are reluctant to express themselves, it gives them freedom."

Only the person holding the object is allowed to speak, so it is understood that no one is allowed to interrupt. The sole exception involves expressions of agreement directed by the group toward whomever is speaking. Some groups say "Ho!" in imitation of Native American councils, but I suggest an appreciative "Mmm-hmmm" or "Uh-huh." On occasion, people may be moved to become even more vocal; I see no reason to outlaw "Tell it, girl!," "Speak the truth!," "You've got *that* right!" or other enthusiastic choruses. As the talking stick process becomes familiar, you may choose to further relax the no-interruption rule. You are establishing an agreed upon norm for your group, not adhering to a mandatory standard. Some salons have gone so far as to ban laughter. To me this policy seems counterproductive. Laughter plays a vital role in binding people together.

Turn taking tends to be more time consuming than open conversation. Most salons therefore establish a time limit when using the talking stick, often three to five minutes per speaker. Even with a time limit, it's best to include no more than six to twelve people if you hope to go around the circle more than once. Twelve people with a five-minute speaking limit require over an hour for each cycle, allowing time for passing the stick, silence, and breathing quietly while preparing to speak. If your group is large, you may want to break into small groups to discuss a particular issue. Each subgroup can reach a consensus, then choose one member to represent its ideas in a larger council at the end of the meeting. During this concluding portion, all members watch and listen, and all are free to assume the talking stick if they wish to speak.

However, if you are truly dedicated to practicing council, ignore time. Try letting the circle function until it reaches its own conclusion, without checking the clock or fretting when someone talks at length. Traditional councils may last all night or continue for several days if an important community action is being considered. Among the Maaori, informal family councils start after dinner and continue until dawn. These late-night discussions become increasingly uninhibited and imaginative. As the night progresses, it becomes each speaker's duty to keep everyone else awake—by singing or playing music if necessary. Or the family may pass the "walking stick," jovially forcing sleepy participants to sit up, move around, and say something.

If you would like to invite children to a salon but fear they would be hard pressed to participate in your conversations, try using a talking stick and discussing a topic relevant to their experiences. You might, for example, talk about what makes for a good teacher. Holding the stick lets young people feel confident that they are being treated as equals. You may be startled by the stories and wise observations they contribute.

Talking sticks and other turn-taking methods are particularly appropriate if your

"The simplicity of the use of the talking stick is deceptive but it's very powerful. People who don't usually listen have to listen, and people who don't usually talk because they're intimidated get the space to talk. Freed from the impulse to interrupt, people are forced to listen. 🙶

—Salonist Bruce Hyde

topic lends itself to personal and experiential discussion. Council rounds are also effective in conflict resolution and decision making. Some salons prefer to use talking sticks only when they have a particular problem they want to resolve or a course of action to consider. However, you can also use a talking stick when no particular discussion topic or issue has been chosen. In this kind of open council, called a "check-in" or "weather report" by some salons, members take turns describing what's going on in their lives. They may tell a story, reflect on something in a current news report, or describe an incident or encounter that moved them. Remarks by one person may trigger comments or reflections from others in the group, and the circle often begins to draw together around a particular theme. This theme then becomes the basis for further discussion.

In lieu of selecting a topic, you might pose an open-ended question that encourages people to draw on their life experiences, eliciting personal stories. An initial round based on such a question can be conducted before a salon begins its customary discussion. Questions that focus on personal experience can be followed by broader questions related to the topic. Activist/facilitator Margo Adair suggests opening with questions like these:

"Can you describe a major turning point in your life?"

"What role model has inspired you?"

"Which activities have you enjoyed lately, and which have been difficult?"

> 66 If Margaret Mead's people of the Manus could sit down and deliberately redesign their culture and bring it in line with the twentieth century, we should be able to do the same. But why bother to try to understand, to empathize, to learn somebody else's culture? Why bother to learn a new set of rules and new ways of communicating? Isn't the job too subtle, too complex, and too ill-defined? Perhaps. But the rewards can be very great, and the alternatives are unthinkable."
>
> —Anthropologist Edward T. Hall, *Dance of Life*

"What is a burning question for you at this time in your life?"

"Which aspects of your heritage do you take pride in?"

"How did the people who raised you make a living, and how did they feel about it?"

Quakers follow a similar format when they pose "queries" meant to stimulate deeper thinking on a matter. The queries often include questions related to childhood or early experiences. I like to open a meeting by posing questions related to the topic that was discussed at the previous session. People often have reflections or experiences to share, adding depth to the previous conversation and providing a sense of continuity from one gathering to the next. At the Ojai Foundation, morning councils are often begun by passing the talking stick and asking people to share dreams from the night before. The collective response creates a montage that mirrors the circle's journey into the dreamworld.

Ritual

Ceremony is the smoke of friendship.
        —Chinese proverb

Both passing a sacred object and opening your meeting with a round of storytelling are ways of adding ritual. Ritual actions may be used to pace the group, focus attention, prepare people for nonordinary interactions, bind community through shared experiences, and add a spiritual dimension to discussions. In particular, a ritual opening helps people depart from their habitual ways of being with one another, and distinguishes the salon from more ordinary activities.

In the salon context, ritual can be as simple as setting aside the first fifteen minutes for introductions or recapping the last meeting. You may also choose to add prayer, short meditation, conscious breathing, or a period of silence to your opening ritual. Quakers believe that starting with five to fifteen minutes of silent worship or meditation helps center people, freeing

A group practicing council

them to speak from a wise and heartfelt place.

Many councils light a fire (if outdoors) or a candle in the center of the circle as part of their ritual. Flame is a traditional symbol of transformation. Hawaiians believe the central fire absorbs negative emotions that may emerge during the council. Consequently, they bury the ashes far away when ho'oponopono is over, symbolically ensuring that the conflicts will not return to disrupt community harmony.

Eating as a group is both a ritual and a celebration of community. Sharing a meal can also change the pace or direction of the discussion. In almost all traditional councils, dining together is as important a part of maintaining community harmony as the discussion itself.

Masks or other objects can be used as ritual representations of different attitudes and viewpoints. The speaker may, by putting on a mask, hat, or cloak, choose to speak for an animal spirit, a god, or some other being. The person becomes open to receiving wisdom from larger or more powerful sources, perhaps gaining access to extraordinary thoughts and impressions.

For most gatherings, a means of closure is even more important than a ritual opening. An abrupt conclusion feels anticlimactic at best; at worst, it may leave people feeling alienated and frustrated. Many traditional councils end with short, explicit summaries of what has been discussed. They may also include a time for closing prayers. During these periods, council members reflect silently on what has been said, hoping that their new level of understanding will benefit the world in the future.

Council Leadership

Like traditional salons and study circles, most councils include a leader who guides the process. The simple expedient of structured turn taking is helpful, but the role of a leader who sets the mood for the group and keeps it on track is essential. Zimmerman and Coyle recommend using two facilitators, or *chiefs*—preferably a man and a woman. By working as a pair, they reinforce the feeling of partnership that underlies the council process itself. Because chiefs are supposed to remain as neutral as possible, most traditional councils designate two or more leaders. One typically acts as backup, in case the other has extremely strong feelings on a particular subject.

The qualities of a good council leader appear to be universally agreed upon.

66 The word is half his that speaks, and half his that hears it."

—Michel de Montaigne, French essayist

Whether the occasion is a Native American council, a Quaker meeting, or ho'opono-pono, those considered the best leaders have a sense of humor; they are emotionally mature, honest, free from self-centeredness, and sufficiently extroverted. They must regard all individuals as partial keepers of truth, and they are simultaneously sensitive to the quality of the discussion and the moods of individuals. In addition, many councils expect leaders to have some religious training, and to view the council process as a spiritual one.

A leader may open a council meeting with prayer or silence, secure the talking stick if one will be used, and remind members of the agreed upon rules of conduct. He or she then introduces the discussion topic or the agenda for the meeting, often beginning the first round by asking a question. The leader may pause for a moment of reflection, then offer the first reponse to the question. Leaders who initiate the circle in this manner should model an appropriate response by being authentic, specific, and succinct. At the Ojai Foundation, a council leader may pass the talking stick immediately to the left after framing the initial question. He or she then becomes the last to speak. Coyle and Zimmerman suggest that leaders should use their turns throughout the council meeting "not only to share on a personal level, but also to respond to what others have said, and to summarize the central themes that emerged during the session." In councils that do not employ a strict round, the leader often refrains entirely from responding to the questions posed. He or she guides the session by asking questions, summarizing what has been shared, and calling on people.

Council chiefs must avoid trying to make outcomes conform to their own expectations or hopes. Indeed, councils may not reach resolution at all. They are often concerned with the authentic search for inner truth, and are not geared to arriving at once-and-for-all answers. Sometimes the most useful role a leader can assume involves being silent at the end of a round, waiting to proceed until each individual is again ready to participate.

Despite their neutral stance, council leaders wield a considerable amount of power. They set the agenda, phrase questions, and offer summaries of the discussion. They may also discipline or rein in people who talk too long or whose comments are irrelevant. In London, Quaker *clerks* (equivalent to council chiefs) stand up silently to indicate when a speaker should relinquish the floor. If someone is regularly disruptive, becomes too theoretical, interrupts others when they are speaking, or is overly aggressive, an experienced, elder Quaker called a "weighty Friend" may take the individual aside and deliver a private admonishment.

Councils, whether focused on interpersonal dynamics or spiritual practice, often add

a designated person who does not speak at all during the meeting. This person, known as a witness, is asked to watch how people change and how the group as a whole is functioning. He or she is asked for insights at the end of the meeting. Witnesses describe what they have observed in general terms, without picking on people by name. In essence, they tell the story of the group, identifying moments when it faltered, how it changed over time, and how close it came to achieving its aim. Witnesses are particularly valuable as mirrors for council leaders, who can use the observations to handle future meetings more effectively. Regular members of the group can rotate in the witness role, or salon visitors can be asked to perform this function. Although witnesses may sit within or outside of the circle, they do not take up the talking stick.

The principles that guide council should be established at the first meeting, and the leader may remind members of these principles at any time thereafter. One guide-

66 A young girl, very solemn with the weight of her responsibility, handed her the Talking Stick, an oak staff beautifully carved, beaded, and feathered, carrying in its tip a small microphone. Powerful speakers were hidden in the branches of the four sacred trees that stood at the four quarters around the outskirts of the bowl."

—Starhawk, *The Fifth Sacred Thing*

line followed by most council groups was developed by the Ojai Foundation: "Speak honestly, be brief, and listen from the heart."

In a booklet entitled *Faith and Practice*, Quakers suggest that each member should address the leader rather than other individuals in the circle, and should "be hesitant about speaking more than once. Each vocal contribution should be something which adds to the material already given." Another common rule in councils stipulates that anyone may choose to abstain from speaking, and no one else may comment on that choice. The right to pass, then, is as sacred as the right to speak.

While members should monitor themselves to be certain that what they say is authentic and necessary, they should also ask themselves whether they are refraining from comments that deserve to be heard. The leader should encourage shy people to express themselves, for their ideas may transform the discussion, add a missing piece, or move the group toward resolution. It is also the leader's responsibility to ensure that no one fears being ostracized as a result of telling the truth. According to activist Joanna Macy, fatalism, indifference, repression, cynicism, and anger can pervade a group when difficult truths are not spoken.

In order to establish a safe environment for the revelation of deep and difficult thoughts, an explicit rule of group confidentiality is necessary. The facilitator should occasionally remind people that all comments shared in council may be discussed with others only in the broadest terms, omitting any details that might identify or harm people in the circle.

From the Heart

A fool's soul is always dancing on the tip of his tongue.
　　　　—Arabic proverb

The concept of speaking and listening from the heart suggests that we become aware of the source of our words. It implies speaking sincerely and with integrity, drawing upon imagination and intuition, and serving the group rather than one's own ego. It generally means avoiding analysis, theorizing, and debate. Speaking from the heart often triggers emotional responses, ranging from eyes filled with tears to voices ragged with anger.

Speaking from the heart requires allowing your internal body signals to guide you as you approach deeper truths. Recognize the twinge that indicates falsehood, the tension that precedes self-aggrandizement. Let these signals tell you that you are not yet ready to speak. On the other hand, if you find your heart beating faster or realize that you are holding your breath, then by all means speak. The risky words you are about to utter are likely to be important ones.

The leader must be prepared to handle emotions as they emerge without allowing the group to lose its focus. Most of the time, handling emotions is a matter of listening to someone with full attention, touching or hugging the person gently if necessary, but without probing or pushing for details. The leader may also suggest that participants direct their intense feelings toward the fire or candle at the center of the circle. Sometimes members may simply need to vent emotion for a little while. If they are listened to rather than ignored or thwarted, they will in most cases pull themselves together and refocus on the group. People who frequently indulge in emotional outbursts, however, crave attention. Whether their feelings are genuine or not, they must come to understand that they are disturbing the council process. The leader can take them aside privately to discuss the situation, perhaps asking for their suggestions and support in keeping the group focused. On occasion, individuals may disclose themselves at a level that is too intimate for the group to handle. The leader can suggest that the issues involved are too large to be dealt with at that time, asking that they be deferred until the group is ready to address them.

For some, speaking from the heart means speaking from the spirit. Quakers aim for a larger truth, believing that a part of the voice of God exists in each individual. If you have doubts about what you are about to share in council, Zimmerman and Coyle suggest asking yourself questions such as these:

"Will my speaking serve me?"

"Will the circle or the community be served?"

"Will the 'bigger picture,' Life, God . . . be served?"

The line of questioning applies doubly to the council chief, who models authentic speech for the entire council.

Speaking from the heart may entail the use of metaphor, poetry, and stories to reveal complex points of view. Myths and personal experiences are riddled with ambiguity and paradox, revealing a great deal about the nature of human reality. A speaker can use anecdotes to exemplify common human experiences. If you are the speaker, you might try describing, in the third person, something that happened to you, using such beginnings as:

"Once upon a time there was a little boy who . . ."

"There once was a woman who . . ."

"Let me tell you a story about something that happened long ago . . ."

By framing your experiences as if they happened long ago or to a fictional character, you may make it easier for others to find relevance and wisdom in your words. You may even arrive at an insight you would not have discovered if you had remained directly identified with the story. Myths, folktales, news tidbits, and childhood fables are relevant and appropriate in the context of council. There is no need to analyze these stories. Allow them to sink into the deeper consciousness of the group. Both traditional tales and modern stories bind the group in shared understanding.

Silence and Active Listening
To be outspoken is easy when you do not wait to speak the complete truth.
—Rabindranath Tagore, *Stray Birds*

While storytelling is an important component of councils, silence and careful listening are also central to the process. In many cultures a silent person is regarded as more trustworthy than a facile talker. The early English Quakers looked down upon talkativeness, considering it an indication of worldliness; silence signaled an admirable suppression of ego and will. In southern India, the Paliyan people consider verbosity abnormal and offensive. In Denmark, Sweden, and Japan, silence among friends indicates that people are at ease with each other, and have no need to fill in conversational gaps. By contrast, most Americans have grown up in a culture that regards any social silence as uncomfortable, if not downright unfriendly.

If your salon or council is open to experimentation, you might even be interested in John Hudak, who founded the Silent Meeting Club in Philadelphia. Members of this discussionless salon convened at various spots around town, but refrained from talking to one another. Hudak started the group so people would have a chance to be together without having to make the usual, obligatory small talk.

Silence can be called during discussions that have become too emotionally heated. Hawaiian council leaders declare cooling-off periods of silence, called *ho'omalu*, giving members time to reflect on the purpose of the process and bring their emotions under control. Quakers also call for periods of contemplation when a meeting is getting out of hand; sometimes the meeting is halted altogether, with an agreement to reconvene in a month's time. Here, too, the break provides time to reflect and to heed the voice of inner wisdom.

"Let thy speech be better than silence, or be silent. "
—Dionysius the Elder, Greek ruler of Syracuse

CHAMPION LISTENERS

The bravest listener I know is Frances Peavey, who undertook a world tour to find out what ordinary people thought about the prospects for our planet. In Tokyo, Bangkok, Delhi, she sat on a bench in a central square with a sign beside her. The sign read: "American Willing to Listen." People lined up in queues so long that often she was there on her bench till one or two in the morning. She did not pretend to be an important official or a famous author; "I'm just an ordinary citizen," she would say, "but I want to know what people are thinking"; and she would take notes. In Delhi she met the representative from Tonga, who was attending the world conference of Nonaligned Nations. The delegate was so struck by the role that Peavey had taken on that she set up a table for her in the lobby of the hotel where the conference was being held. Peavey came every afternoon at four, when the Tonga representative brought up one delegate after another for the simple but rare opportunity to talk to an "American willing to listen."

[Another] champion listener is Norie Huddle of the New Committee on National Security. With her tape recorder she travelled the U.S. to interview people from all walks of life. "What do you think would make America strong?" she would ask. Sometimes the immediate answers were knee-jerk reactions about building our defenses and being ready to "nuke" the Russians. But Huddle would just listen with avid interest: "And then?" As people experienced themselves being *heard*, without rebuttal or interruption, they would go on talking and find their ideas moving in new directions. "This is crazy," a truck driver would say, who had been ready to nuke the Russians, "What a world to leave our kids. You know, maybe we could have an exchange with the Soviets—their young people coming over here, ours going over there—to know each other better and reach some kind of agreement so we could survive." If Huddle had approached him to sell such an idea ... that same person might have rejected her, branding her as a "pinko." By virtue of her listening, he heard it from himself, gained respect for his own ingenuity.

—Joanna Macy, *Despair and Personal Power in the Nuclear Age*

The many inflections of silence are integral to the group voice. Silence can be pointed—for example, when people refuse to respond to an outrageous comment. It can be respectful, as when a long pause follows a particularly moving statement. It can indicate accord, pleasure, surprise, and depth of feeling, as well as sarcasm, humor, hostility, and punishment. But most importantly, silence gives people permission to speak thoughtfully and sincerely. When a speaker remains silent for a time, it indicates that he or she is waiting for the right moment or idea, not choosing words flippantly or hastily. In council, each speaker is expected to pause before beginning, waiting for inner truth to reveal itself.

Listening is the foundation of conversation. There is no such thing as a storyteller without an audience, nor a speaker without a listener. In council, a willingness to fully engage in listening ensures that use of the talking stick becomes something more profound than an exotic method of raising hands. Through listening to others carefully, we are able to step imaginatively and empathetically into their shoes, and to experience the world from an entirely different point of view, if only for a few moments. Californian Shelley Kessler, who has taught council methods to elementary school students, advocates listening "between the lines" of the person speaking, "hearing the feelings and the intentions as well as the words. It requires tremendous discipline." This sort of rigorous attention to other people's speech is variously known as creative listening, active listening, or deep listening.

Active listening is not easy. For one thing, most people think about four times faster than they speak. This means a listener can tune a speaker out three-quarters of the time while pondering his or her own ideas. If you find yourself doing this, practice watching the speaker as well as listening to what is being said. Note each word and nonverbal signal, allowing your mind to be at rest during the pauses between words. If you regularly jump to conclusions about where someone is headed and then stop listening, discipline yourself to pay attention long enough to find out whether your assumptions are correct.

"Begin low, speak slow;
take fire, rise higher;
when most impressed be self-possessed;
at the end wax warm, and sit down in a storm. 99

—Anonymous

Active listening also requires setting judgments and reactions aside. While listening, make no attempt to prepare what you might say in response. Instead, try internally summarizing the essence of what you are hearing. Ask yourself how the speaker feels about the subject, and whether his or her words are congruent with visible body language and expressions. Look for underlying meaning rather than superficial information.

Notice which words trigger automatic reactions in yourself. People often assume that everyone uses the same words to mean the same things; however, emotionally charged opposites like democracy/communism, feminine/masculine, crime/safety, and community/individualism are examples of words that mean quite different things to different people. When you find yourself reacting to what a speaker has said merely because a certain word was used, listen to determine whether the speaker is using the term the same way you use it. If you aren't sure, ask for clarification rather than arguing about what it means. You might also devote a council session to a particular word or concept that often produces misunderstandings in the group. Ask each person who holds the talking stick to state the problematic word three times, then to say whatever comes to mind (an anecdote, image, or feeling). By the end of the round, repetition will have diminished the word's impact. The images, feelings, and stories will tell your group much about what the word implies to different people.

Sometimes people become too overwhelmed to listen to one another. Perhaps the words have become repetitive, or the group has been sitting for too long and members have begun daydreaming. In councils, this is most likely to happen if the circle is a fairly big one, as no individual will have an opportunity to speak more frequently than once an hour. Psychologists suggest that forty minutes is about optimal for learning—that the mind shuts down if it's forced to take in too much at once. Therefore, it's a good idea to stretch and shift positions every forty minutes or so. Singing, meditating or praying, telling jokes, shouting, and other changes of pace help refresh participants as well.

I recommend that you practice listening skills as a group. Educate your ears by listening to books on tape, news, poetry, and rap music for five to fifteen minutes. Listen to the dialogue in older movies. A fringe benefit of listening to beautiful or unusual language is that your own spontaneous speech will become more lively and articulate.

❝ Having two ears and one tongue, we should listen twice as much as we speak.”

—Turkish proverb

You may also need to exercise your ability to understand what someone else is saying without simply picking it apart for the sake of a good argument. Try breaking into groups of three. Choose a controversial topic. Ask one person to state his or her position on the subject for roughly five minutes, then ask the second person to summarize what the first person said. To complete the round, ask the first person to talk about whether the second person's summary was accurate. Now reverse the process, asking the second person to make a statement, the first to summarize, and the second to provide feedback on the summary. Finally the third person, who has thus far been listening and observing, should comment on what he or she noticed while the others were speaking and listening.

Alternatively, you might ask two people to go into the fishbowl. First one person speaks; then the other reports to the larger group what the first person said. The group assesses the accuracy of the summary before the fishbowl process is reversed.

As another exercise, groups of about six people might allow each person to speak for two to three minutes on an emotionally charged subject. The others listen without comment. Then, without singling out individuals, the group discusses what it is about language, speaking styles, and mannerisms that makes listening easier or more difficult. In this way they are learning about both speaking and listening.

As your salon or council members become adept listeners, you may find it hard to accept new people in your group. You are, in effect, creating your own sub-culture—complete with unique rules to which other people are not accustomed. California salonist Bert McNutt reported that newcomers to Salon Visalia often seem "very talkative and have a lot to say, but are restless when it is their turn to listen. They tend to interrupt a lot, and most never make a second meeting." In your first contact with potential new members, explain what you are trying to do as a group and the styles of speaking and listening that you have developed. If necessary, conduct a listening exercise each time a new person visits.

When you listen deeply to others, you may find yourself without anything clever or moving to say when your turn comes around. But this lack of preparedness allows access to spontaneous and heartfelt words. Whether you're engaged in council or conversation, remember to take a deep, slow breath when it's your turn to speak. Allow several seconds to pass before speaking. Restate the central question or topic in your mind, so you aren't unduly limited by the previous person's comments. Now say whatever springs to mind, instead of trying to recapture the thoughts you had while others were speaking. If nothing comes to mind, take another deep breath, and another, until something wells up. As all of your group members become accustomed to active listening and unprepared speaking, you will find that your words hold great feeling, meaning, and impact.

ELEVEN

Creativity Salons:
Conversation at Play

The poem, the song, the picture is only water drawn from the well of the people, and it should be given back to them in a cup of beauty so that they may drink—and in drinking, understand themselves.
　　　—Federico García Lorca, Spanish poet

Playfulness and artistic expression have always been part of the salon experience. At one time or another, almost every salon turns to a creative activity, whether it's putting together a newsletter, playing charades, reading aloud, or musical jam sessions. Many salons devote at least one annual gathering to some kind of creative group project. Some dabble in clay or sing; others go to concerts, dance performances, plays, or museums. Salonists commonly quilt or play card games during and around conversation.

One inventive salon, the Ax Murderers of Columbia, South Carolina, while dedicated to fruitful talk, has also met alongside a lake to roast marshmallows and tell stories; gone fishing; engaged in creative writing exercises; swapped old magazines and catalogs; played favorite CDs and cassettes during meetings; taken lessons in aikido, the Japanese art of self-defense; played intimacy and get-to-know-you games; and brought favorite books to read aloud. The salon's colorful motto reflects its members' eagerness for new experiences: "Ax murderers are never satisfied."

Members of a salon in California's Silicon Valley became so interested in adding creative projects to their salon that they ended up holding two monthly meetings—one for the "Silicon-versationalists" and another for "Silicreationists." Other groups have also expanded their meeting schedules. A salon in Southern California added two writer's groups, a postmodern reader's group, a general reader's group, and a political action group to its regular session.

> **" A village which has no organized music or neglects community singing, drumming, or dancing is said to be dead."**
>
> —J.H. Kwabena Nketia, African musician

Salons often include performances, along with discussions and creative activities. Marharbour, founded by Mary Marr in Denver, Colorado, for example, included classical music programs, workshops, poetry, dance, and art and photography shows. A creative writing group met on Tuesday nights, and discussion salons were held every third Wednesday of the month. This vigorous salon illustrates the range of activities that can occur in a modern salon.

Performances and lectures by artists can inspire group members to try things themselves. Salon-keeper Lana Turner sometimes surprises members of her Harlem, New York, salons with a writer or musician, who interacts and presents his or her work following dinner. Of these evenings, Turner said: "It's a nice departure, a way for people to talk to the artist. The things that become the most important are the things that are most personal. You don't get the same feeling when you leave a major concert at the Paramount Theater or Radio City. You may think 'That was wonderful,' but you very rarely have a lasting sense of coming into contact with somebody. My guests hear directly about ways that someone can construct a frame or movie or script, a novel, someone who performs well, who sings. Those talents should be shared on many bases. By the time they leave, they're all sailing out of here thinking, 'Oh God! What was that?!' They leave and think about how wonderful it would be to do it in their own home."

Entertainment and art projects often stimulate meaningful discussion, especially if the activities deliver a message or adhere to a theme. This is the basis of Chautauqua-style gatherings, which combine entertainment with discussion. In June of 1991, for example, the *Utne Reader* held an outdoor Chautauqua salon from 6 P.M. to midnight. Comedy, dance, and music alternated with minisalons. During half-hour periods between performances, those in the audience were asked to form small groups and talk about topics inspired by the performances.

If you're part of a salon or thinking of forming one, don't underestimate the importance of having fun. Playing together is a healthy way of socializing, one in which people can get to know each other safely, easily, and without feeling they must perform or impress others. When salonists do not feel free to play and laugh, when the conversational tone has become too weighty and earnest, when rules limit the range of activities and expression, the demise of the salon may result.

I enjoy holding conversations while I'm doing something creative. I frequently find that, when my hands are occupied, my speech seems to become more eloquent and patient. Rhythmic physical actions such as drumming, knitting, sewing, and even drawing, can help the creative unconscious find a voice. Buried ideas may suddenly rise to the surface during such activities. Many people find extreme satisfaction in working on a project while talking with friends. When someone is partially occupied by a creative endeavor, the focus is deflected from the individual. The moment-to-moment pleasure of being together prevails, and gaps in the conversation are more companionable. I have often thought that salon hosts should routinely provide blocks and puzzles, crayons and paper, clay, or craft tools for guests. These diversions keep hands moving while minds catch up.

Organizing a Creativity Salon

The logistics of forming and hosting a creativity salon are potentially complex, but the rewards can be immense. While many creative activities (especially those involving language play) require little in the way of special supplies or space, others are noisy and supply-intensive, and work best in a large, open room. Most creative projects last longer than the average discussion. Plan on setting aside at least four hours for a creativity salon, and perhaps six or seven hours for some projects. Certain events, such as the Foto Safari or sandcastle building, can consume an entire day and are best conducted outdoors.

Creative activities may require initial explanation, warm-up exercises, or training. Therefore, you might ask people to come on time or allow an hour at the beginning for socializing while latecomers arrive. I usually include a tea break after the first couple of hours have passed. The "intermission" allows people to interact, or to go home if they must leave early. It may also serve as a transition period before attempting complex or improvisational activities. I rarely serve meals, because I don't want to add more labor to the setup and cleanup required for creative activities.

It's important to plan warm-ups for unfamiliar or performance-oriented activities. Warm-ups ideally set people at ease, teach basic skills, and allow salonists to access their playful impulses.

The Creativity Salon in Berkeley, California

> **" We have no art. Everything we do is art."**
>
> —Balinese saying

Warm-ups should be easy activities in which no individual is singled out. Any necessary skills should be broken down into quickly assimilated steps. People who have been told that they lack talent in a particular area will balk or leave if they're expected to do too much too quickly. If the warm-ups are silly and elicit laughter, so much the better.

An example of a barrier-breaking warm-up for theatrical activities was developed by the Loose Moose Improvisational Theatre in Calgary. It has been described as follows: (1) Everyone keep eyes popped open and round, as big as possible; (2) Everyone (on signal) march around the room, pointing at any and every object and shouting as loudly as possible the wrong name for it (call a rug a bus, call a chandelier a dog, and so on).

Fifteen to twenty seconds of the chaos engendered by step two is plenty. For participants in this simple exercise, everything suddenly looks fresh; habitual interpretations of objects and people are swept aside, as are customary inhibitions.

A creativity salon should generally begin with the most structured activities, proceeding to those that require greater looseness or improvisation. This applies particularly to musical or theatrical undertakings. If you are going to improvise music, you might start by assigning the numbers one through eight, then asking your members to make a noise each time their number comes up in an eight-count beat. Only after an hour or two of such structured exercises should you attempt pure improvisation; otherwise you're likely to end up with pure cacophony.

Occasionally an activity is too boring, too easy, too sedentary, or too competitive—or it simply won't work with the number of people in attendance. If you have no other ideas to propose, take a break. During the break, ask people what they think about the project so far. Solicit suggestions for variations or rule changes. Sometimes you'll find that everyone is quite content with the activity as is; at other times, members will come up with better ideas.

A creativity group can be much larger than a conversational group, provided there is room for everyone to dance, paint, and so on. My creativity salon often includes fifteen to twenty people, and sometimes thirty or more show up. Men often make up the majority of creative groups, while women may comprise the majority at discussion groups. I suspect this is because many women are told they aren't good at creative endeavors, and have had less opportunity to use their hands freely as children. Surprisingly, people who consider themselves artists initially express the most reluctance to attend creativity salons. Some are reluctant to try something outside of their area of expertise; others don't want to do something they are "good at" with nonartists. The participants who quickly loosen up and have fun are often those who are not artists. They're likely to work in a job or enjoy a creative hobby that's usually called a craft: carpenters, sign painters, weavers, and the like.

Children can be included in creativity salons. My thirteen-year-old foster daughter at first invited her friends over on salon night so they could laugh at the crazy adult antics from the sidelines. However, the teenagers inevitably joined us as the evening progressed. Younger children will join in quickly or, if the activity is too difficult, they will play by themselves or fall asleep amidst the bustle.

Dynamics of the Creativity Process
People who do not break things first will never learn to create anything.
　　—Tagalog (Filipino) proverb

Creativity salons focus on providing an atmosphere that fosters spontaneous, uninhibited, inspired behavior. If you are the salon leader for a particular project, your role is to set the stage for an experience to happen; you need not direct the experience itself. Organize the setting, provide any necessary props, then let whatever happens take place without interference. If you attempt to control, organize, and time your activities, real and spontaneous expression is unlikely to emerge.

Nevertheless, you'll need to be aware of the issues that people confront in creative play groups. Almost everyone feels hopelessly inept in at least one area of creative endeavor. Some will insist that they can't sing. Others will say "I'm not funny," or

"Every child is an artist; the problem is how to remain an artist once he grows up. **99**
　　—Pablo Picasso

"I'm not very coordinated," or "I couldn't act my way out of a paper bag."

You can reduce participants' anxieties in several ways. First, offer varied projects that draw upon a wide range of abilities. This ensures that each member will feel comfortable with some percentage of your activities. Second, occasionally choose obscure activities that are new to all members. If no one knows how to do something very well, all are equally incompetent. This can be quite comforting. Third, rotate your activity leaders. Utilize the ideas and experiences of everyone in your group, in part to avoid setting up teacher-student dynamics. Fourth, plan simple warm-ups, as explained above. Fifth, don't allow criticism in your group. And finally, make all activities as collaborative as possible.

The No-Critique Rule

Never tell anyone he has no talent. That you may not say. That you do not know. That is the one absolute prohibition laid down.

> —Martha Graham,
> dancer and choreographer

On the first invitation to my creativity salon, I wrote: "Perfection is unnecessary, Criticism is stifling, Creativity is not a god. ART IS PLAY." This is the essence of my philosophy about creative projects. The only rule I establish in creativity salons is this: There shall be no criticism, little feedback, and very little praise. The no-critique rule makes it possible for newcomers to participate freely with people they've never met

GUIDELINES FOR REDUCING FEAR OF CREATIVITY

- Offer varied projects that draw upon a wide range of abilities.
- On occasion, choose obscure activities that are new to all members.
- Rotate your activity leaders.
- Plan simple warm-up exercises.
- Don't allow criticism.
- Make all activities as collaborative as possible.

before. It helps shy people and those who consider themselves uncreative play fearlessly.

In my experience, even compliments stifle people. Approval can make a creator begin to judge and stand outside of his or her creations. Playing with utter abandon may cease. Natural, spontaneous creativity occurs in the absence of rewards and punishments. I don't worry when people look at each other's work and make appreciative noises, but I do try to prevent positive feedback if it's focused on one person at a time. At open poetry readings, for example, it's fine for listeners to hum or nod in satisfaction after a good poem, but I ask them to refrain from telling the poet which lines or images particularly moved them. Why? Because analysis instantly ruins the mood of a creative salon. When members know they will be expected to provide a critique, many stop listening to the poetry. Instead, they focus on framing their analytic comments. Meanwhile, other writers in the group may decide not to read at all, fearing that the response will be bland or dismissive.

Martha Graham

Contrary to popular belief, art blossoms in the absence of critique and analysis, and even the most playful activities can yield precious results. For example, finger painting turned into performance art one night at my salon, as we began transferring the paint to our bodies. Guests left the actual paintings behind when they departed, but I decided to use them as wrapping paper. Several ended up enclosing Hanukkah gifts to an artist friend. He liked them so well that he hung them on his studio wall. And so these paintings, made unselfconsciously, had first been rejected and left behind. Then they were used for a practical purpose. Finally, they were displayed as works of art.

When people make art themselves, they become less intimidated by, and more appreciative of, professional art pieces. As they come to understand the medium, the effort involved, and the creative process itself, they become better-informed viewers or listeners. As they create things themselves, they become more supportive of creativity in others. Ultimately, being creative gives everyone the opportunity to develop their abilities and the freedom to exercise them.

Collaborations

Making every creative project a "jam session" is another way to take the pressure off of individuals. When people concentrate on working together, they worry less about being judged. With a little ingenuity, almost any creative activity can become a collaboration. I sometimes spend time in the library or ask friends for ideas to help me turn whatever I'm planning into a larger group activity.

For example, you don't have to sit in isolation writing or reading poetry at a poetry salon. During one of my favorite salon nights, we took turns reading poetry aloud while the group improvised dance and music to accompany the spoken words. Later, two of us began reading two entirely different poems aloud, each reciting a few lines at a time as though acting out two parts of a scripted dialogue. The result made a strange kind of sense. In fact, it was surprisingly beautiful.

At another session, each salonist composed a four-line poem. We then numbered the lines, cut up the poems, and passed the lines out randomly so that each person received four unrelated lines. Recipients then assembled the lines in any order, altered the grammar slightly if necessary, created a title, and read the new poems aloud. Again, the results were gratifying.

Collage is another art form that lends itself easily to collaboration. I've held two kinds of collage sessions. At the first, I placed an enormous pile of magazines, photographs, fabric scraps, and
miscellaneous found objects in the middle of the floor. I asked each salonist to cut out and glue a few pieces from the pile onto a piece of blank paper or poster board. Then, at regular intervals, I instructed everyone to move one position to the left around the circle of collages, adding new elements to each collage. We continued all the way around the circle, until everyone reached their original pieces. Each person then finished the piece and took it home. However, no one was forced to collaborate. Those who preferred to preside over their own collages from start to finish simply sat outside of the circle.

The second project was bigger. First I made a color photocopy of a favorite art print and cut it into twenty equal squares, numbering each square on the back so I could reassemble the painting later. I then cut out ten-by-ten-inch pieces of cardboard. When guests arrived, I asked them to form twenty groups of two or three people (it was a large group). I gave each group a square from the painting and a larger square of cardboard, asking them to reproduce what they saw in collage form. None of them were familiar with the original painting, and some didn't even realize it was a painting.

Each small group then proceeded to paint, paste, draw, sew, and staple objects and colors onto its piece of cardboard. At the end, all pieces were reassembled. People stood in awe as the collage suddenly came together, thrilled by the interpretations. I eventually glued the cardboard pieces to a large canvas. The collage version of the painting hangs on my living room wall, and it is much admired by visitors.

Some projects really do require individual attention—primarily those that call for a great deal of equipment and focus on creating a small object (such as modeling in Femo or Sculpy Clay or enamel beadmaking). In the absence of collaboration, a feeling of community, friendliness, and acceptance should be encouraged as people chat with one another while making their pieces, walk around the room to see other people's work, ask for advice, or borrow tools. A few people will inevitably feel disappointed with the result of their efforts, so it's a good idea to schedule an interactive group project for your next session.

I discourage competitive activities. Competition brings out the worst in some people. They may gloat, cheat, threaten, posture, worry, or withdraw. However, if your group is exceptionally good-natured and closely knit, laughs a lot, and refrains from all forms of personal judgment, you may be able to enjoy competitive activities. On occasion, the best way to frame an activity is to build it around a game that involves winning and losing. If you've decided to play competitively, set up teams rather than competing on an individual level. The game should require several different skills, so that everyone can contribute and no individual will become the star of the team.

Rousseau-inspired collage
created by the Berkeley Creativity Salon

Choosing Projects

Unless your group wants to limit itself to one particular kind of artistic activity, variety is the key criterion for choosing creative projects. In most cases, avoid repeating activities. Remember that a creativity salon is not a workshop devoted to enhancing and perfecting skills in a particular art form. Rather, creative salons are places where members play with different media, tools, and techniques, and in so doing become less inhibited.

Keep a running list of potential projects as they occur to you or are suggested by others. I often group activities arbitrarily into three categories, then rotate salon sessions among the three categories. The headings I use are performance, product, and language and logic. *Performance* projects are those that require people to perform as a group or for an audience. Music and dance activities are performances, even if everyone in the group participates. *Product* activities include all arts that employ physical media to produce things you can take home with you. *Language and Logic* projects include all literary endeavors and many games.

You can, of course, divide activities into any number of categories. If you'd like to take the classical approach, you could schedule activities according to each of the nine Greek muses, rotating between: Calliope (epic poetry and eloquence); Euterpe (music and lyric poetry); Erato (love poetry); Polyhymnia (oratory or sacred poetry); Clio (history); Melpomene (tragedy); Thalia (comedy); Terpsichore (choral song and dance); and Urania (astronomy). Or you might take the psychological approach, choosing activities that will stimulate each of five intelligences: bodily/kinesthetic, including all dance forms; musical; linguistic/verbal for writing and reading; visual/spatial for most visual arts; and logical/mathematical, the basis of many games. Collaborations and theatrical games also serve to develop interpersonal intelligence.

Here's an entirely different, time-honored approach: Choose a theme, then come up with as many activities as possible that are connected to your theme. Theme evenings were quite popular at the turn of the century. At these gatherings, a speaker or demonstration was accompanied by related music, pictures, food, and games. While many of the activities might strike us today as corny or forced, the salonists at least demonstrated no end of ingenuity in devising things to do. Here are instructions for one such event from a book entitled *Eighty Pleasant Evenings*, published in 1898. The theme is "A Building Evening," and the author advises would-be organizers to:

"Begin with instrumental music, followed by a paper, talk, or reading on some interesting phase of architecture, ancient or modern. Pictures of famous buildings may be displayed on walls or tables. . . . Conduct the company on an imaginary tour to visit some of the most remarkable of them. Holmes's 'Chambered Nautilus,' Longfellow's

'Building of the Ship,' or some other 'building poem' may be sliced or dissected and the fragments passed for those present to arrange in proper sequence, comparing notes and finding seats accordingly. The poem may then be read. . . . Another game which may either follow or precede the 'dissected poem' is the 'tower of excuses.' The leader relates his imaginary experiences in building a tower, first having assigned to the other players the parts of mason, carpenter, glazier, plumber, electrician, etc. When he tells how each workman failed to fulfill his contract, the player alluded to must interrupt the story with an instant excuse before the next workman is mentioned. Those who fail thus to give an excuse may be sentenced . . . [to] banishment to an adjoining room until they shall have succeeded in building a tower of some kind. The tower may be built of anything at hand, such as books, hats, umbrellas, chairs, newspapers, etc. Serve refreshments of layer cake, and ice-cream in bricks; and close the evening with two or three vocal selections. Two especially good ones would be 'I Built a Bridge of Fancies,' and 'Building for Eternity.'"

The simplest way to decide what to do at each meeting is to throw the question open to everyone in the salon. Rely on others to suggest projects they can explain to the group. The skills and hobbies of members can become terrific group projects. On my own, I would never have thought of many of the creative activities my group enjoyed in Berkeley; nor would I have suspected that my friends were so eclectic. For example, I would never have experienced making enamel beads, as a friend taught us to do one night. Now I regard handling molten glass as one of life's great pleasures.

To some extent, your meeting place may limit the scope of your projects. If you don't have a large, open space, valuable body movements will be difficult. If you have fussy neighbors, loud jam sessions may not be feasible. If you own an expensive home that contains delicate and expensive objects, you may not be willing to let people melt glass with blowtorches or spread finger paints all over your rugs. On the other hand, you can make most spaces work with a little effort and plastic tarps. I once organized a pumpkin-carving party in a beautifully furnished home by pushing all the furniture to the side, covering the upholstery with large towels, and protecting the floors with drop cloths and newspaper. I set buckets around the room to hold all the pumpkin seeds. At the end of the session we rolled up the newspapers, containing the mess inside them. After we rearranged the furniture, the room was as pristine as it had been before our activity.

Finally, in making your choices, don't limit yourself to narrow definitions of what's "creative" or "artistic." Visit any modern art museum and you will quickly realize that

SALONISTS AT PLAY

Once your salonists begin thinking about creative activities and projects, you're likely to come up with dozens of ideas. However, if you're stuck or you'd like some initial inspiration, the following list may help. Regard the suggestions as seeds that can in most cases be improvised upon, hybridized, and adapted to the inclinations of your members. The harvest will be uniquely your own.

Performance
   Soapbox ranting (standing on a crate and declaring your peeves)
   Poetry reading
   Communication without speech
   Show and tell
   Free-style spoken poetry such as rap
   Children's rhymes, clapping, jump rope
   Mime
   Improvisational comedy
   Parlor games (charades, others)
   Puppet theater

Language and Logic
   Writing limericks, haiku, spoof lyrics on well-known tunes
   Timed writings based on cue words or pictures
   Formal debate
   Creating a code or language
   Political discourse (taped or videotaped and edited)
   Epigrams, quotes, non sequiturs (make them up or recite favorites)
   Fictionary, Scrabble, Boggle, Trivial Pursuit, other word games

Music and Dance
   No-instruments instrumental music
   Belly, jazz, contact, African, hula, Cajun, and other dancing
   Drumming, percussion, wind instruments
   Karaoke (rent a machine)
   A cappella chanting, folksongs, blues, improvisation
   Making an instrument

Exploring and Making Art
   Postcard art (create, mail them out anonymously)
   Tactile art gallery (exploring art while blindfolded)
   News clipping collages
   Field trips to art museums
   Mask making
   Multimedia collage
   Ukrainian egg dyeing

Pencil, charcoal, pen and ink, pastel, watercolor, crayon art
Finger painting, oils, acrylics, fabric paints
Clay, Femo plastic clays, Silly Putty, Play-Doh
Making finger puppets, shadow puppets, marionettes
Pop-up cards (art pops up when card is opened)
Pictionary
Wood, soapstone, soap, potato, and wax carving
Candle making
Wire sculpture
Mobiles from found objects
Embroidery, macrame, quilting, basket weaving
Making lamp shades
Decorative cookies, pancakes, other food art
Painting a mural
Making paper
Making hats
Body or face painting
Hair and beard decorations
Collage capes

Nature and Science

Bird-watching
Tidal pool exploring
Wildflower identifying
Astronomy
Field trips to science and natural history museums
Picnics
Nature hikes
Protesting environmental abuse
Conducting experiments
Investigating why things work

Hard to Classify

Fortune-telling (palm reading, tarot, I Ching, other)
Team treasure hunts with clues composed in rhyme
ESP experiments
Designing an alien planet, alien race, culture, or spaceship
Watching home movies
Hypnosis
Feeding each other while blindfolded
Balance/timing games, wrestling
Healing walk, levitating, trust games
Blowing giant soap bubbles
Extinct animals, monsters, mythical creatures
Dungeons and Dragons and spin-offs
Designing a city, building, room, or clothing

> **66** Make art life, and life art, with no gulf between the artist and the people."
>
> —Rafael Alberti, *Alianza de Intelectuales*

almost anything can be considered art. If you put a frame on something, give it a title, and display it in a flattering manner, it *is* art. I don't mean this to be critical. I mean it to be a statement of liberation. Creativity lies in the process and the attitude, not in the final outcome.

Language and Logic Games

All was done gaily and without grimaces. No one bit his fingernails, and no one stopped laughing or speaking. All that was heard were challenges and answers, assaults and the return sallies.
—Mademoiselle de Scudéry, describing rhyming games in her salon

It's easy to add linguistic play to your regular salon conversations. Language games are the least messy, the least expensive, and the least physical of creative projects. They may result in a product, such as a poem, story, or letter. Some, like reading aloud or acting before the group, involve aspects of performance. They may in fact be completely ephemeral and almost indistinguishable from regular salon conversation. They are the most intellectual of all creativity salon activities.

Good sources for these activities include books of parlor games and writing manuals, especially English as a Second Language (ESL) textbooks, which often offer group writing exercises and games. You might also visit game stores. Many games now on the market, such as *Pictionary*, *Fictionary*, or *Password*, were adapted from simple parlor games that originally required nothing more than pen and paper. You may be able to play them without buying the packaged versions.

Because linguistic projects often require performers and listeners, they provide fewer opportunities for group participation. For this reason, you need members who are already at ease with one another. They should be able to create freely, perform, ad lib, and read aloud without shame or paralyzing inhibitions. To develop this sort of comfort, remember to start with light warm-ups; avoid pressuring members to read aloud what they have written; seek opportunities for teamwork; and intersperse language activities with others that focus less on individuals.

Playing linguistic games will improve the overall quality of salon conversations. Jokes, poetry, and other delights to the ear and the mind are the product of skills that wither away unless they are practiced regularly. If we are to use words well, we must listen to them through reading aloud, declaiming poetry, and playing freely with rhythm, rhyme, and meaning. One simple activity involves reading aloud to one another from favorite books of poetry and prose. This can evolve into group performances, as others play music or act out the text. I enjoy listening to people read long poems aloud, changing their voices as others in the group call for different characterizations. Long poems with a strong rhythm are best (poems by John Keats work wonderfully). Try changing from a cowpoke to a drunk, a little old lady, a Southern belle, a sex maniac, a stuffed shirt, or a fussy teacher without dropping a beat.

Next you might play old-fashioned verbal games during breaks in your conversations. Try setting a theme and asking everyone to quickly write one- or two-line poems or epigrams on the subject. Then read the poems aloud. Another popular game dating back to the fifteenth century involves making up terms for groups of objects. The names should be amusing phrases or collective nouns that reflect the nature of the thing itself. Thus, "a pride of lions" describes the group and comments on the animal's proud bearing. Others examples might include: "A flush of plumbers," "a sprawl of malls," "a huddle of players," "a rack of sadomasochists," and so on. The game is known as "venery," and these examples are drawn from James Lipton's book, *An Exaltation of Larks*.

Punning was considered déclassé in the more recent French salons, but the practice was revived in nineteenth-century America through such games as "A Tour of Nations." This exercise in verbal play involves making up definitions for words that contain the -nation suffix. For example, "germination" is the nation from which we start; "impersonation" is an actor's nation; and "consternation" is a nation for astonished people.

After World War I, surreal word games became popular. One such game was called "The Exquisite Corpse." The antecedent was probably a drawing game in which someone folded a piece of paper into thirds, drew a head on the top third, then folded it back, leaving just indicator lines showing before passing it to the next person. That person would draw the torso, and a third participant finished with the hips and legs. The stunning creation would then be revealed in its entirety.

The Exquisite Corpse accomplishes the same thing with poetry and prose. Participants start by writing an article and an adjective on a piece of paper. They then fold the papers so the words can't be seen, and pass them along to other members of the circle. Next each person writes a noun, folds the paper, and passes it. The game continues with a verb, another article and adjective, and another noun or noun phrase.

"To express the emotion of life is to live;
to express the life of emotion is to make art. **"**

—Margaret Anderson, *My Thirty Years' War*

When completed, the papers are unfolded and the sentences thus created are read aloud. A typical example gives the game it's name: "The exquisite corpse shall drink the new wine." This surreal game and many others are beautifully described in the Shambhala/Redstone box *Surrealist Games*, available in many game shops and bookstores.

Performance and Improvisation
If you can walk, you can dance. If you can talk, you can sing.
　　　　—Proverb from Zimbabwe

Performance activities are often the most physical, ephemeral, and exuberant of creative projects. They include music, singing, dance, and theatrical games. I also consider sensory and scientific explorations and field trips performances, in the sense that each participant becomes part of an audience that delights in the performances of the natural world. But creative performances don't require an audience. Many of these activities involve all members in the group. The best sources of performance ideas are theater texts, parlor and party game books, and science and game books written for children.

Performances can be simple or ordinary activities to which some twist has been added. For example, you might host a potluck dinner at which guests are not allowed to feed themselves, but must wait to be fed by someone else. Or you might ask your guests to bring only finger foods and eat blindfolded. Another activity with a sensory twist is called Color Transformations. To try it, hold a regular discussion salon or arrange to play a simple game. Ask everyone to come dressed in one color from head to toe, and to bring a second outfit of a different color. At a designated point, take a break while everyone changes into the second outfit and observe how the color shift affects the mood of your group.

Most indoor performances work best when you can move all the furniture to one side and free plenty of floor space. These tend to be noisy activities, so let your neigh-

❝ Put a commonplace expression in its right place, clean it up, rub it hard, bring it to light in such a position that it strikes with its youth, and with the same freshness, the same upspring that it had at its birth—and you will act as a poet."

　　　　　　　　　　—Jean Cocteau, *Le Rappel à l'ordre*

bors know if you expect to be running loud or late. If you plan to conduct many such activities, begin gathering a collection of strange objects, clothing, and instruments.

Like word games, theatrics are a salon staple. From highly stylized tableaus to uninhibited comic improvisation, theater games have been central to salons throughout history, perhaps because they are the ultimate community activity.

In its many forms, charades is one of the classic salon activities, and for many it is the least intimidating form of improvisation. The earliest version of the game was called tableaus (or tableau vivants), a form that peaked in popularity during the 1830s. To create tableaus, break into several teams of four or five people. Send each team into a different room, asking each group to decide on a famous painting or sculpture, a short scene from a movie or book, or a well-known commercial or billboard advertisement. The selection should be a visual picture or action with which everyone in the salon is familiar. The teams then return to the main room. Using props if necessary, each team in turn strikes a pose reminiscent of its chosen scene. The rest of the group members try to guess what the team is portraying.

"We're not sure what it is, but it's inspired by Salvador Dali."

Another early version of charades involved no acting at all, instead employing riddles that separated and described parts of words. In his excellent rule book and historical study entitled *Charades*, James Charlton offers the following example:

My *first is a part of the face*;
My *second is a kind of jam*;
My *third is a pleasure boat*;
My *whole is a well-known English authoress*.

To solve the riddle, add the syllables described in the first three lines (jaw, jelly, yacht) and speak them quickly. The answer is novelist George Eliot.

Modern charades combine tableaus and riddles. The English version of the game, called acting charades, was extremely popular in the late nineteenth and early twentieth centuries, and is still played.

In acting charades, participants speak their clues and deliberately try to make them obscure. When played in England, the larger group divides into two teams that separate to plan their charades. Each charade is comprised of one long word broken into several syllables, and each syllable stands as a word on its own. For example, "insinuate" would break into "in, sin, you, ate"; "superconductor" could become "sue, per, con, duck, tour." The team then returns to perform a series of small theatrical scenes, one for each syllable. During each scene, someone in the group uses the cue word for that syllable in the dialogue. When all syllables have been performed, a final scene is presented, including dialogue with the entire word inserted. The often bewildered but thoroughly entertained audience attempts to guess the word.

Activist and author Joanna Macy

According to one story about the introduction of charades to the United States, British dramatist Noel Coward saw the game played in England, later describing it to his friends at the Algonquin Round Table. He was uncertain of the rules, so the Round Tablers made up their own, eventually developing the miming game that Americans now call charades.

Musical activities can be a great success, even if there are no professional musicians in your group and no real instruments are used. My favorite musical salon experience happened one night when I asked people to bring any kind of noisemakers to the session—beans in glass jars, springs, wine glasses with water in them, sticks, and pots. This collection of utensils, along with our voices and hand clapping, provided our music. We simply began to make noise. By midnight my roommate, a musician who had originally declined to attend because "it's no fun playing with nonmusicians," was drumming ecstatically on a turned-over paint bucket. The rest of us were dancing, hollering, and singing.

Art Projects

At one salon we made gift wrap. I wrote one of my favorite quotes on it by Brenda Ueland, about not grinding when you're trying to be creative and just letting it flow out of you. I have it up on my wall and I just love it. I look at it and I think about the night I made it. Those were great times.

— Judy Bell, member of the Loring Café Salon

Art projects include anything made by hand that you can keep. These projects are usually easy to think up, but you may have to go to some trouble to arrange them. They may be expensive, as they often require tools and supplies. I always ask for contributions from salonists if I've spent a significant amount on supplies. I also ask people to bring things from home—interesting objects, paper, scissors, glue, fabric, and anything else we might need. To find project ideas, visit art stores and peruse craft and activity books for children. I get a great deal of inspiration from visiting modern art exhibits.

One art project was inspired by an exhibition of the work of Brazilian artist Hélio Oiticica. On display were short, collaged capes made of many materials and known as *parangolés* (a term derived from a Brazilian slang word meaning "animated situation"). To create similar capes in your salon, simply glue, sew, staple, and tie together fabric pieces of varied textures and colors. The creations should be in the shape of a short poncho with ragged, strange shapes and openings. Next you can paint them and sew

"There is a vitality, a life force, an energy, a quickening that is translated through you into action, and because there is only one of you in all of time, this expression is unique. And if you block it, it will never exist through any other medium and it will be lost. The world will not have it. It is not your business to determine how good it is, nor how valuable, nor how it compares with other expressions. It is your business to keep it yours clearly and directly, to keep the channel open. You do not even have to believe in yourself or your work. You have to keep yourself open and aware to the urges that motivate you. **"**

— Martha Graham, dancer, teacher, and choreographer

beads, bells, and ribbons to them. If you like, add pockets and fill them with poetry, letters, flowers, pebbles, and found objects. The parangolés are clothing, sculpture, and painting all in one. Invented with the samba in mind, they are not complete until you have danced in them.

Art creations are often amenable to a theme orientation. Activist Joanna Macy suggests making collages for a peaceful world. Using the usual collage materials, simply pose the question: "What would a world of peace and justice look like?" Then let your imaginations inspire a powerful vision. Holiday themes also work well. You might do Ukrainian-style egg dyeing around Easter; mask making around Halloween; or create gift wrap at the winter solstice. For gift wrap, assemble large sheets of all kinds of paper, including newspaper, brown paper bags, a big roll of butcher-block paper, and even some thin, cheap fabrics. Ask people to bring their paints, from acrylics to water colors, plus scissors, glue, sparkles and stickers, and anything else that might serve as colorful adornment. Then just let people decorate the large pieces of paper. When the glue has dried, everyone is free to take their creations home.

Another favorite project, one that moves your salon outdoors, is the Foto Safari. This salon generally takes all day, so you may want to schedule it for a Saturday or Sunday morning and hope for warm, sunny weather. Before the session, prepare a list of short sentences and quotes. Television and advertising are lucrative places to find punchy phrases. Comedic or offbeat sentences that lend themselves to several interpretations are best. You should have one or two pages full of phrases, photocopied so that each participant has a copy of the list. Ask people to bring cameras and rolls of film. When they arrive, split your salon into groups of three or four, allowing just one camera per group. Instruct the groups to go for a walk and take pictures, keeping the list of phrases in mind as possible captions for the pictures taken. They are welcome to pose, to use props, or to set up shots. After completing a roll of film, they should drop it off at a one-hour developing center. Reconvene later that day and ask each group to paste their photos onto cardboard, with the appropriate captions underneath. When this process is finished, circulate the cardboard pieces. Be prepared to laugh, and to marvel at the ways in which your groups interpreted the captions.

I am endlessly rewarded and fascinated as I watch how people relate to their own products at creativity salons, especially those who consider themselves nonartistic. One woman keeps everything she has made—every poem, sculpture, mask, drawing, and photograph—in a shrine of sorts at her home. Taken as a whole, her pile of "junk" is a fascinating installation piece, and an ever-changing visual journal of her years in the salon.

E-Salons:
Conversations on the Net

I profit a great deal from the discipline of imposed listening enforced by a medium like the WELL. My verbal intelligence is *very* quick, and in conversation I *far* too often find I'm responding before I've really mulled over what I've heard. It's a continual revelation to discover how much more deeply I see into problems if I force myself to take the time to carefully consider, in written form, positions with which I disagree.
—Michael D. Thomas, e-salonist

Communicating on-line often has fewer repercussions than face-to-face conversation with people you see on a regular basis. As a result, you may feel free to discuss things in more depth on-line, and to reveal attitudes and experiences you might otherwise keep private. However, many people find that there is less emotional content in on-line communications, perhaps because the people talking are unlikely to meet each other face to face. There is a social paradox involved, often noted by people unaccustomed to talking via computer: The process combines openness, even intimacy, with a sense of emotional and physical distance. Some find this disconcerting; others take comfort and are liberated.

The e-salon, or electronic salon, has been made possible by computer-mediated communication technology. E-salons, small groups of people who discuss chosen topics through private e-mail lists or conferences, are just one of many formats for conversing on-line. Other alternatives include the following:

Chat. Real-time chat is a popular form of communication on both the Internet and commercial on-line services. Primarily a means for socializing, chat is not well-suited to the in-depth, deliberative discussions that characterize salons. Like a telephone conference call, everyone chatting must be simultaneously connected, no matter which time zone they're in. The exchanges tend to be short—generally no more than one or two lines of text per person.

Usenet Newsgroups. Newsgroups are single-topic bulletin boards or discussion forums that take place on the Internet. Thousands exist, devoted to virtually every conceivable subject. Messages are stored on hundreds of "host computers" around the world, and users can read and post new messages at any time, day or night. It is possible to set up a private newsgroup that is limited to a small group of participants.

Internet mailing lists (listservs). Likewise, thousands of single-topic, discussion-oriented mailing lists are found on the Internet—both public and private lists. Each time a participant sends a message to a central list server (or host computer), the server e-mails a copy of the message to all list participants. Many Internet service providers can set up an inexpensive mailing list for a small group of users who wish to start an e-salon.

Computer Conferencing Systems. The Cafe Utne <http://www.utne.com>, the WELL <www.well.com>, the MetaNetwork <www.tmn.com>, and ECHO <www.echonyc.com> are among the computer conferencing systems on the Internet. These systems employ special software on a single host computer, accessible via a Web browser. They require users to register, and most charge a monthly or annual fee. The primary attraction of conferencing systems is that participants often feel as though they're contributing members of a community, not just subscribing consumers. Conference hosts (or moderators), staff, and users get to know one another, and each system develops its own social norms. Like members of newsgroups and mailing lists, conference users can read and post messages at any time, to any topic that interests them. Many conferencing systems allow a small group of users to create private conferences, which can function as an e-salon.

"Finn's Law of On-line Discussions:
Every on-line discussion, no matter what the original topic,
ends up being an argument about gun control. **99**

—Robert Finn, e-salonist

CMC: Talking in the Virtual World

Computer-mediated conversation (CMC) offers some advantages over meeting face to face (F2F). People are not limited by geography in getting to know one another. Unless users join a real-time chat line, they can log on to read and post messages at any time, ignoring sleep schedules and time zones. Like F2F salons, on-line groups are generally inclusive meritocracies, in which intellect and clever use of language are valued, but physical and demographic characteristics are invisible or irrelevant. Economic class is one of the few factors that limit on-line participation. Anyone who cannot afford or gain access to a computer, a modem, and an on-line account does not have a voice in the virtual world.

CMCs can be as lively and rewarding as vocal conversations. Although they are typed and take place over days or even months, they are experienced as talking, rather than reading. Participating regularly can establish friendships and provide intellectual stimulation. Depending on the area of the Net and the kind of group you participate in, anywhere from ten to ten thousand people may be reading your words. In this sense, CMCs resemble "publication" of your comments, which can add excitement to the experience.

For most people, though, the on-line environment is not a means for establishing deep friendships or connecting to the local community. Its power lies in providing access to a broad range of people and information throughout the world. It's a splendid place for intellectual conversation and a certain amount of creative play. It can be a helpful social environment for people who, for one reason or another, have not found acceptance in the local community or are physically isolated.

While many people join computer conferences because they want access to information and a variety of views on a subject, there is a place in the virtual world for general conversation between a limited group of users who interact regularly. These groups represent the form of conversational gathering known as the e-salon.

The E-Salon
This is a SALON . . . something different from a focused listserv discussion group. The reason I chose to partake in it to begin with was because I was intrigued with the possibility of

people forming community (virtually) without relying on a known or anticipated common cause or interest. We are experimenting with the concept of a virtual neighborhood.
—Ronin the Barbarian (aka P. D. Marsh), private e-salon member

E-salon members are not bound together by an interest in one topic, but by their interest in communication itself. The groups are generally small, comprised of ten to twenty participants, and the list or conference is private. Each member sees everyone else's responses to whatever topics the group chooses to discuss.

The small number of members, the relative privacy ensured by exchanging responses via e-mail or closed conferences, and the open subject matter make the e-salon resemble a face-to-face salon. The first e-salons were private Internet mailing lists created experimentally by the Neighborhood Salon Association. On a random basis, the NSA simply grouped together any twenty-five people who signed up, making some adjustments to include international participants and ensure gender balance. Some users who were involved in large public conferences devoted to specific subjects scoffed at the effort, saying that no one would be interested in talking to a couple of dozen strangers who had no common interests. In practice, though, e-salons have demonstrated much the same potential as traditional salons, and hold some advantages over large networks. The original groups remain active in Cafe Utne on the Web.

While e-salons cannot provide the range of information and worldwide contacts offered by public computer networks, they succeed on different terms—largely because they are private and intimate. Nearly fifty percent of e-salon participants are women, compared to just twenty percent on most public user services. There are fewer

HOW TO COMMUNICATE EFFECTIVELY ON-LINE

- Compose off-line
- Use emotive punctuation
- Avoid sarcasm and irony
- Be brief
- Be tolerant of spelling and grammatical errors
- Post regularly
- Ask permission to quote

instances of flame wars and other socially inept or nasty behaviors in e-salons. Members tend to be polite because they know each other; there is no horde of invisible people reading their words without comment or commitment. People who have spent a great deal of time in public networks report that e-salonists are, on the whole, friendlier than public users. This is probably because, within a matter of weeks, e-salonists learn the identities of members, whereas it can take months or years to become familiar with others in large conferences.

It is important to establish personal identities quickly in an e-salon, so members know who they're talking to. In my e-salon, we asked each participant to write a one-paragraph biography. After a few months we also assembled a list of addresses and birthdates, and began sending each other birthday cards and small presents. Several of us ended up talking on the phone and meeting one another face to face as business trips took us to members' hometowns. All of this contributed to a feeling that we were participating in a safe group comprised of real and decent people.

Along the continuum of interpersonal contact, the e-salon sits in the middle, somewhere between the anonymity of large computer groups and the face-to-face closeness of small traditional salons. Graham Storrs, a British e-salonist, described to members the level of intimacy he experienced in an e-salon: "We are neither an ultra-intimate community of electronic lovers nor disembodied consumers of each other's messages. I think we're something in-between, pretty intimate in our own way, but also very detached from one another. I don't sit at my desk all day and daydream about what each of you is doing. I probably would not even be gregarious enough to introduce myself in person were I in the hometown of any salon member. But on the other hand, I really cherish the opportunity to look in daily on the conference and offer whatever thoughts might seem appropriate in reaction."

Membership in an e-salon requires a greater time commitment than participation in larger computer venues. Lurking (read-only participation) is discouraged in small e-salons. For the group to remain viable, each person should probably write a response at least once a week. On the other hand, messages that are too long or too frequent can be a problem. One of the difficulties we experienced in the early months of our e-salon was the extraordinary amount of output. Some people didn't have time to keep up with the conversation, and began dropping out altogether. As member Kenneth Simon explained, "It's very scary to sign on and find thirty or forty new messages in a single day. I worry that, in order to participate at this rate, I'm sacrificing a lot of what I need to be doing: research is waiting, and there's a sun to go out and feel the warmth of." However, Kenneth decided not to leave the e-salon, because "at this point it would be too much of a loss. I'd miss learning so much; I'd miss you all and the way we communicate." But the crisis meant that we had to find a way to limit our responses. For many e-salons, the volume of messages is one of the first problems that emerges. After debating several alternatives, we simply decided that those of us who were too vociferous should pay attention and post less frequently; those of us who tended to lurk should speak up more often. A happy equilibrium was reached when our postings dropped from nearly a hundred per week to more manageable dozens. Your e-salon may have to decide between limiting the length and number of postings (much like setting time limits in a traditional salon) and simply allowing attrition until the group is small and the volume of messages is reasonable.

At this writing, the ideal structure for e-salons is still being hashed out—and in any case it may vary according to the needs of each group. In my opinion, our e-salon conversations were most engrossing when we rotated facilitators regularly and selected topics. Our facilitators were volunteers from the group who indicated their availability and interest. Their tasks involved polling members for potential topics, taking a vote, then initiating the chosen topic with an introduction or a focused question. During the month's tour of duty, each facilitator tracked the direction of the conversation, helped reroute digressions and resolve misunderstandings, reinvigorated the discussion with new questions, and summarized the opinions of the group toward the end of the month. The job was then handed over to the next volunteer.

Later, we tried dropping formal facilitation and topic choosing, in favor of a more unstructured approach to conversation. Salonists brought up whatever was most interesting to them at the time, and those who shared the interest responded at will. Some members wanted to be able to follow the discussion wherever it led, rather than arbitrarily changing topics each month. Other members felt strongly that we should participate equally, regulate ourselves, and process any problems as a group, rather than depending on a facilitator. The result was a more relaxed, friendlier atmosphere, but the conversations tended to have less depth and complexity. We would touch lightly on a topic, then move on. I continue to believe that using facilitators, at least during the first several months of an e-salon and again whenever problems arise, greatly contributes to the group's viability. Other e-salons have failed primarily because no one took the initiative and got the salon organized in the beginning.

One of the unique aspects of on-line communications is that several conversations can be carried on simultaneously, especially if a conferencing system is used. You might find that, at the end of a month, some people in your group want to continue talking about that month's topic, while others want to select a new one. Both can happen in the e-salon.

E-Salon Topics

Because e-salons lack the information-gathering capacity of large computer networks, the best topics are generally those that focus on personal or social concerns, rather than obscure political, technological, or legal subjects. Relationships, work, education, the environment, and similar subjects placed the members of our e-salon on an equal footing; we were eager to tune in every day to see what others had written. When some members took risks and revealed intimate experiences, their disclosures helped our group achieve an unusual level of warmth and concern for one another. Other computer networks have also found this to be the case. Cliff Figallo, former director of the WELL, reported that "being vulnerable with each other is the most effective hook. Next to that might be everyone gaining access to a consistent and valuable flow of information. But real human connections, with the occasional hurts that go with them, are much sought after on- and off-line."

It's also important to engage in lighthearted, personal conversation in your e-salon. One of the men in our group initiated a "check-in topic" that helped revive us during a slump. I recommend this as a regular feature, running parallel to the topic of the month. During the check-ins, members report on whatever is happening in their personal lives—the thoughts, feelings, and events that are uppermost in their minds. Check-ins help people feel involved with one another. As author and CMC participant Howard Rheingold has written: "In a virtual community, idle talk is context-setting. Idle talk is where people learn what kind of person you are, why you should be trusted or mistrusted, [and] what interests you." The check-ins can also be a source of new topics for the primary conversation.

Another side discussion that may be useful is the "process topic." Within this conversation, e-salonists discuss what is and is not working for them in the e-salon; which topics they'd like to discuss in the future; and any interpersonal problems they are experiencing in the salon. Such discussions should not be considered an interruption, but part of the process that leads to a greater level of involvement and interest. The facilitator of the group should take an especially active interest in this topic.

Virtual author Howard Rheingold

> 66 Once you learn your way around, don't be afraid to pose new topics of discussion: plant informational seeds and watch discussions grow around them, and study the ways knowledge emerges from discourse."
>
> —Howard Rheingold, "Virtual Communities"

In my experience, computer conference hosts and facilitators have often been unusually sensitive to the nuances of communication and the pitfalls of relying on the written word. For the most part, they are also fascinated by new expressions and new ways of conveying emotion on-line. Consequently, e-salons may spend more time discussing facilitation and the process of communicating than most face-to-face conversational groups, where standards of behavior and communication are assumed or unconscious. If you'd like tips for doing a better job of facilitating your e-salon, try logging on to larger networks under the hosting/facilitation/mediation topic.

The process topic becomes most important when members start to consider leaving the e-salon, or when your group considers inviting new members. As with traditional salons, either situation can be disruptive, and should be handled as smoothly as possible. When people drop out, the remaining core group often loses heart. Departure also tends to diminish the flow of new topics, because fewer active members means fewer points of view. You may have to come up with creative ways of keeping people involved and maintaining their interest. Sometimes the simple expedient of trying entirely new topics helps immensely; in other cases, you may want to redesign the structure of the e-salon itself.

If attrition has become a significant factor, your group may decide to add new members. This can be a tricky proposition, as trust and standards of behavior have already been established. It can be disruptive if a new person holds radically different ideas about how the e-salon should proceed, but it can also be quite stimulating. Members may be thrown into stormy relations as adjustments are made, but the group will ultimately become stronger as the wider range of voices enriches the conversation. If you've stopped having volunteer facilitators, it's generally a good idea to reinstate the role for a few months after adding new people. The facilitator can focus on helping the new members adjust to the e-salon and vice versa.

I believe that private e-mail between members should be kept to a minimum, unless the communication is solely for the purpose of following up on a topic that doesn't interest others in the group. Private e-mail too often involves gossip about other people in the group. It's far preferable to bring up difficulties within the e-salon's process topic, or to discuss them with the facilitator. When e-salonists rely on private e-mail to vent their feelings, they are avoiding precisely the kind of communication that could establish a sense of unity within the entire group.

In any kind of salon, including e-salons, commitment to remaining involved is crucial. On-line relationships proceed cyclically, just as they do when conducted face to face. There are periods of greater and lesser intimacy. Cliff Figallo observed relationship cycles on the WELL: "This led to some personal crises and periods of despair, which were followed by healing and rejuvenation. This repeating cycle, I think, taught those of us who were paying attention a lot about the resilience of on-line community. It's easy enough to log out and never log in again, but others keep coming, and there are good people among the new arrivals who come with hope and willingness to be open to others." In the end, caring enough to outlast difficulties is what brings people to genuine closeness and understanding, whether on-line or off.

Netiquette

People who enter the virtual world are encountering each other in a still-new medium of communication, one without precedent that (sometimes unfortunately) imposes few constraints on social behavior. For many people, going on-line is somewhat like visiting an unknown culture, one in which the rules are never quite explained and are consequently often ignored. A number of netiquette guides have been published in the last several years; however, on-line newcomers are likely to discover that guidelines vary from network to network and group to group. Discussing and reaching a consensus on standards of behavior for your e-salon remains the best way to minimize future blow ups, dropouts, and irreconcilable personality clashes.

As a fundamental step, establish what level of politeness (amounting to self-censorship in written communications) your members feel is necessary. Some people prefer to maintain the same level of politeness and respect on-line that they would expect face to face. One adamant e-salonist, Donald Kreis, wanted "no part of any electronic salon that does not regard civility as among its highest ideals. . . . I am keenly aware that by participating in this electronic salon we are effectively in each other's living rooms.

"Do you think e-mail attracts weirdos? The possibility of lurking, the anonymity, the social distance it maintains, do these encourage the socially inadequate? "

—Graham Storrs, e-salonist

LURKERS, BOZOS, FLAMERS, AND STALKERS

People on-line interact under a peculiar set of circumstances. They are often anonymous; they are communicating on an almost purely intellectual level; there are few consequences to their actions; and the rules for behavior are neither fixed nor readily understood. These circumstances sometimes encourage difficult personality types and uncomfortable interactions. On-line communicators have developed four terms to describe undesirable interlopers.

Lurkers

Lurkers join a computer network to read, but rarely or never post responses. Although they are not particularly annoying, they are much discussed by those who write regularly and feel the weight of a silent audience.

As the most anonymous of all users, lurkers are often accused of voyeurism. This is especially likely if the topic could be considered titillating—a conference on sexuality, for example.

In fact, lurkers are seldom sitting in judgment on the writers. They are more often people who haven't yet learned their way around, lack confidence in their writing skills, or simply don't have time to write. They may lurk during some topics but participate in others, depending on whether what they have to say is relevant to others.

Lurkers are found in most large networks. Given the number of participants, their presence makes little difference. However, bystanders can negatively affect small conferences and private e-salons. It can be difficult to share thoughts and feelings in the presence of silent, unknown watchers.

Bozos

"Bozo" is the on-line term for a person who is considered annoying. A bozo may be someone whose viewpoint or on-line personality inspires dislike; consequently, he or she may be ignored. Bozos are usually people who have few social skills and no apparent interest in learning them. They tend to misrepresent and misunderstand other people's words, argue without paying attention to what anyone else is saying, interrupt the flow of the conversation with irrelevant comments, and harp endlessly on one or two pet subjects. Most bozos favor intellectual posturing, game playing, and manipulative conversations. They may be proselytizers of one sort or another. However, few of them are universally shunned. They are irritating but not necessarily hateful people.

Flamers

"Flaming" is on-line jargon for heated arguments and vicious personal attacks. Most flame wars start with an intellectual argument that degenerates into name-calling. In most instances, a participant's emotional buttons have been pushed unintentionally by another person's opinions. After a few insults have been traded, others usually jump in and calm things down by noting that a flame war has started and urging the combatants to end it as quickly as possible. Alternatively, users may tell the adversaries to "Take it to e-mail."

Some people flame just to stir things up and get attention. Flamers, as described by author Howard Rheingold, may be "people who use vicious on-line verbal combat as a way of blowing off steam from the pressures of their real life—'sport hassling'—and others who use it voyeuristically, as a text-based form of real-life soap opera. To some people, it's a game."

In my experience, flaming or gross insults don't occur nearly as often as many people think. The best defense against flame wars is an assumption that goodwill exists among all users and a general ability to ignore insults.

Stalkers

Stalkers are the only truly evil characters found on-line, although they rarely participate openly in public conferences. These users are immature, sometimes emotionally sick people (often young men) who use private e-mail to harass, annoy, and frighten others (often women). Stalkers may attempt to obtain the addresses and phone numbers of the women they have decided to hassle or attack. Threatening or disgusting e-mail should be reported to the network staff as soon as possible, as stalkers can be barred from most on-line services. As an added precaution, many on-line women assume non-gender-specific pseudonyms.

We are guests in each others' homes—and yet we are wholly unable to draw on whatever reserve of warmth and trust people develop through actual in-person acquaintanceship. So, much of what I read on the salon seems like great stuff for a book or a newspaper or a debate in a legislative committee, but would be very unwelcome pouring out of the mouth of a potential friend whom I had, say, invited over for a beer and some conversation. Not offensive, mind you, just unwelcome."

Other e-salonists believe that good communication means total, spontaneous honesty on-line. They favor live-and-let-live, argumentative discussions; they may consider a more restrained approach somewhat boring, or even dishonest. Ruth Trimble, a member of our e-salon, expressed this attitude by encouraging other participants to: "Get rude—if you like. If being rude is being 'honest' and being truly yourself, then do it. Who will mind? This is only a computer screen! No one will arrive at your house, huffing and puffing with offense."

I tend to fall more in the first camp. I appreciate people who take the time to read other people's postings carefully, and who rewrite their own so their remarks are as thoughtful and clear as possible. The most difficult problem faced by e-salonists and others on-line is that they must rely on language to provide all contextual and physical cues. The facial expressions, body language, and tonal emphasis present in face-to-face encounters, which help us understand meaning, are utterly absent on-line. In one sense this is liberating. As e-salonist Graham Storrs puts it, people are not being judged by "the physical manifestations of age, sex, attractiveness, race, weight, height, mannerism, and all those other things that evoke our innate or learned prejudices." But the only available conveyor of nuance is the written language. Not everyone can be expected to write clearly and brilliantly, but they can at least review and reflect upon their writing, consider the potential impact of their words, and take the time to determine whether they really understand what was written by other members. As with all conversations, asking for clarification can prevent misunderstandings.

Emotions On-line

As you might expect, it's relatively difficult to convey emotion clearly on-screen. Everything you read or write appears to have equal weight, so a flippant remark may be taken seriously; an emotional comment may elicit intellectual arguments; or an intellectual comment may provoke vehement emotional comebacks. As one rule for communication, I suggest *composing off-line* whenever you are about to issue an emotional response. This will save you money, but more importantly it gives you a chance to review your words before you fire them off irretrievably.

"Having your ID bozo filtered and topics you initiate forgotten is punishment of sorts. After less than a month on the WELL, I've picked up on a few names I don't have much 'truck' with, some I'm wary of, others I eagerly look forward to reading postings from. **99**

—Salonist Carol Anne Ogdin

It's also helpful to become familiar with and *use emotive punctuation*. Typing in UPPERCASE can convey shouting and excitement, although it is discouraged otherwise as difficult to read. The sideways smiley face :-) indicates lightheartedness and good intentions. The smiling wink ;-) implies a gentle teasing nudge, a shared joke, or "no hard feelings." These symbols and their variants are increasingly well known and accepted around the world.

Despite the new kinds of punctuation, humor that relies on tone of voice doesn't translate clearly on-line and often leads to misunderstandings. Therefore, it's a good idea to *avoid sarcasm and irony* unless you're communicating with people who are already accustomed to you, your opinions, and your written tone. Punning and other forms of verbal play are, however, highly sought after on-line. They are often applauded with acronyms like LOL (Laughing Out Loud) or, better yet, ROTFL (Rolling on the Floor Laughing). Other acronyms include IMO (In My Opinion) and BTW (By the Way).

The use of symbols and abbreviations is fairly common on-line, although they can render conversations unintelligible if taken to an extreme. Part of their value lies in their succinctness, underscoring my belief that it's important to *be brief* when on-line. As in traditional salons, saying your piece and letting others have a chance is a valued practice. Succinctness demonstrates that you respect other people's time and money. It also works to your advantage—short entries (less than half a page) are generally read more carefully. Long passages may be downloaded and read at leisure, but they are more often skimmed or skipped altogether. As a group, your e-salon members may want to limit the length of messages. Some software systems afford you the option of hiding lengthy entries, then indicating how participants can look it up. If you compose responses that are directed only at a few people, it is considered good netiquette to send your comments via private e-mail, rather than subjecting the entire group to irrelevant remarks.

Although writing skills are valued on-line, try to *be tolerant of spelling and grammatical errors*. Even skilled, intelligent people make errors when they compose hastily on-line, and not all among us are good typists. In addition, some participants may not share the same first language with others. Focus on content rather than presentation,

Rules for Flame Wars

E-salonist Joel Sax developed these tongue-in-cheek guidelines for the civil enactment of the highly uncivil excercise known as a flame war:

These rules are issued in the spirit of clearing up some preconceptions about the waging of flame wars. Flame wars do not require profanity, as commonly misbelieved. The following list demonstrates ways to undertake "clean" flame wars:

1) Accuse the other party of your worst faults.

2) Insist that you are an avatar of the Truth and that the other person is Falsehood incarnate, or at least "misled."

3) Dwell on errors. Correct them in others at every opportunity.

4) Never apologize unequivocally. If forced to apologize, justify yourself in a way that makes it sound like the other party was responsible for your actions.

5) Write in such a way that the other party looks stupid if they don't respond.

6) Try to be many things at once, so that you can deny everything that is said about you.

7) Say the same thing over and over again.

8) Always strive to get the last word.

9) Never let a debate rest. Never allow the other party to withdraw without making it clear that they have lost.

10) Insist that you are misunderstood.

11) If you can't find something to flame the person about, make something up. Convince yourself that you see the "real" motives.

12) Remember: Winning is everything.

Rule for Those Who Do Not Want to Get into Flame Wars: Ignore them.

and enjoy the occasional, serendipitous typographical errors that add humor to the interaction. On occasion, typing errors end up becoming new words that are affectionately adopted by the community. "Gopod," the result of one such typo, became the gender-free term for the Universal Being on the WELL.

Your group should also decide whether to tolerate lurkers. Some groups are at ease with members who contribute on an occasional basis, perhaps as seldom as once a month. However, many e-salons establish minimal levels of involvement. For a number of reasons, it's generally important to *post regularly*. In traditional salons a silent person can remain an active presence; in the e-salon, a nonwriter is completely invisible—a virtual nonentity.

Because anyone can download and print out your on-line words, privacy and copyright issues have become a major concern to many virtual community members. Another common netiquette rule arises from this concern: always *ask permission to quote* if you'd like to use the comments of someone you've read or corresponded with on-line. In addition, it is generally considered very bad form to publicly reveal identifying features such as real names, home addresses, and phone numbers. In some groups, violating someone's privacy in this manner is grounds for being barred from the network.

Those who behave inappropriately on-line are chastised primarily by being ignored. On-line involvement, to an even greater degree than face-to-face conversation, is generally prompted by a desire to be heard. Those with other motivations become lurkers. Consequently, behavior is checked by telling people what they are doing wrong, refusing to respond, or eliminating them from the group by denying access. The late Kathleen Creighton described how she responded when she encountered someone she considered a bozo: "There are people who make the most outrageous and untrue claims—some of which I just can't let pass (although I ignore most of them). Typically, what will happen is that the person will then respond to me, twisting my words and my argument with a response so patently ridiculous it doesn't bear answering. So I don't. I simply don't."

Refusing to respond and skipping over entries written by people you dislike is one way to avoid confrontations. Some programs allow you to exercise more systematic methods of ignoring flamers and bozos, through the use of kill files or bozo filters. These allow you to instruct your computer not to show you anything written by a particular person. In a sense, bozos are shunned by those who don't get along with them, though they may still be accepted by the larger group. If they are shunned by the hosts or facilitators of a particular conference, however, they are likely to feel the consequences more deeply. Hosts sometimes ask all participants in a group to filter out entries from a particular person. The impact of such an imposed silence should not be underrated. Nor should this action be taken lightly. It is akin to declaring someone dead and turning all eyes away in a traditional society.

Some conferences (though not e-salons) utilize software allowing facilitators the option of hiding or even erasing entries they deem deeply offensive or seriously disruptive. The option hides a particular entry from everyone else, but it's a message-by-message solution that does not ignore everything written by a particular individual. The conference host will usually contact the offender via e-mail and explain why the message was censored. It is almost never done arbitrarily, as on-line participants tend to be ardent protectors of free speech.

Overall, very few people are excluded completely from participating in a conference or a system. Exclusion is analogous to barring someone from attending a salon. It has wide implications for everyone involved. Nevertheless, hosts can generally remove people from private conferences, and network administrators can deny access to identified stalkers.

Exhibiting knowledge of how to behave on-line is part of what establishes a sense of community. Every on-line group has its habits and preferences. Newcomers are often apparent due to their ignorance of these conventions, but in most cases they are tolerated or appreciated for the freshness of their views. Old-timers are generally willing to instruct them, or to point out agreed upon standards.

If you're new to the world of on-line salons, ask questions. Don't be too inhibited in your responses, and feel free to tell people what you want. You will help the e-salon come alive.

PART IV

The Open Circle:
Salons and Community

Extended Family:
Building Community in Your Salon

A true community begins in the hearts of the people involved. It is not a place of distraction but a place of being. It is not a place where you reform, but a place you go home to.
—Malidoma Patrice Somé, *Ritual: Power, Healing, and Community*

Amerícan society encourages and professes to admire a certain kind of isolation—the isolation of self-sufficiency. The importance of community is de-emphasized, but the need for a sense of belonging does not go away. In fact, if the need is unmet, people may experience a profound sense of loss or disturbance. Robert Gonzales, a psychotherapist in Southern California, became interested in salons because he thought they would be helpful to his clients—almost all of whom reported "some form of isolation or disconnection from community."

Perhaps it's not surprising, then, that most people who join modern salons do so out of a desire for community. For the population at large—from single mothers to senior citizens and average adults—the absence of community is a serious issue. People turn to salons not just for intellectual stimulation, but to share their lives with their neighbors, and to find a way out of isolation. They seek to belong to their neighborhoods. Whether your salon meets this need depends upon to what degree it functions as a community.

Characteristics of Community

As a result of observing and becoming involved with many communities, I have developed nine characteristics of vital, healthy communities. If, over time, your salon embodies these characteristics, it will serve as a community for your members.

The fundamental characteristic of community is *shared time*. If a community is to be created and sustained, members must meet one another regularly. Shared time ensures shared experiences, which in turn foster emotional links between people. When I spend enough time with others in a common endeavor, I grow to love and care about them—even if I don't see them socially or count them as close friends. Conscious community requires a commitment to participate, which means that people must take the time to hash out problems as well as playing together and chatting casually. A salon becomes a community only if a majority of the members are committed to spending time together regularly over the course of many months or years.

The second characteristic of community is *shared space*. Meeting repeatedly in a familiar house or café builds a bond between your members as they come to share a sense of "home." But even if your salon meets in varying locations, members will perceive themselves as part of a community if they encounter each other regularly outside the salon. The neighborhood itself may become your salon's shared space.

Over time, salonists should become increasingly familiar and at ease with one another. For this to happen, the group must be a *manageable size*—neither too large nor too small. If the salon is too large or its membership is unstable, names and faces cannot be recalled from one meeting to the next. Few people will develop a sense of belonging. Social scientists have found that groups are not experienced as communities if they become larger than six hundred people (much larger than any salon), because too many people are strangers to one another.

At the same time, I believe that a certain minimum size is necessary to sustain community. While members of a very small group may become good friends, such groups are easily dispersed, because they are heavily dependent on the personalities of a few individuals. They also lack the diversity of true community. If you would like to develop a sustainable feeling of community, your group should be at least the size of an extended family—roughly a dozen people. But in practice, your salon community is more likely to be viable if you have thirty or more members.

Like everything else, building community takes practice. As a medium-sized group meets regularly, it comes to exhibit a sense of *shared history*. Those who demonstrate

❝ Community is a place where the connections felt in the heart make themselves known in bonds between people, and where tuggings and pullings of those bonds keep opening up our hearts.❞

—Parker Palmer, Quaker

an ongoing commitment to being involved with one another begin to develop standards of behavior; they create and pass down rituals and traditions; and they tell stories about their shared experiences. In a sense, they create a culture.

In the midst of this created context, people come to understand that they belong to a particular group, time, and place. It is this *sense of belonging* that people seek when they long for community. Of course, most of us identify ourselves as belonging to many groups—perhaps to humanity, and to a family, nation, tribe, or neighborhood. A salon provides a smaller, more clearly defined community, supplementing but not supplanting other groups. Your salon begins to do this as soon as members invent a name for the group, and community is confirmed when the salon establishes a presence in the larger neighborhood.

"Belonging" is sustained by each individual's willingness to invest in relationships with others in the community. As members come to feel part of your salon, they should also become more responsible for maintaining the group. They will in turn reap the benefits of group support. This sort of *interdependence* is the single most definitive feature of community. A true community is a safety net for every member, a mutual aid network comprised of people and their resources. Interdependence becomes apparent when members of a group help each other find jobs; collaborate on creative efforts; swap tools, music, and books; attend each other's social events; watch each other's kids; help each other move; and so forth. When each person willingly supports the other members of the salon, the salon acts as a community.

However, *room for individuality* must exist alongside interdependence. People often insist that they can maintain freedom of choice and social liberation only as individuals; and that support during crises, making decisions by consensus, and a sense of belonging mandate conformity and loss of individuality. But community does not stand in opposition to individuality. Rather, community is the opposite of anonymity. When people

AN EQUATION FOR COMMUNITY

Shared time
+ shared space
+ manageable size
+ shared history
+ sense of belonging
+ interdependence
+ room for individuality
+ ability to mediate problems
+ consensus

_____

COMMUNITY

> 66 The only individuality a person has to give up in community is the 'right' to take advantage of others, to be dishonest, or to attempt to obtain from others or from the community more than s/he is willing to give them.
>
> —*Builders of the Dawn*

have neither community nor an internal sense of self, they become invisible, unable to act, belonging nowhere. People who are deeply community-minded are never anonymous. In practice, interdependence teaches tolerance of one another's foibles. A healthy salon should encourage individuality, tolerate eccentricity, and relish unusual ideas. The voice of the nonconformist should be welcomed as the conscience of the group, forcing people to acknowledge their preconceived notions and make decisions carefully.

Combining interdependence with individuality means that disputes will sometimes occur. Another aspect of community is its *ability to mediate problems*, minimizing the risk of permanent estrangement between members. Community mediation assumes that any problem within the group is the entire group's problem; that problems always involve more than one person; and that rarely is one person completely in the right. Salons work to maintain community when they create their own guidelines for behavior, are willing to make and learn from mistakes, and succeed in resolving disputes in a manner that preserves the integrity of the group without ignoring or discounting the needs of any individual.

Finally, a community reaches a *consensus* when making major decisions—especially those that relate to the larger world. The effort to reach an agreed upon decision before taking action distinguishes community from other groups of people. When your salon has learned and practiced democratic decisionmaking processes, defining itself as a unified group, it has become a living, multidimensional community.

Stages of Community Building

If the community is completely honest, it will remember stories not only of suffering received, but of suffering inflicted—dangerous memories, for they call the community to alter ancient evils. The communities of memory that tie us to the past also tie us toward the future as communities of hope.
  —Robert Bellah, *Habits of the Heart*

Discussion groups that meet for a year or more discover that new questions and problems perpetually present themselves. The structure of the salon may need continual fine tuning; new people advocate new ideas, while founding members suddenly move away. A crisis may arise that forces the group into greater intimacy than anticipated. If your salon is to survive for more than a short time, you must be flexible and responsive to change. It's helpful to understand the stages a typical group experiences as it struggles to establish community, so your salon members don't simply give up when difficulties arise. For a thorough background in community building, I recommend reading M. Scott Peck's well-known *The Different Drum: Community Making and Peace*, as well as the comprehensive *Creating Community Anywhere* by Carolyn R. Shaffer and Kristin Anundsen (who is also a salonist).

The first stage for most groups is, logically enough, the stage of "Beginnings." Shaffer and Anundsen refer to this as the "Excitement Phase," or "Getting High on Possibilities." It is the period of decision making, establishing behavioral guidelines, and getting to know one another. Because people are often polite, tolerant, and eager to make the group work, serious conflict rarely emerges during this period. Your group may initially feel remarkably warm and friendly, but Peck calls this phase "Pseudocommunity," because people do not reveal much about themselves and generally avoid disagreements. A salon comprised of like-minded individuals may happily stay in this phase for years, as long as people remain content with social conversation and have no desire to forge a deeper connection.

"Conflict is the fastest way to create community, something a group needs in order to understand itself—provided you catch the forbidden edge of the issue that's almost unspeakable. **" **
  —Arnold Mindell, *The Leader as Martial Artist*

COUNCIL AND CONFLICT

Traditional cultures often have highly developed methods of dealing with conflicts and strong emotions. For example, the Hawaiian ho'oponopono are councils held specifically to work out problems that must be safely but completely exposed, then resolved in order to restore harmony. Traditionally, these councils are held after any traumatic event to prevent future problems from arising in the community. As one participant put it, "When you suppress and repress hostilities, pretend they do not exist, then sooner or later they are going to burst out of containment, often in destructive, damaging ways." Through the controlled release of strong feelings, ho'oponopono councils maintain a healthy community.

As healer and ho'oponopono scholar Mary Kawena Pukui explains it, the process works through self-scrutiny and a commitment to absolute truthfulness and sincerity. Participants must willingly thrash out "every grudge, peeve, or resentment." Such deep emotional scrutiny is made possible by the interventions of the leader, who questions each person involved and does not allow others to interrupt. Responses are directed only at the leader. When all emotions and circumstances have been expressed, the leader summarizes. Members ask one another for forgiveness, and ideally the matter is never discussed again—thus assuring both confidentiality and prevention of future recurrences of the problem.

The ho'oponopono, then, is not merely a piece of cultural exotica, but a sophisticated example of how council methods can be used in communities. As defined by the Ojai Foundation, councils have been adapted for use in schools through the Mysteries Program in Southern California, where students pass the talking stick, tell stories, meditate, create ceremonies, and otherwise work together to examine family relationships, sexuality, drugs, and other topics critical to children in our times.

If you want to move your group out of this phase, you may need to encourage frankness and choose topics that evoke emotion or highlight human differences. For example, you might address issues of class, culture, or gender, asking questions that encourage people to respond out of personal experience. In any case, your salon may discover a strong area of disagreement on its own, which will also move the group into the next stage of community building. This period of "Power Struggles" is called the "Autonomy" phase by Shaffer and Anundsen, while Peck labels it "Chaos." Jane Mauchan described the dynamics succinctly when our e-salon entered this phase: "The polite get-to-know-you phase is over. The 'real' personalities are starting to show." This is a difficult time. Many groups break up or splinter when power struggles arise.

You'll know you've moved into this stage when members begin questioning the standards and goals of the group. Some may call for stronger leadership and demand that someone take charge; others will advocate rigid rules and agendas; still others may insist on dispensing with all guidelines and structure. To survive this phase, your members must be willing to deal with conflict. In fact, they should regard arguments as an indication that the group is heading toward greater intimacy and solidarity. All voices should be encouraged, yet facilitators must work to ensure that arguments don't devolve into name-calling. During this time, group leaders should avoid making sweeping decisions or pronouncements; instead, they should continue to support members' efforts to express their true feelings and ideas. Facilitators may even need to relinquish control and cease all efforts to organize or fix the group.

Peck believes that, in order to attain true community, the entire group needs to undergo a giving up period, which he calls "Emptiness." Members must relinquish all barriers to communication, as well as all expectations, prejudices, ideologies, and controlling habits that would otherwise prevent them from accepting one another. For many, this is a painful process. However, deeper friendships will form as a result. As one salonist noted, you may lose a few acquaintances along the way, but you'll gain a family.

During the "Power Struggles" phase, it's often helpful to shake up the established structure by trying new ways of interacting. It's an appropriate time to try some of the exercises suggested in the chapters on conversation and council, especially those designed to draw out less talkative people. Turn-taking methods, rituals, and even creative games can help your members focus on the community-building process. As they become more aware, they will work through most clashes of opinion and personality.

As your group gains respect and sensitivity for each member and for the dynamics of interaction, it will move into Anundsen and Shaffer's "Stability Phase," or what Peck regards as "True Community." A stable group is one that has become comfortable with agreed upon roles and structures. Stability is a cheerful period. Members feel they have cohered. Leadership issues are resolved, and the need for a facilitator may simply disappear, because people have learned to trust one another. Each member gains a sense of identity within the community.

Like other human conditions, stability is often temporary or imperfect. Your salon may occasionally lapse into its old, chaotic behaviors. Don't be dismayed if the same problems are discussed over and over. Healthy communities continually revisit past policies and are in a state of constant flux as the needs of community members change. It's far better to accept and move through these changes than to become rigid or intolerant of dissension.

If your group remains stable for some time, while maintaining enough flexibility to accommodate individual development and community evolution, it will eventually enter the phase that Anundsen and Shaffer call "Synergy." The period is one of unfolding and growth. Synergy is signaled by the emergence of new roles and leaders in the group; by deeper self-expression during discussions; and by the members' willingness to act in ways that support and sustain the group. This is a highly productive stage—a time when you can accomplish many of your group's goals, if you have established any. People trust one another, express their feelings accurately, feel safe, and are highly committed to the group. The only problems associated with this phase involve resistance to change when new people or ideas influence the community.

Eventually, all committed groups face the stage of "Transformation." Anundsen and Shaffer suggest that groups can transform in any of three ways. They may segment, expand, or disband. Many salons end up segmenting, perhaps forming secondary groups to concentrate on writing, creative play, or new methods of interacting. Other salons expand, either because members long for greater diversity or because they want to connect with society at large. The urge to become more actively involved in politics or social issues is a form of expansion. When salonists decide as a group to tackle a social problem, they are in a transformative phase.

Whether in five months or fifty years, every salon will reach its natural end. If a group disbands

Benjamin Franklin

> "We must all hang together or,
> most assuredly, we shall all hang separately. **"**
>
> —Benjamin Franklin

because it failed to meet expectations, it probably never quite became a community. Helen White summed up the prevailing attitude at one salon that dissolved after a short time: "I suspect we had a problem that may be more acute in university-laden areas like ours. Many of us have plenty of folks to discuss issues with in our everyday lives; we were drawn to the salon idea more because of the community-building aspect. And when COMMUNITY didn't envelop us after three or four months—well, the whole thing was taking too long! Where was the payoff? So, many of us dropped out to take a running leap at some other activity that may provide that elusive sense of belonging—and *fast!*"

However, salons that take the time and have the courage to transcend superficial dislikes and attractions in the group—salons that have established community—end for other reasons. They end when the people in them grow older, move away, or die. They end when they cease to serve their purpose in people's lives. They often end at times of cataclysmic social change, as during a war. But your salon can extend its lifetime by remaining open to new members, and by providing a relaxed, realistic environment. Perhaps the healthiest attitude is one of keen interest in what happens next, without fretting unduly about the future.

Community Consensus
One tree cannot make a forest.
> —Nigerian proverb

Community is best supported by consensus, but finding consensus within multiple viewpoints is no easy task. Your members must devote themselves to considering all sides of a problem and recognizing that people view the problem itself differently. But rigorous, open discussion eventually leads to a kind of cohesion, and the best course of action generally becomes apparent. When your group moves beyond opposing viewpoints to a collectively acceptable answer, solution, or attitude, you are building the strongest possible bonds of community.

Consensus is a decision with which all members agree. There are no majorities or minorities, no votes, and no representatives. Everyone in the group works together to form a working conclusion that all members can live with. Employing some variant of the council process (see Chapter Ten) is generally the best way to achieve this kind of group agreement. Every person has an equal voice in a group attempting to arrive at consensus. This does not mean you assume that each member is equally knowledgeable or possesses the same level of insight into a problem. It *does* mean listening to each member in the belief that, at any moment, he or she may offer the element that was missing from your discussion. Clarissa Pinkola Estes explains the rationale in an essay entitled "Consensus Ingredients": "One person may know more of the truth at one time, while another person may know more at another time. Even when we have all the facts before us, it may be the spirit is lacking; and this may come forth from yet another who sees the whole better than anyone else." In the quest for consensus, it is necessary to welcome wisdom from every quarter.

Reaching consensus is a slow process, but it is the surest and truest form of democracy. It consumes more time than voting or electing representatives, because everyone participates directly in each decision. It requires openness and tenacity, because consensus cannot be reached if there is any strong "nay" in your group. One dissenter blocks the decision or conclusion. However, each individual is expected to be mature and responsible, avoiding attempts to manipulate or obstruct the group process to such a degree that decisions cannot be made. Each group member must learn to trust that every other member has the insight to know when it is proper to stand against or question the group view. In the process, mutual respect flourishes, and individuals come to understand their responsibility to the group.

No matter how much trust and perserverance your group exhibits, there will be times when opinions are at odds and reaching a decision or conclusion seems impossible. There are several ways you can deal with such impasses. First of all, remember to take breaks, and to allow your members time for reflection. Secondly, remind the group that, because there is no general sense of agreement, perspective may be lacking. Step further back from the problem or approach it from a different direction—perhaps by discussing the values that form the basis of each opinion. A third option involves reaching consensus on a partial or temporary decision and setting a date to reopen discussion. This provides resolution without closing the issue.

Do not blame one or two people who prevent the group from reaching a decision. The facilitator should remind group members that these individuals are operating with integrity, and out of deeply held beliefs. At the same time, the facilitator can ask the dissenting individuals to be certain they aren't acting out of self-interest, but out of a strong sense that the group viewpoint is wrong. In many cases, the best way dissenters can serve the group is by continuing to dissent.

Some groups agree that if an individual does not strongly oppose a decision, but is merely neutral or uncertain, he or she can stand aside so the consensus can move forward. Other groups practice what is known as "consensus minus one." That is, a single dissenter can be overridden, but two dissenters cannot. One observer believes that this

"Already in my personal life I am beginning to feel
a sense of community—coming together—connecting
with my fellow New Yorkers. Just the other day my neighbor
had a blackout in her building, so we offered the use
of our apartment for the evening (we had plans) so she
could do some work. Last week I returned home to find
a wonderful note and a package of scarves (she had inherited
a collection from her grandmother) to replace one I had lost
during an anti-fur demonstration with a fellow salonista.
I've actually had people 'drop by,' unannounced, just
to say hello. Community can happen—even in NYC. **"**

—Elisabeth Mead, salonist and regional salon coordinator

practice protects the group against "unaccountable insanity or temporary bouts of grumpiness." Clarissa Pinkola Estes agrees that, in a society accustomed to adversarial interactions, consensus minus one may be the only way some groups can reach decisions. The drawback to this approach is that the dissenter may feel disregarded; however, it should become clear over a period of time that he or she is not being singled out or picked on. The dissent of other members will also be overridden by the group.

The way you frame your consensus is as significant as the discussion preceding it. At some point, the group's agreement must be summarized, and the summary should be reviewed by all members to determine whether it conveys the essence of your decision. This can happen quite informally. The group member that first notices a consensus view emerging from the discussion can articulate it, asking if everyone agrees. Alternatively, you might experiment with the method used by some aboriginal people in western Australia. There, when one person states an acceptable opinion or idea, the other community members pick it up, repeating it rapidly in summary. The background chorus serves to indicate consensus. In Quaker communities, consensus is arrived at through "minutes" prepared by the clerk. The minutes express "the sense of the meeting" in succinct, accurate terms. When the minutes are finished, the clerk reads them aloud, then checks with the other committee members to ensure that all are in agreement. Anyone is free to suggest revisions or further discussion.

OPHELIA'S PALE LILIES: A SALON HISTORY

"Three of us friends were sitting around talking about the state of the gallery scene and publishing," recalled salon founder Kelly Shea. "We thought it would be nice if there were some place where people could just go and do their own thing. It wouldn't cost any money, you wouldn't have to join anything, you wouldn't have to pass any examination to belong. It would be a gathering place for people who did writing or painting or sculpture or people who didn't write but maybe just wanted to come and listen, or actors who wanted to read other people's writings. It would be an open discussion group. We'd sit down and talk about the arts." From this discussion, the creative salon known as Ophelia's Pale Lilies was born.

The group began to meet twice a week, on Wednesday and Saturday mornings, to discuss the arts. For the first six months, the conversations were a great success. "We had a sculptor bring his pieces and talk about them. We had a painter who painted while we talked. We had a photographer that would bring her work and people would write about it. People were saying, 'This is so incredible! There's no place else in town where you can do this unless you take a class, pay a lot of money, and apply to be accepted.'"

However, as with all groups, growth and change occurred. The original five or six members became a dozen. As more people came, the visual artists dropped out and the salon became primarily a writer's group. Members stopped discussing the arts in general, instead reading and talking about pieces they were writing. The group began meeting only once a week, on Saturdays. As Kelly described it, the salon became "a living entity that had to respond to the desires of everyone who came to it."

After a little over a year, most of the people in the group had accumulated a body of written work. They began to talk about trying to get published. In her role as initiator of the group, Kelly responded by researching and supplying the group with places where they could submit their poetry. After these new writers began to get rejection slips, she came up with the idea of publishing a one-page, throwaway flyer containing poetry written by group members. The flyer would provide a place to publish her friends' poetry but, more importantly, it would reach people who normally didn't read poetry. The publication was christened *Ophelia's Pale Lilies*.

Conflict intensified as the flyer became the group's primary focus. The name itself became a source of power struggles. People attempted to assert themselves by suggesting more rules for the group. Some members questioned Kelly's role as leader; others demanded that she take stronger stances and participate more fully. The original core group of friends left, although for reasons having nothing to do with the group.

The remaining members had joined as a result of publicity. They seemed to demand order and structure, and did not share Kelly's desire for a free-flowing, leaderless, creative group. As is common during periods of intense power struggles, they advocated greater rigidity. "It became this thing that needed to be administrated," Kelly reported. "I started getting a little annoyed around then, because this was supposed to be fun." At this point, she was doing all the work and financing the publication herself.

Kelly responded by trying to find ways of sharing responsibility, relinquishing some of her control as the group's founder. "The second or third year, we decided to take turns having someone be the head of the meeting that day. We also took turns rotating a group of editors that would work for three months. But people didn't like the tone the broadsheet would have for three months. So then we had three editors, each one in for three months, with one dropping out and a new one coming in each month. A poem was published if it had two out of three votes." For a time, Ophelia's Pale Lilies achieved stability.

The expectations surrounding the publication of *OPL* began to vary widely. On the one hand, said Kelly, "People really liked *OPL*. It got to the point where writers who had received awards were submitting stuff. I didn't know who they were, so I treated them the same way I treated everything else I got." As *OPL* became more successful, group members became fussier about maintaining their stability, and perhaps insufficiently concerned with common goals and mutual respect. In addition, members had conflicting ideas about where the publication was headed. "*OPL* began to suffer because it had to live up to people's personal expectations. Those expectations were all different. Some people wanted it to make money. Some people wanted its name to be known and lots of people to attend its functions. Other people wanted the publication to come out like clockwork and be a respected publication. I thought that was all fine, but it was steering away from the main intention. At one point it even got elitist.

People would ask newcomers, 'Well, are you a writer?' I'd have to remind people that anyone could come."

The group had returned to chaos, perhaps in part because deep communication had never occurred. But in some ways, Ophelia's Pale Lilies did become synergistic. Everyone had a voice in running the group, and it attempted to meet everyone's needs. But Kelly had not been able to let go of her original designs for the group; nor was she willing to go where the group was taking her. She didn't like the way newcomers to the group were treated by old-timers, who were leery of any changes they did not instigate. She didn't want to remain the head of the group, but the group kept demanding her leadership. She realized that she needed to make a decision.

Kelly decided to leave the group. She was pregnant, but in any case the effort of trying to appease everyone had worn her out. It wasn't an easy decision. The publication was on the verge of becoming a successful magazine. "At first I was so gung ho and full of energy. But when all that administrative stuff starts to settle on you, it's really revolting. I didn't want to do it, because I already had a full-time job and I wasn't finding time to write anymore. You've got some choices to make. What's the purpose? Why are you meeting? Even if you meet to sew quilts, after a while you're going to have two or three quilts, and then you have to decide who's going to take the first one home."

Kelly's decision to leave was the transformative stage for the group. OPL continued to meet without her, sporadically publishing the broadsheet. Kelly has thought about moving to another city and initiating another creative salon. "What I would do differently is take one of two avenues. I would from the beginning reject any authority, any 'I am the leader of the group' role. I'd make sure I took care of myself, got a chance to do my own work, and didn't speak up that much. Or, if I took the other avenue, I would from the very beginning make sure I was leading the group and guiding it the way I thought it should be done. I can argue both ways to this day. I also think I would do things more slowly next time. OPL got big overnight."

In the end, Kelly was also transformed by the group. "OPL mattered to me. The best thing about it for me was knowing that, if you want to do something, you can just do it. And that it does take on a life of its own. You give birth to this thing, it grows up, and like any child, it doesn't become exactly what the parent intended it to be."

Final and interim summaries can be utilized by any salon as a means of ending a meeting and ensuring common understanding. As your salon draws to a close, the facilitator can take a few minutes to describe what has been said, then ask if the summary captures the sense of the discussion. A summary is even more effective if it's written down, with provision for others in the group to add or change words as appropriate. Summaries can organically lead to the framing of the next session's topic, and they often point the way toward a deeper level of discussion. If you choose, you could use the summarizing process to link your topics from month to month, allowing one discussion to flow into the next.

Inhabiting Regions: Salon Networks

As salons become increasingly widespread, they enable people to establish connections in any community. Salonists are often interested in visiting other groups in the area, thus expanding the number and variety of people they know, and potentially enlarging the salon community.

From time to time, a dedicated salonist decides to track all salons in a given region. The endeavor may be spurred by hearing about other nearby salons, or by looking through NSA's nationwide directory. The individual may publish a newsletter letting all salonists in the area know when and where meetings are held and which topics or activities are planned. A number of past or present regional salon networks have functioned in this manner.

Regional networks have operated in parts of northern and southern California, Washington, Virginia, New York, New Jersey, and Washington, D.C. Some networks have included up to forty salons, which have maintained some degree of regular contact with one another. Salonists may visit other groups; two or three salons may get together for joint weekend retreats; facilitators may meet in order to swap tips on salon leadership.

Informal weekend retreats have been a favorite way to promote inter-salon connections. For example, four or five salons in New York have assembled for a retreat twice every year. On Friday evenings, the salonists get to know one another, choose topics and activities for the rest of the weekend, and set an agenda for focused conversation that usually involves breaking into smaller, mixed groups. The agenda is generally dropped or revised on Saturday, as participants discover that one topic is of overriding interest to everyone. Between long hours of conversation, they eat, dance, watch obscure videos, play games, or take hikes in the Catskill Mountains. Extended saloning of this sort between people who wouldn't otherwise meet could become a powerful aspect of the salon movement.

> 66 Without a community you cannot be yourself.
> The community is where we draw the
> strength needed to effect changes inside of us."
>
> —Malidoma Patrice Somé, *Ritual: Power, Healing, and Community*

Regional gatherings are also useful for people who live in remote rural areas and can't meet on a frequent basis. Many are willing to drive a considerable distance for an opportunity to engage in extended conversation. The Roguettes of Rogue River, Oregon, have met seasonally at their Country Salon. During the first of these "marathon salons," which lasted nine hours, the salonists discussed the arts in talking stick rounds; reviewed books; exchanged erotic limericks; discussed murals and children's book illustrators; and critiqued foreign and American films. Following dinner, they answered the question, "What does art in everyday living mean to you?" The conversation ultimately became a discussion of spiritual well-being and problems related to the isolation of rural living.

In some cases, salons organize regionally for the primary purposes of consolidating information and creating a facilitation support network. This involves a somewhat more complicated organization. The information must be gathered and distributed, and salon representatives who will attend network meetings should be designated. Contact people from the salons in a region may assemble once or twice a year to discuss what's going on in their salons, to help each other locate new members, and to inspire one another with success stories. However, regional organizations don't have to be elaborate. A simple newsletter, sent to all contact people and including meeting and activity information, can be sufficient to maintain contact.

Perhaps the greatest benefit of regional and national salon networks is that they provide opportunities to visit other groups. Within a year or two after formation of the Southern California network, it became possible to attend a salon in the greater Los Angeles area six days a week. If you could tolerate the driving, you might visit a Pasadena salon on Sunday afternoon and another in Culver City that night; spend Monday night with a group in Venice-Marina Del Rey; travel to Topanga and the South Bay on Wednesday; hang out Thursday with either the Forty-niners or the Beach, Beach, Beach Salon; and on Friday, enjoy a chat with the Decade-nts in Palos Verdes. Presumably, Saturday would be a day of rest and vocal recuperation.

The salon network in Washington, D.C., organized by Larry Schuster, combined regional networking with salon-hopping by presenting a "Salon Showcase." At the event, a contact person from each salon in the area made a short speech, describing the salon he or she represented to an audience of eighty. The attendees included veteran salon-goers as well as many people who had never attended a salon in their lives. It was an innovative way to get the word out, and it provided a smorgasbord of testimonials and information to those in attendance.

Regional coordinators serve best when they provide accurate, up-to-date information on when and where salons are meeting in the area, which are seeking new members, who is available to mentor new salons, and what special events will be conducted by network salonists. A regional coordinator can also help specialized or topical salons form and find members. The Southern California Salon Community Network's newsletter, *Dialogue*, has listed both would-be salons and ongoing special salons. One issue listed five existing specialty groups: a feminine spirituality salon; a creativity salon; a postmodernism salon; a creative writing salon; and a readers' salon. Several specialty salons not yet underway were listed as well. An effective regional network can also provide hosts who are willing to house salonists visiting from out of town, or even foreign travelers eager to attend and speak at salons while in the United States.

As a rule, regional coordinators should avoid overorganizing and offering unsolicited advice. Salons tend to prefer autonomy. They will drop out of a network if they feel that someone is pushing them to get involved in a bureaucracy or asking for too much of a commitment. Most people want a network to help interested newcomers find their salon, or to provide a forum for facilitators to exchange information. Salonist Jeanne Melvin's attitude is fairly typical: "It's great for salon contacts to get together, maybe once a quarter, to see what other salons are up to. But we're resistant to more organization. There's enough work for contact people without more information coming in to pass along. A regional coordinator has to understand that, because groups are formed organically, they are very strong on their own."

Regional organizing requires at least one salonist who is so devoted to the task that he or she invests a great deal of imagination and time in the effort. The entire community should support coordinators financially, at least to the extent of covering mailings, but coordinators cannot expect to be otherwise paid. They should scrutinize their own motivations carefully, and should avoid proselytizing or attempting to dictate

"So we, who are united in mind and soul,
have no hesitation about sharing property
All is common among us—except our wives. **"**

—Tertullian, Carthaginian theologian

practices. Their reward comes from being involved in a large community and contributing to the creation of new salons.

When your salon arrives at a full-fledged sense of community—a sense of its internal strength, energy, and consensus beliefs—it may begin to look outward. Your members may contemplate ways of interacting with the larger community. Many salon groups have volunteered at soup kitchens, participated in demonstrations, held public consciousness-raising events, met with local boards of education, or initiated letter-writing campaigns. While community involvement is by no means mandatory, the salon movement as a whole could potentially influence the quality and character of community life throughout the United States and elsewhere.

As David Mathews, president of the Kettering Foundation, has observed: "Democracy is born in conversations."

FOURTEEN

Salons in Society:
Making a Difference

It's a mistake to think of salons as action groups, but it's not a mistake to think that action can arise from salons.
       —Erika Sukstorf, guerrilla salonist

S alons and salonists have repeatedly demonstrated the capacity to move from talk to action. Following the April 1992, riots in Los Angeles, many salonists there were "shocked into the awareness that our community was going up in flames," as regional coordinator Ronny Barkay put it. Salon members began to discuss what community really meant to them, and many became interested in actively responding to the needs of the city. Individuals from various groups in the region formed the Creative Action Salon, which directed its efforts toward getting people to vote and establishing a Time Dollar bartering co-op. The members also sent an open letter to the media, suggesting the formation of a Citizens Broadcasting Commission.

Barkay and guerrilla salonist Erika Sukstorf then contacted community members through computer bulletin boards and founded The Next Step, a multicultural, non-profit organization seeking permanent self-help solutions to longstanding problems in the inner city. Several salon members joined The Next Step, contributing their expertise in writing, public relations, and fund-raising to set up a program that helped businesses affected by the riots obtain loans. They also conducted classes for teenagers and business-people in financial survival, computer applications, and other means to empowerment.

Conversational groups that are formed in order to discuss specific social or political issues often take action more quickly than general salons. This is why the study circle model has been so effective around the world—particularly when the circles have focused on citizenship, human rights, health education, or literacy. In the civil rights arena the Citizenship School, developed by Esau Jenkins and Bernice Robinson in South Carolina, focused on literacy for African-Americans. The study of fundamental documents of government, such as the Declaration of Independence and the United Nations Declaration of Human Rights, sparked extraordinary discussions of what citizenship is all about. By organizing small community study groups, participants learned an array of skills that were later put to use in forming civil rights groups. The communities involved experienced a "dramatic decline in the levels of crime and social pathology," according to a subsequent study.

From 1930 through the late 1960s the Metis, an indigenous people from Canada, created their own materials for study circles, discussing and proposing solutions to the economic and social problems that beset them. The circles did much to revitalize their history and values as a people. They also helped the Metis analyze treaties with the Canadian government.

Swedish study circle organizations have supported successful programs abroad. In Tanzania, for example, Swedes trained discussion leaders, provided study materials, and helped facilitate circles that encouraged Tanzanian citizens to read, debate, and vote. Between the late 1960s and 1981, the literacy rate in Tanzania rose from twenty percent to eighty percent—in good part because of these study circles. In addition, a health and sanitation campaign was initiated in the early 1970s that trained seventy-five thousand study circle leaders over a three-month period. Radio programs and printed booklets were then used as the bases for study. An estimated two million people participated in weekly discussions throughout the country.

More recently, National Issues Forums programs for corrections institutions have produced issue books in abridged form for literacy students. The topics include "The Drug Crisis," "Growing Up at Risk," and AIDS. Inmates, who participated voluntarily, experienced an increase in self-esteem as they improved their reading and speaking skills. They also gained a stronger sense of

Salonist Ronny Barkay (at left) organized efforts to aid inner city residents after the 1992 L.A. uprising.

> "You should never wear your best trousers
> when you go out to fight for freedom and truth. "
> —Henrik Ibsen, *An Enemy of the People*

belonging to and participating in society.

Discussion and study groups throughout the world have brought literacy and political savvy to rural people. They have often helped people decide whether technological and social changes should become part of village life. Cohousing groups in Denmark and the United States have built small, living communities whose viability is maintained through conversation. Local councils such as African palavers demonstrate the political importance of developing public speaking skills, listening attentively to every member of a community, and drawing upon the wisdom of elders.

Salon activism may begin after a group has been together for several years, when each member has come to trust the views and personalities of the other members. The salonists may then arrange to work together on small, coordinated projects, such as letter-writing campaigns or volunteer work at a homeless shelter. Jim and Nicole Fary, members of a Maryland salon, reported that their salon participated in Montgomery County's annual volunteer day by preparing food packages for homeless people. Kevin Spitler from Arlington, Virginia, is part of a salon that has painted the stairwell for a day care center, cohosted a picnic for homeless children, and marched in a pro-choice demonstration in Washington, D.C.

Your salon is most likely to act in a unified manner if the minds and hearts of all members are engaged by a particular issue. This may happen following a natural or community disaster. New laws or political candidates coming up for a vote may also galvanize salon members. If a salon returns time and again to its concern about one subject, the members may at some point form a politically active subgroup. Such groups should in most cases limit themselves to efforts that are short-term, specific, and focused, grounding each of their actions in consensus. To enhance their influence, the subgroups might consider joining forces with established, financially supported nonprofit organizations that tackle the same issue. Salonists generally find that their interpersonal and organizing skills are highly valued by grassroots networks and other activist groups.

Having said all this, I do not mean to suggest that salons *should* become politically or socially active. In fact, some salons form specifically as an antidote to activist burnout. Mary Ruthsdotter has been a member of one such group. "Another action-oriented group wasn't what we were after," she explained. "And one ground rule was quickly articulated: Our discussions would not leave us frustrated, stymied, negative, or depressed about the world!"

Activists may turn to the salon as a respite—as a place to discuss issues other than those in which they are directly involved, to form friendships, and to benefit from a feeling of community. These salon-goers often regain inspiration in salons, returning to the tasks of building a better world with renewed vigor. The Southwest Area

Roundtable Group in Minneapolis has been fairly typical in this respect. Salonists run their monthly meetings as study circles. Each member takes a turn at developing a study guide ahead of time, then facilitates the meeting. The group is issue-focused rather than philosophical. All members are involved in a neighborhood association, a political party, or a grassroots organization, but they set their political affiliations and preconceptions aside when they attend the Roundtable.

Individual salons should be cautious about tackling projects that do not have the support of the whole group, or that seem too challenging for the group's resources. Without shared history, a durable sense of community, and the solidarity of consensus, groups that begin as conversational gatherings may be unable to withstand the pressures of political involvement. Many salons prefer to stick with the entirely legitimate function of providing a haven for egalitarian conversation. As you might expect, taking concerted action on a regional basis is even more difficult. Rarely are all members of all salons in a region ready to take the same action at the same time. Many salonists feel highly protective of the distinctive role of their salon, and rightly so. If your salon is contemplating action on an issue, perhaps the best advice is to start small, then take the time to assess the effect of your efforts on the salon itself. Take your community involvement seriously, because social change is often triggered by incremental actions, which gather momentum and eventually become a movement. Therefore, the smallest project undertaken by your salon could have unforeseen and significant implications.

Salons and Global Citizenship
In the last century, the most important issue which has faced humankind has been figuring out the mechanisms of production. In the next one hundred years, it will be the mechanisms of cooperation.
    —Adam Jacobs, salonist

Imagine a world in which salons meet regularly in every inhabited square mile. Imagine people visiting salons as frequently as they buy or gather food. Imagine all of us talking, searching for solutions to social problems, and gaining the support of colleagues and friends when we attempt to realize our ideas. Imagine governments turning to salonists for counsel on decisions that affect community life. Imagine everyone voting. Imagine sharing tools, meals, and cars up and down the block. Imagine a society in which no one fears criticism when they open their mouths to sing, lift their skirts to dance, set their pens to paper, or stand before a crowd to speak.

These imaginings may be more realistic than you think. Salons stand to learn much from the world, but the world has also learned much from salons and the skills that salons

> "I know I write my elected officials much more as a result of hashing things out on-line, and that I've joined the literacy volunteering thing as a direct result of being on-line. If there is such a thing as the Well being a social movement, and not just part of the move toward on-line living, it would be in how it spurs us to genuine action. Perhaps a drop in the bucket sort of action, but action nonetheless. **"**

—*The WELL as a Social Movement*

instill. In all likelihood, these skills will become the foundation of responsible global citizenship in a sustainable future. There are signs, in fact, that such a future is imminent.

An innovative application of consensus decision making is Sweden's newest export. In 1989 Karl-Henrik Robert, former head of the country's leading cancer institute, had grown tired of the seemingly endless scientific bickering over insignificant aspects of environmental problems. He likened scientists to monkeys who were arguing over withering leaves in a dying tree, instead of paying attention to facts they can agree upon—i.e., that the tree is dying. Hoping to cut through scientific doublespeak and encourage business and government action on environmental realities, the scientist founded a business-and-life philosophy called The Natural Step.

"Actually, my hero is George Bush."

Robert first developed a paper on the fundamental conditions he considered necessary for a sustainable society. He then sent it to Sweden's entire scientific community for comment. When he received the scientists' suggestions, Robert incorporated them into his paper and recirculated the document. After repeating this process

66 The most powerful instrument of
intellectual community organizing is the salon."

—Stewart Brand, editor of *CoEvolution Quarterly* (1974)

twenty-one times, he formally introduced his consensus paper to the nation.

At the root of Robert's environmental theory is the cyclic principle, which states that reconstruction of material must equal consumption of material, and that waste must not accumulate in nature. Robert elaborated four conditions necessary for sustainability:

1. Nature cannot withstand a systematic buildup of dispersed matter mined from the earth's crust (such as minerals and oil).

2. Nature cannot withstand a systematic buildup of persistent compounds made by humans (such as PCBs).

3. Nature cannot withstand a systematic deterioration of its capacity for renewal (such as fish harvests that exceed replenishment levels and the conversion of fertile land to desert).

4. Therefore, if we want life to continue, we must (a) be efficient in our use of resources and (b) promote justice—because ignoring poverty will lead the poor, for reasons of short-term survival, to destroy resources (such as the rainforests) that we all need for long-term survival.

Robert's paper ignited a Swedish national phenomenon. The scientific community had reached consensus, and the Swedish government quickly endorsed the report at the highest levels. An educational packet (including booklets and audiotapes) based on the paper was prepared and sent to every household and school, enabling citizens and students to learn the basics of sustainability. Seminars were conducted for members of Parliament. Study circles proliferated. An Environmental Youth Parliament was established, and a Natural Step journal targeted at business readers was founded. A number of famous artists and celebrities appeared on television to promote and celebrate the birth of this remarkable national project, and much of Sweden's business community signed on. As a result of Natural Step training, more than twenty five of the country's largest corporations have since changed their operations and production processes to support the productivity of the earth. For example, IKEA, a leading Swedish furniture company, now offers a line that complies with Natural Step conditions. The products contain no metals, and are made of wood harvested through sustainable forestry practices. The ultimate purpose of the program is to establish common ground upon which all sorts of people—employers and employees, right- and left-wingers, atheists and believers, and so forth—

can meet. When they are able to arrive at scientifically based consensus, the way is cleared for concrete action. In the long term, the project promises to completely reorganize the nation's way of life in order to bring it into alignment with the laws of nature.

An isolated phenomenon? Probably not. In the United States, business visionary Paul Hawken agreed in December of 1994 to become president of the fledgling American Natural Step program, which formed an advisory council comprised of U.S. scientists, businesspeople, and professional organizations. U.S. businesses, including Monsanto Company, the chemical manufacturing giant, and Odwalla, an all-natural juice company headquartered in California, have

Anthropologist Margaret Mead

begun studying the Swedish Natural Step program. At this writing, these companies and others await completion of the domestic version. According to Odwalla co-CEO Greg Steltenpohl, "Natural Step . . . is not a politically charged agenda where you're bad or evil for cutting down trees. Rather, the approach removes the emotional charge of the environmental base and puts us on a common-ground basis. It's a nonthreatening way to communicate the need to be rational in how we make decisions."

Of course, the Natural Step program did not emerge from the salon movement. But the values, skills, and processes that have been celebrated for decades in salons clearly support such responsible global citizenship. As more and more citizens seek ways to influence social and political decision making—and as many of these decisions assume great urgency—consensus action, public speaking skills, council methods, mediation, and community building will become ever more important. Many movements, voices, philosophies, and circumstances will undoubtedly contribute to the global changes that loom on the horizon. But revolutions large and small can originate in a living room or café, where a handful of people have gathered to examine the state of their neighborhood, their community, and their world. You might well find yourself among that handful.

Salonists who wish to make a difference might take heart from the words of anthropologist Margaret Mead: "Never doubt that a small group of thoughtful, committed citizens can change the world. Indeed, it is the only thing that ever has."

APPENDIX A
The History of Salons:
Recommended Readings

Among the many biographies and historical studies I read during my research, these are my personal favorites. You'll find full publication information in the bibliography.

Janine Bouissounouse, *Julie: The Life of Mademoiselle de Lespinasse: Her Salon, Her Friends, Her Loves.* Translated by Pierre de Fontnouvelle.

Margaret Case Harriman, *The Vicious Circle*

J. Christopher Herold, *Mistress to An Age: A Life of Madame de Staël*

Amelia Gere Mason, *The Women of the French Salons*

Peter Quennell, ed., *Affairs of the Mind: The Salon in Europe and America from the 18th to the 20th Centur*

APPENDIX B
Salon Literature and Memoirs:
Recommended Readings

This is a listing of novels, plays, and memoirs that are at least partially set in the salon milieu.

Natalie Barney, *Pensées d'une Amazon* ("Thoughts of an Amazon"). Author's memoir.

Sylvia Beach, *Shakespeare and Company*. Memoir.

Lord Byron, *The Blues: A Literary Eclogue*. A comedy satirizing the British Bluestockings and their salons.

Ramón de la Cruz, *Sainete Las Tertulias de Madrid*. A late eighteenth-century play satirizing the Spanish salons known as tertulia.

Max Eastman, *Venture*. This novel includes a description of Mabel Dodge's salon.

Benito Pérez Galdós, *Episodio Nacional La Estafeta Romántica*. An 1899 novel including references to tertulia.

Benito Pérez Galdós, *La Fontana de Oro* ("The Golden Fountain"). An 1890 novel with a humorous description of a revolutionary tertulia.

Ramón Gómez de la Serna, *Pombo*. Recollections of the tertulia at Café de Pombo, written in 1918.

Langston Hughes, *The Big Sea*. An autobiography including descriptions of the personalities and gatherings of the Harlem Renaissance.

Aldous Huxley, *Crome Yellow*. This novel includes a caricature of the salon hosted by Ottoline Garsington.

D. H. Lawrence, *The Plumed Serpent*. Includes a character based on Mabel Dodge.

D.H. Lawrence, *Women in Love*. Includes a caricature of Ottoline of Garsington.

Marty Martin, *Gertrude Stein Gertrude Stein Gertrude Stein: A One-Character Play*. A play based on Gertrude Stein's autobiographical writings.

Molière, *Les Précieuses Ridicules*. A play satirizing salon society.

Charles Palissot, *Les Philosophes*. A satirical play featuring Madame Geoffrin and the Encyclopedists.

Michel de Pure, *La Prétieuse*. A novel based on poet Madame de la Suze's salon.

Marcel Proust, *Remembrance of Things Past*. A novel.

Mesonero Romanos, *Memorias de un Setentón*. An 1880 autobiography including an account of public tertulias in the 1830s.

Gertrude Stein, *The Autobiography of Alice B. Toklas*. Includes descriptions of the Stein salon/studio in Paris.

Wallace Thurman, *Infants of the Spring*. A novel set in the milieu of the Harlem Renaissance.

Carl Van Vechten, *Nigger Heaven*. A novel about the Harlem Renaissance period.

A P P E N D I X   C
Creativity and Play:
Resources

Here are some of the books and resources I have found useful in my creativity salon:

Thomas Armstrong, *7 Kinds of Smart: Identifying and Developing Your Many Intelligences*. Includes lists of games and exercises that could easily be adapted to creativity salons. Readable and practical.

Alastair Brotchie, compiler, Mel Gooding, editor, *Surrealist Games* (Shambhala/Redstone Editions, 1991). This wonderful box of word and drawing games invented by the surrealists is available at many museum gift shops and some book and game stores.

James Charlton, *Charades: The Complete Guide to America's Favorite Party Game*. Truly complete, easy to follow, and humorously written.

Exploratorium Teacher Institute, *The Exploratorium Science Snackbook*. A great sourcebook for creative science play.

Magnetic Poetry Kit. Distribute handfuls of magnetized words and see what happens. Available at many gift shops and bookstores.

Stephen Nachmanovitch, *Free Play: Improvisation in Life and Art*. Inspiring essays on creativity and play, together with a few exercises.

Milton E. Polsky, *Let's Improvise: Becoming Creative, Expressive, and Spontaneous Through Drama*. Theater exercises.

Jo Miles Schuman, *Art from Many Hands: Multicultural Art Projects*. An excellent book explaining how to do a wide range of unusual and beautiful art and craft projects from around the world. Written for teachers working with kids, so the instructions are easy to follow.

Viola Spolin, *Improvisation for the Theater: A Handbook of Teaching and Directing Techniques*. Written for those who teach professional acting skills. Filled with exercises for theater games that could easily be adapted for use in the salon.

Barbara Steinwachs and Sivasailam Thiagarajan, *BARNGA: A Simulation Game on Cultural Clashes*. Available through the Intercultural Press, P.O. Box 700, Yarmouth, ME 04096. The nature of the game and its purpose must be kept a secret from everyone except the person setting it up. Allow plenty of time for a long and vigorous discussion following the game.

Ukrainian Gift Shop, 2422 Central Avenue NE, Minneapolis, MN 55418. Mail-order catalog available. Best inexpensive source of Ukrainian egg-dyeing kits and instructions.

World Game Institute, University City Science Center, 3508 Market Street, Philadelphia, PA 19104 (215-387-0220). Stocks many interactive games, maps, and workshop materials for increasing understanding of global resources.

Community Connections:
Readings and Resources

Books for Familiarizing Yourself with American Community

Robert Bellah, Richard Madsen, William M. Sullivan, Ann Swindler, and Steven M. Tipton, *Habits of the Heart.* A fascinating sociological overview of the nature of society and community in the United States.

Exploring/Exploratorium Quarterly. The Spring 1992, issue includes an article by Robert Pincus on exploring city streets to discover the history of your community.

Increasing Group Diversity and Understanding

Rick Simonson and Scott Walker, editors, *The Graywolf Annual Five: Multicultural Literacy: Opening the American Mind.* Essays on diversity and racism accompanied by an excellent list of what everyone should know about cultures around the world. This would make a great basis for a reading group. It's also an excellent starting point for salon members who want to increase the diversity of their group, but first want to improve their understanding of the multicultural experience.

Clyde W. Ford, *We Can All Get Along: 50 Steps You Can Take to Help End Racism.* A list of ideas useful for a group that wants to expand membership diversity and/or increase members' understanding of racism.

Foundation for Community Encouragement, Inc., P.O. Box 50518, Knoxville, TN 37950-0518 (615-690-4334). Founded by author, therapist, and community scholar M. Scott Peck.

National Council for International Visitors, 1420 K Street NW, Suite 800, Washington, DC 20005-2401 (800-523-8101). Provides guides for contacting international visitors in your state.

Utne Reader Neighborhood Salon Association, 1624 Harmon Place, Suite 330, Minneapolis, MN 55403 (612-338-5040) or e-mail at <salons@utne.com>. Maintains nationwide directory of U.S. salons and offers support services.

Study Circle Organizations and Guides

American Institute of Discussion, Box 103, Oklahoma City, OK 73101 (805-840-9681). Primarily active in Texas and Oklahoma, suggests books for three- to ten-week discussion programs.

Chautauqua Institution, Chautauqua, NY 14722. Historical information on Chautauquas, also conducts a host of summer education and entertainment programs.

Choices for the 21st Century, Center for Foreign Policy Development, Brown University, Box 1948, Providence, RI 02912 (401-863-3465).

National Issues Forums, 100 Commons Road, Dayton, OH 45459-2777 (800-433-7834). Organization devoted to making study circles accessible and widespread. Provides English and Spanish language study materials, and conveys opinions of study circle participants to policymakers.

Study Circles Resource Center, P.O. Box 203, Pomfret CT 06258, (860-928-2616). Provides materials, support, and technical assistance, primarily to community-wide study circle programs.

The Union Institute Office of Social Responsibility, Center for Public Policy, 1731 Connecticut Avenue NW, Washington, DC 20009-1146 (202-667-1313).

On-line Communities

Cafe Utne, 1624 Harmon Place, Suite 330, Minneapolis, MN 55403 (612-338-5040) or <http://www.utne.com>. Coordinates e-salons and other on-line activities.

Echo, Echo Communications Group, Inc., 97 Perry Street, Suite 13, New York, NY 10014 (212-292-0900) or <www.echonyc.com>

MetaNetwork, (703-243-6622) or <www.tmn.com>.

The WELL (Whole Earth 'Lectronic Link), 27 Gate 5 Road, Sausalito, CA 94965-9976 (415-281-6500, 800-935-5882) or <www.well.com>.

A P P E N D I X   E
Communications and Group Dynamics:
Readings and Resources

Auvine, Densmore, Extrom, Poole, and Shanklin, *A Manual for Group Facilitators*.

Avery, Auvine, Streibel, Weiss, *Building United Judgment: Handbook for Consensus Decision Making*.

Sedonia Cahill and Joshua Halpern, *The Ceremonial Circle: Practice, Ritual, and Renewal for Personal and Community Healing*.

A Great Books Primer: Essays on Liberal Education, the Uses of Discussion, and Rules for Reading. Available from The Great Books Foundation, 35 East Wacker Drive, Suite 2300, Chicago, IL 60601-2298 (800-222-5870).

Study Circles Resource Center, *Guidelines for Organizing and Leading a Study Circle.* Available from SCRC, P.O. Box 203, Pomfret, CT 06258 (860-928-2616).

Institute for the Arts of Democracy, 700 Larkspur Landing Circle, Suite 199, Larkspur, CA 94939 (415-453-3333).

M. Scott Peck, M.D., *The Different Drum: Community Making and Peace*.

Joanna Macy, *Despair and Personal Power in the Nuclear Age*.

The Center for Conflict Resolution, 731 State Street, Madison, WI 53703 (608-255-0479). Offers workshops and materials on mediation and dispute resolution.

The Ojai Foundation, P.O. Box 1620, Ojai, CA 93023. Provides booklets and workshops on using council methods.

Michael J. Sheeran, *Beyond Majority Rule*. An excellent book on the ins and outs of the Quaker methods of decision making and interacting at meetings.

Bibliography

Abrahams, Roger D. *The Man-of-Words in the West Indies.* Baltimore and London: The Johns Hopkins University Press, 1983.

Adair, Margo. *Working Inside Out: Tools for Change.* Berkeley, CA: Wingbow Press, 1984.

Adair, Margo, and Sharon Howell. *The Subjective Side of Politics.* San Francisco: Tools for Change. Pamphlet.

Aldis, Janet. *Madame Geoffrin: Her Salon and Her Times, 1750-1777.* London: Methuen & Co., 1905.

Alexander, Christopher, Sara Ishikawa, and Murray Silverstein with Max Jacobson, Ingrid Fiksdahl-King, and Shlomo Angel. *A Pattern Language.* New York: Oxford University Press, 1977.

Altmann, Alexander. *Moses Mendelssohn: A Biographical Study.* Tuscaloosa: University of Alabama Press, 1973.

Anderson, Margaret. *My Thirty Years' War.* New York: Covici, Friede Publishers, 1930.

Anderson, Margaret. *The Strange Necessity: The Autobiography, Resolutions and Reminiscence to 1969.* New York: Horizon Press, 1970.

Andrews, Robert. *The Concise Columbia Dictionary of Quotations.* New York: Avon Books, 1987.

Apple, Michael W. *Official Knowledge: Democratic Education in a Conservative Age.* New York: Routledge, 1993.

Apte, Mahadev L., *Humor and Laughter: An Anthropological Approach.* Ithaca, NY: Cornell University Press, 1985.

Arendt, Hannah. *Rahel Varnhagen: The Life of a Jewish Woman.* Translated by Richard and Clara Winston. New York: Harcourt Brace Jovanovich, 1974.

Ariés, Philippe and Georges Duby, general editors. *A History of Private Life,* Vols. I-IV. Cambridge, MA: The Belknap Press of Harvard University Press, 1987-1990.

Armstrong, Thomas. *7 Kinds of Smart: Identifying and Developing Your Many Intelligences.* New York: Plume Books, 1993.

Aronson, Nicole. *Mademoiselle de Scudéry.* Translated by Stuart R. Aronson. Boston: Twayne Publishers/G.K. Hall & Co., 1978.

Auvine, Brian, Betsy Densmore, Mary Extrom, Scott Poole, and Michel Shanklin. *A Manual for Group Facilitators.* Madison, WI: The Center for Conflict Resolution, 1978.

Avery, Michel, Brian Auvine, Barbara Streibel, and Lonnie Weiss. *Building United Judgment: A Handbook for Consensus Decision Making.* Madison, WI: The Center for Conflict Resolution, 1981.

Ayer, A. J., and Jane O'Grady, eds. *A Dictionary of Philosophical Quotations.* Oxford, UK: Blackwell Publishers, 1992.

Barker, Robert G. *Ecological Psychology.* Stanford, CA: Stanford University Press, 1968.

Barreca, Regina. *They Used To Call Me Snow White...But I Drifted: Women's Strategic Use of Humor.* New York: Penguin Books, 1991.

Bauman, Richard, and Joel Sherzer. *Explorations in the Ethnography of Speaking.* London: Cambridge University Press, 1974.

Beck, Peggy V., and A. L. Waters. *The Sacred: Ways of Knowledge, Sources of Life.* Tsaile, AZ: Navajo Community College, 1977.

Bellah, Robert, Richard Madsen, William M. Sullivan, Ann Swindler, and Steven M. Tipton. *Habits of the Heart: Individualism and Commitment in American Life.* New York: Harper & Row, Perennial Library, 1985.

Berendt, John. "The Clever Retort." *Esquire.* October 1991.

——"The Salon." *Esquire.* November 1990.

Bianco, Frank. *Voices of Silence: Lives of the Trappists Today.* New York: Anchor Books, Doubleday, 1991.

Blennerhassett, Lady. *Madame de Staël: Her Friends, and Her Influence in Politics and Literature,* 3 vols. London: Chapman and Hall Ltd., 1889.

Bloch, Maurice, ed. *Political Language and Oratory in Traditional Society.* New York: Academic Press, 1975.

Bohm, David. "On Dialogue." *Noetic Science Review.* Autumn 1992.

Bohm, David and Mark Edwards. *Changing Consciousness: Exploring the Hidden Source of the Social, Political and Environmental Crises Facing our World.* San Francisco: HarperSanFranciso, 1991.

Bohm, David, and F. David Peat. *Science, Order, and Creativity*. New York: Bantam Books, 1987.

Bostick, Alan. "Word of Mouth." *The Tennessean*. Sunday, May 16, 1993.

Bouissounouse, Janine. *Julie: The Life of Mademoiselle de Lespinasse; Her Salon, Her Friends, Her Loves*. Translated by Pierre de Fontnouvelle. New York: Appleton-Century-Crofts, Inc., 1962.

Bradbrook, M.C. *The School of Night: A Study in the Literary Relationships of Sir Walter Raleigh*. New York: Russell & Russell, 1965.

Breggin, Peter R. *Beyond Conflict: From Self-Help and Psychotherapy to Peacemaking*. New York: St. Martin's Press, 1992.

Brown, Dorothy M. *Setting a Course: American Women in the 1920s*. Boston: Twayne, 1987.

Cahill, Sedonia, and Joshua Halpern. *The Ceremonial Circle: Practice, Ritual, and Renewal for Personal and Community Healing*. San Francisco: HarperSanFrancisco, 1992.

Campbell, Paul Newell. *Rhetoric: A Study of Communicative and Aesthetic Dimensions of Language*. Belmont, CA: Dickenson Publishing Co., Inc., 1972.

Carbaugh, Donal, ed. *Cultural Communication and Intercultural Contact*. Hillsdale, NJ: Hove and London, Lawrence Erlbaum Assoc., 1990.

Carr, Phillip. *Days With the French Romantics in the Paris of 1830*. London: Methven & Co., Ltd., 1932.

Concise Columbia Encyclopedia. New York: Avon Books, 1983.

Craveri, Benedetta. "Conqueror of Paris." *The New York Review*. December 17, 1992.

Crocker, Lester G. *The Embattled Philosopher: A Biography of Denis Diderot*. Michigan: Michigan State College Press, 1954.

Curiel, Roberta, and Bernard Dov Cooperman. *The Venetian Ghetto*. New York: Rizzoli, 1990.

Czikszentmihalyi, Mihaly. *Flow: The Psychology of Optimal Experience*. New York: HarperPerennial, 1990.

De Bono, Edward. *Future Positive*. London: Penguin Books, 1979.

——. *Practical Thinking*. London: Penguin Books, 1971.

Diaz, Adriana. *Freeing the Creative Spirit: Drawing on the Power of Art to Tap the Magic and Wisdom Within*. San Francisco: HarperSanFrancisco, 1992.

Drennan, Robert E., ed. *The Algonquin Wits*. Citadel Press, 1975.

Duncan, Hugh Dalziel. *Communication and Social Order*. London: Oxford University Press, 1970.

Eastman, Max. *Enjoyment of Living*. New York: Harper and Brothers, 1948.

Eisler, Benita. *O'Keeffe and Stieglitz: An American Romance*. New York: Penguin Books, 1992.

Emigh, Phyliss. "Kindred Souls or Kissing Cousins?: SCRC's Interpretation of Study Circles Does Not Always Match the Swedish Model." *FOCUS on Study Circles: The Newsletter of the SCRC*. Winter 1991.

Epstein, Seymour. *You're Smarter than You Think: How to Develop Your Practical Intelligence for Success in Living*. New York: Simon & Schuster, 1993.

Estes, Caroline. "Consensus Ingredients." *In Context*. Fall 1983.

Farb, Peter. *Word Play: What Happens When People Talk*. New York: Vintage Books, 1973.

Fein, Esther B. "A Best-Selling Author Settles in the Hot Seat to Meet Her Readers." *The New York Times*. May 13, 1993, section B.

Feldman, Reynold, and Cynthia A. Voelke, editors. *A World Treasury of Folk Wisdom*. San Francisco: HarperSanFrancisco, 1992.

Feraca, Jean. "Riches to Rags." *Women of Spirit*. Wisconsin Public Radio. Program one, 1991.

Ferrero, Pat, and Elaine Hedges. *Hearts and Hands: The Influence of Women and Quilts on American Society*. San Francisco: The Quilt Digest Press, 1987.

Fielding, Daphne. *Those Remarkable Cunards: Emerald and Nancy*. New York: Atheneum, 1968.

Fitch, Noel Riley. *Sylvia Beach and the Lost Generation: A History of Literary Paris in the Twenties and Thirties*. New York: W.W. Norton & Company, 1983.

Ford, Clyde W. *We Can All Get Along*. New York: Dell Publishing, 1994.

Furbank, P. N. *Diderot: A Critical Biography*. New York: Alfred A. Knopf, 1992.

Galdós, Benito Pérez. *La Fontana de Oro*.

Gang, Philip S., Nina Meyerhof Lynn, and Dorothy J. Maver. *Conscious Education: The Bridge to Freedom*. Atlanta: Dagaz Press, 1992.

Garvey, Timothy J. *Public Sculptor: Lorado Taft and the Beautification of Chicago*. Urbana: University of Illinois Press, 1988.

Gatto, John. *Dumbing Us Down: The Hidden Curriculum of Compulsory Schooling*. Philadelphia: New Society Publishers, 1992.

Gerard, Glenna. "Dialogue: A Communication 'Practice Field.'" Gerard Global Concepts: February 1992.

Gómez de la Serna, Ramón. *Greguerias: The Wit and Wisdom of Ramón Gómez de la Serna*. Philip Ward, ed. New York: Oleander Press, 1982.

Grauman, Brigid. "The Mobile Guide: The Thinking Person's Hotel." Facts Delivered—The Clipping Service for *Wall Street Journal*. February 5, 1993.

Grillo, Paul Jacques. *Form, Function, and Design*. New York: Dover Publishers, 1975.

Gross, Ron. "Salons Belong in Libraries." *Adult and Continuing Education Today*. August 26, 1991.

Hall, Edward T. *Beyond Culture*. Garden City, NY: Anchor Press/Doubleday, 1976.

Hall, Mildred, and Edward Hall. *The Fourth Dimension in Architecture: The Impact of Building on Man's Behavior*. Santa Fe, NM: The Sunstone Press, 1975.

Hapgood, Hutchins. *A Victorian in the Modern World*. New York: Harcourt, Brace & Co., 1939.

Hargrave, Mary. *Some German Women and Their Salons*. New York: Brentano's, 1912.

Harkins, William E. *Karel Capek*. New York: Columbia University Press, 1962.

Harriman, Margaret Case. *The Vicious Circle*. Rinehart & Co., Inc., 1951.

Hart, John E. *Floyd Dell*. New York: Twayne, 1971.

Heath, Lillian M. *Eighty Pleasant Evenings*. Boston: United Society of Christian Endeavor, 1898.

Heider, John. *The Tao of Leadership: Lao Tzu's Tao Te Ching Adapted for a New Age*. Atlanta, GA: Humanics New Age, 1985.

Herold, J. Christopher. *Mistress to An Age: A Life of Madame de Staël*. Indianapolis: Bobbs-Merrill Co. Inc., 1958.

Hillman, James, and Michael Ventura. *We've Had a Hundred Years of Psychotherapy and the World's Getting Worse*. San Francisco: HarperSanFranciso, 1992.

Hipp, Earl. *The Caring Circle: A Facilitator's Guide to Support Groups*. Centre City, MN: Hazelden, 1992.

Hofmann, Paul. *The Viennese: Splendor, Twilight, and Exile*. New York: Anchor Press, 1988.

Hope, A., S. Timmel, and C. Hodzi. *Training for Transformation: A Handbook for Community Workers*, 3 vols. Zimbabwe: Mambo Press, 1984.

Hudson, William J. *Intellectual Capital: How to Build It, Enhance It, Use It*. New York: John Wiley & Sons, Inc., 1993.

Ilardo, Joseph. *Risk-Taking for Personal Growth*. Oakland, CA: New Harbinger, 1992.

Jay, Karla. *The Amazon and the Page: Natalie Clifford Barney and Renee Vivien*. Bloomington: Indiana University Press, 1988.

Johnstone, Charles M., M.D. *Necessary Wisdom: Meeting the Challenge of a New Cultural Maturity*. Seattle, WA: ICD Press, 1991.

Kalweit, Holger. *Shamans, Healers, and Medicine Men*. Translated by Michael H. Kohn. Boston: Shambhala, 1992.

Karpeles, Gustav. *Jewish Literature and Other Essays*. Philadelphia: The Jewish Publication Society of America, 1895.

Keating, L. Clark. *Studies on the Literary Salon in France, 1550-1615*. Cambridge, MA: Harvard University Press, 1941.

Kessler, Shelley. "The Mysteries Program: Educating Adolescents for Today's World." *Holistic Education Review*. Winter 1990.

Lakoff, George, and Mark Johnson. *Metaphors We Live By*. Chicago: University of Chicago Press, 1980.

Levaillant, Maurice. *The Passionate Exiles: Madame de Staël and Madame Récamier*. Translated by Malcolm Barnes. New York: Farrar, Strauss and Cudahy, 1958.

Leviton, Richard. "Reconcilable Differences." *Yoga Journal*. Sept./Oct. 1992.

Lougee, Carolyn C. *Le Paradis des Femmes: Women, Salons, and Social Stratification in Seventeenth-Century France.* Princeton, NJ: Princeton University Press, 1976.

Luhan, Mabel Dodge. *Intimate Memories,* 4 vols. New York: Harcourt, Brace and Co., 1933 to 1937.

Lund, Jens. ed. *Folk Arts of Washington State: A Survey of Contemporary Folk Arts and Artists in the State of Washington.* Tumwater, WA: Washington State Folklife Council, 1989.

Luvmour, Sambhava, and Josette Luvmour. *Towards Peace: Cooperative Games and Activities Selected for Conflict Resolution, Communication Enhancement, Building Self-Esteem.* North San Juan, CA: Center for Educational Guidance Books, 1989.

Luyster, Isaphene M., editor and translator. *Memoirs and Correspondence of Madame Récamier.* Boston: Knight and Millet, 1867.

Macy, Joanna. *Despair and Personal Power in the Nuclear Age.* New Society Pub., 1983.

Maggio, Rosalie. *The Beacon Book of Quotations by Women.* Boston: Beacon Press, 1992.

Marchese, John. "From Muffin Shop to Salon." *The New York Times.* May 30, 1993.

Maré, Patrick de, Robin Piper, and Sheila Thompson. *Koinonia: From Hate, through Dialogue, to Culture in the Large Group.* London: Karnac Books, 1991.

Mason, Amelia Gere. *The Women of the French Salons.* New York: The Century Co., 1891.

May, Henry F. *The End of American Innocence: A Study of the First Years of Our Own Time, 1912-1917.* New York: Alfred A. Knopf, 1959.

Mills, Eugene S. *The Story of Elderhostel.* Hanover: University Press of New England, 1993.

Mills, Stephanie. "Salons and Their Keepers." *CoEvolution Quarterly.* Summer 1974.

Mindell, Arnold. *The Leader as Martial Artist: Techniques and Strategies for Resolving Conflict and Creating Community.* San Francisco: HarperSanFrancisco, 1992.

Modena, Leon. *The Autobiography of a Seventeenth-Century Venetian Rabbi: Leon Modena's Life of Judah.* Translated and edited by Mark R. Cohen. New Jersey: Princeton University Press, 1988.

Morgan, Kelly Blake. *Beyond Potential: A Revolution in Management Thought.* New York: Warner Books, 1993.

Morrell, Ottoline. *Ottoline at Garsington: Memoirs of Lady Ottoline Morrell, 1915-1918.* Robert Gathorne-Hardy, ed. New York: Alfred A. Knopf, 1975.

Myers, Sylvia Harcstack. *The Bluestocking Circle: Women, Friendship, and the Life of the Mind in Eighteenth-Century England.* Oxford: Clarendon Press, 1990.

Nachmanovitch, Stephen. *Free Play: Improvisation in Life and Art.* Los Angeles: Jeremy P. Tarcher, Inc., 1990.

Natanson, Maurice and Henry Johnstone, eds. *Philosophy, Rhetoric and Argumentation.* University Park, PA: The Pennsylvania State University Press, 1965.

Oldenburg, Ray. *The Great Good Place.* New York: Paragon House, 1989.

Oliver, Leonard P. *Study Circles: Coming Together for Personal Growth and Social Change.* Washington, D.C.: Seven Locks Press, 1987.

Oliver, Leonard P. "Study Circles and Union Democracy: Study Circles in the International Union of Bricklayers & Allied Craftsmen." Washington, D.C.: Oliver Associates, 1993. Pamphlet.

Pacific Yearly Meeting. *Faith and Pratice of Pacific Yearly Meeting of the Religious Society of Friends: A Quaker Guide to Christian Discipline.* San Francisco: Pacific Yearly Meeting, Friends Center, 1985.

Peck, M. Scott, M.D. *The Different Drum: Community Making and Peace.* New York: Simon and Schuster, 1987.

Plant, Judith, and Christopher Plant, eds. *Putting Power in Its Place: Create Community Control!* Philadelphia: New Society Publishers, 1991.

Quennell, Peter, ed. *Affairs of the Mind: The Salon in Europe and America from the 18th to the 20th Century.* Washington, D.C.: New Republic Books, 1980.

Rapoport, Amos. *Human Aspects of Urban Form: Towards a Man-Environment Approach to Urban Form and Design.* Oxford: Pergamon Press, 1977.

Rheingold, Howard. *They Have a Word for It: A Lighthearted Lexicon of Untranslatable Words and Phrases.* Los Angeles: Jeremy P. Tarcher, Inc., 1988.

———. *The Virtual Community: Homesteading on the Electronic Frontier.* Reading, MA: Addison-Wesley, 1993.

Sanger, Margaret. *Margaret Sanger: An Autobiography*. New York: W.W. Norton & Co., 1938.

Shaffer, Carolyn R., and Kristin Anundsen. *Creating Community Anywhere: Finding Support and Connection in a Fragmented World*. New York: Jeremy P. Tarcher, 1993.

Sheeran, Michael J. *Beyond Majority Rule*. Philadelphia, PA: Philadelphia Yearly Meeting, 1983.

Shepherd, Chuck. "News of the Weird." *Funny Times*. October 1992.

Shook, E. Victoria. *Ho'oponopono: Contemporary Uses of a Hawaiian Problem-Solving Process*. Honolulu, HI: Published for the East-West Center by the University of Hawaii Press, 1985.

Slater, Philip. *A Dream Deferred: America's Discontent and the Search for a New Democratic Ideal*. Boston: Beacon Press, 1991.

Sokolov, Raymond. *Native Intelligence*. New York: Harper & Row, 1975.

Sommer, Robert. *Personal Space: The Behavioral Basis of Design*. New Jersey: Prentice-Hall, Inc., 1969.

Starhawk. *Dreaming the Dark: Magic, Sex and Politics*. Boston: Beacon Press, 1982.

Steffens, Lincoln. *The Autobiography of Lincoln Steffens*. New York: Harcourt, Brace & World, Inc., 1937.

Stein, Gertrude. *Autobiography of Alice B. Toklas*. New York: Vintage, 1933.

Stein, Ruthe. "Book Clubs in the TV Age." *San Francisco Chronicle*. March 23, 1989.

———. "Don't Expect Them to Read It Your Way." *San Francisco Chronicle*. May 23, 1989.

Steinwachs, Barbara, and Sivasailam Thiagarajan. *BARNGA: A Simulation Game on Cultural Clashes*. Yarmouth, ME: Intercultural Press, Inc., 1990.

Stupar, Camille M. "Cafe Salons." *CUPS, a cafe journal*. November 1992.

Sylvander, Carolyn Wedin. *Jessie Redmon Fauset: Black American Writer*. Troy, NY: Whitston Publishing Co., 1981.

Talbot, Michael. *The Holographic Universe*. New York: HarperPerennial, 1991.

Tannen, Deborah. *You Just Don't Understand*. New York: Ballantine Books, 1990.

Thompson, Charles "Chic." *What a Great Idea!: Key Steps Creative People Take*. New York: HarperPerennial, 1992.

Thompson, Robert Farris. *Flash of the Spirit*. New York: Random House, 1983.

Tinker, Chauncey Brewster. *The Salon and English Letters*. New York: Macmillan Co., 1915.

Trouncer, Margaret. *Madame Récamier*. London: MacDonald, 1949.

Van Erven, Eugéne. *The Playful Revolution: Theatre and Liberation in Asia*. Bloomington: Indiana University Press, 1992.

Vaughan, Frances E. *Awakening Intuition*. New York: Anchor Books/Doubleday, 1979.

Vidal, Mary. *Watteau's Painted Conversations: Art, Literature, and Talk in Seventeenth- and Eighteenth-Century France*. New Haven: Yale University Press, 1992.

Walker, Scott, ed. *The Graywolf Annual Ten: Changing Community*. St. Paul, MN: Graywolf Press, 1993.

Webster, T. B. L. *Athenian Culture and Society*. Berkeley: University of California Press, 1973.

Webster's New Biographical Dictionary. Springfield, MA: Merriam-Webster, Inc., 1988.

Wedgwood, C. V. *Richelieu and the French Monarchy*. New York, NY: Collier Books, 1982.

Wells, Richard A. *Manners, Culture and Dress of the Best American Society*. Springfield, MA: King, Richardson & Co., 1891.

Westley, Dick. *Good Things Happen: Experiencing Community in Small Groups*. Mystic, CT: Twenty-Third Publications, 1992.

Whitmyer, Claude, ed. *In the Company of Others: Making Community in the Modern World*. New York: Jeremy P. Tarcher, 1993.

Winokur, Jon, ed. *True Confessions*. New York: Plume Book, 1992.

Wintz, Cary. *Black Culture and the Harlem Renaissance*. Houston: Rice University Press, 1988.

Wurman, Richard Saul. *Information Anxiety*. New York: Doubleday, 1989.

Young, Bob. "Cashing in on Indian Spirituality." *Casco Bay Weekly*. From the Internet, April 1, 1993.

Art Credits

vii   Keri Pickett

xi   William Bonk

8   Artist unknown

9   Corbis-Bettmann

10   Corbis-Bettmann

14   Corbis-Bettmann

16   Corbis-Bettmann

20   Hulton Getty

24   Image by Man Ray ©Man Ray Trust

25   Mary Foote/Beinecke Library, Yale

27   Corbis-Bettmann

28   Hirschfeld. Exclusive Representative:
      The Margo Feiden Galleries, NY

29   Springer/Corbis-Bettmann

31   Peter M. Mann

39   Drawing by Wm. Hamilton ©1980 The New
      Yorker Magazine, Inc.

41   David Best

47   Photographer unknown, supplied by salon

48   Photographer unknown, supplied by salon

56   Photographer unknown, supplied by salon

59   Beth Herzhaft

61   Photographer unknown, supplied by salon

63   Robert de Michiell

96   Drawing by Koren ©1987 The New Yorker
      Magazine, Inc.

107   Paul Hardy

110   Whitney Sherman

118   Corbis-Bettmann

128   Donna Kelly

130   Mary Lawton

135   Jan Standerfer

136   William Vazquez

138   Corbis-Bettmann

169   Courtesy of Study Circles Resource Center

176   Scott Anderson

179   Rob Lee

182   Andy Levine

193   Photographer unknown, supplied by salon

197   ©Barbara Morgan, 1940. Morgan Archives,
      Hastings-on-Hudson, NY

208   Catherine Allport

212   David Wariner

217   marcellus amatangelo

232   Photographer unknown, supplied by salon

236   Corbis-Bettmann

248   *Los Angeles Times*

253   UPI/Corbis-Bettmann

Cartoons by Fred Bell
    Pages 55, 75, 80, 91, 93, 99, 137, 145, 174,
    194, 207, 220, 221, 251